WHEN
LIFE
DOESN'T
SEEM
FAIR

WHEN LIFE DOESN'T SEEM FAIR

BRUCE AND JOYCE
ERICKSON

Bookcraft
Salt Lake City, Utah

To Michelle, Lara, and Heidi for their many sacrifices and unselfish caring for their three handicapped siblings, Cindy, Heather, and Mark; and to the many people who have helped us bear our burdens.

Library of Congress Catalog Card Number: 94-73627
ISBN 0-88494-971-0

First Printing, 1995

Printed in the United States of America

Contents

Preface

Joyce often heard me say: "Why does life seem so unfair? Why doesn't God love me? Why doesn't God answer my prayers? What did I ever do to deserve this? Why do bad things keep happening when I keep the commandments? Where is the joy in this life? How can I find peace and comfort?"

Those were just some of the questions that consumed my thoughts after three of our healthy children, one by one, became totally dependent, deformed, and severely handicapped. Other questions plagued me, and my pain, heartache, and despair increased as I encountered additional trials that included financial problems, loss of employment, and serious marital difficulties. Because our children weren't healed by the power of the priesthood, and because we faced continued adversity despite keeping the commandments, a bitterness grew in my heart which sapped my emotional strength and eventually caused me to question the value of living.

This book is an account of finding peace in the midst of adversity. It's the book I wanted to read but could never find as I struggled to understand the seeming unfairness of life. More specifically, this book is about Joyce, me, and our six children and how we each found a degree of peace, each in our own way and each in our own season. It presents a contrast between despair and hope, discouragement and happiness, bitterness and peace. Our story is written from two perspectives: Joyce's, which includes thoughts and feelings of our healthy daughters, and mine. It tells how our trials left Joyce softened, stronger, and with peace, and how they initially left me bitter, unhappy, and full of despair. This book also is about our difficult marriage relationship, which often seemed to call for divorce but which eventually became solidly based on friendship, love, romance, happiness, and unity. In short, this book is about our family's search for understanding and peace, interwoven with our innermost feelings and new perspectives that we gained as we struggled through our trials.

Additionally, this book is about faith, love, and repentance, combined with the insight, guidance, and counsel of ancient and modern prophets. Their counsel is abundantly quoted in this work, not because we are trying to support a thesis as with a research paper, but to demonstrate how understanding came to us line upon line through the scriptures and the words of the Brethren. We also quoted them because their words have universal application, even though each person's trials are unique.

Finally, this work is a blueprint to *enjoying,* not just surviving, the latter days. It is a story that culminates in the sure testimony that Elder Boyd K. Packer was correct when he said, "There is more equality in our testing than we would believe" ("The Choice," p. 21). And, most important, it is a testimony that because of the Atonement, lasting peace will come to each of us, regardless of our adversity, if we follow the counsel of the prophets.

In appreciation to those who have shared their love, time, and resources to lift our heavy burdens, we share our lives with you in the hope that this account will help you better understand yourself, God, and the world around you. And we hope that this work will help you know the promise of the Lord: "Peace be unto thy soul; thine adversity and thine afflictions shall be but a small moment" (D&C 121:7).

Acknowledgments

We wish to thank all who made this work possible. We are grateful to Jean Ernstrom for loving Heather and caring enough to write her testimony "Jesus, Listening, Can Hear." We are most appreciative to Janice Kapp Perry for writing the song of the same title for Heather and then giving us permission to use it in this work. And we are indebted to Michael Ballam for sharing Heather's story with BYU Education Week audiences and for helping us realize that our family experiences could be of value to others.

We appreciate the many wonderful people who reviewed our manuscript and offered suggestions, direction, and the motivation to continue. We are especially grateful for Brookie Peterson, Laurel Rohlfing, Mary Ellen Edmunds, and William O. Nelson, who provided many suggestions and great encouragement and urged us to pursue publication—even after reading early drafts. We are also thankful to Cory Maxwell, editorial manager of Bookcraft, and Rebecca Taylor, editor, for their patience and support during the latter stages of writing.

We express our sincere gratitude to Elder Neal A. Maxwell for sharing stories of Heather and Mark with many congregations. We received motivation and strength from many who heard him and contacted us.

Finally, special appreciation is expressed to President Boyd K. Packer for allowing us here to use many of his stories and experiences in their entirety.

PART I

Joyce's Reflections and Perceptions

Joyce J. Erickson

CHAPTER 1

Walking by Faith

It was the last week in November, 1972. Michelle was four years old, Lara was two, and we were stationed at March Air Force Base (AFB), near Riverside, California. Cindy, our youngest, was eight months old and developing normally. She had learned to scoot around on the floor, sit up, grasp objects in both hands, and stand next to furniture. Then, one Monday morning, I took her to the doctor because she had developed a bad cold. He diagnosed her problem as "a minor case of bronchitis" and prescribed some medication.

I remained fairly unconcerned about Cindy's health until the following Saturday. That day she was very restless, but seemed okay as long as I held her. However, that evening, when I laid her on the floor to care for Michelle and Lara, instead of crying as she had done during the day, her body was motionless, and her eyes stared at the ceiling. I waved my hand in front of her face, but there was no reaction. My heart sank! I called Bruce, and after tense minutes of wondering what we should do, we took her to the base hospital.

Bruce and I nervously waited for the doctor to examine Cindy. He finally came and, after checking her eyes, ears, nose, throat, and reflexes, said he could find nothing medically wrong with her. Confused, Bruce and I protested and asked that he call a pediatrician. When he refused, Bruce and I took Cindy to a hospital in Riverside. There, the emergency room doctor checked her and asked us many questions. He told us he didn't know what was wrong, but because she looked like older children he had seen who were on drugs, he thought she might have reacted negatively to the medication prescribed to treat her bronchitis. He then contacted the doctor we had seen at March AFB Hospital and recommended that Cindy be admitted and observed for the rest of the night.

It was 1:30 A.M. when we arrived back at the base hospital. Cindy was still crying and had not slept for almost twenty hours, and we expected the doctor there to admit her as the Riverside doctor had suggested. To our disappointment, however, the military doctor would neither admit her to the hospital nor consult a pediatrician. Instead, he sent us back home—again insisting that there was nothing wrong.

What should we do? What could we do? On our way home, we discussed the possibility of calling our neighbor who was a doctor—but decided against it because it now was nearly 2:30 A.M. When we arrived home, however, we noticed that lights were still on at the doctor's house. After discussing whether we should disturb him, Bruce finally called and told him what we had been through. We were desperate! Thankfully, he came to our house, checked Cindy, and then contacted a pediatrician who agreed to meet us at the base hospital. Finally, we found someone to help us!

At the hospital, the pediatrician examined Cindy and then summoned other doctors, who worked with her for the remainder of the night. When her condition remained unchanged, she was finally admitted to the hospital at 8:30 A.M. Sunday, at which time Bruce and I returned home to get some much-needed rest. That day our bishop assisted Bruce in giving Cindy a blessing.

We hoped Cindy would recover quickly, but after five days the base hospital doctors were still unable to diagnose her problem. We were heartsick as she was transferred to Los Angeles Children's Hospital, where some of the country's best pediatric neurologists practiced. Upon our arrival there, a team of medical experts asked us dozens of questions and examined Cindy. One took a safety pin and gently ran the sharp point across the bottom of her foot. She didn't even flinch! Bruce and I wondered if there was something wrong with her central nervous system. But, of course, the doctors wouldn't speculate.

The next three weeks were one big series of tests—brain scans, spinal taps, blood samples, an EEG, and dozens more. While the doctors were testing Cindy, Bruce and I spent countless hours making the seventy-five-mile trip back and forth between Riverside and Los Angeles to visit her. The traffic was always heavy and the trip took about two hours each way, which greatly compounded the stress and frustration we felt each day. As we traveled we were always hopeful that Cindy had made some improvement, but each time we arrived at the hospital, all we encountered was bitter disappointment. It was almost more than I could bear to watch Bruce walk up and down the hospital corridor while he held Cindy and sang her name over and over again. "Cin-dy, oh Cin-dy," he would sing, but she never seemed to recognize her name or us. All she did was whimper or cry, and her muscle tone seemed to be weaker than that of a newborn baby. My heart ached for her.

One day, as I watched Bruce holding Cindy, I couldn't help but think, *This certainly isn't what Bruce and I expected when we married in 1967.* We expected to struggle then because Bruce had four years of college to complete, I had one year left, and we had two children by the time we both graduated in 1971. We expected difficulty then. But not now. Not this way, anyway.

Not only was it painful for me to see Cindy hurting every day, but it was difficult trying to give Michelle and Lara the attention they needed, trying to get ready for Christmas, and having Bruce work rotating shifts. In fact, it was so hard juggling our schedule with those things in between all our trips to the hospital that I thought, *If only we could take Cindy home, our lives would be so much easier.* It wasn't long before I discovered how wrong I was!

Although the doctors could not tell us the cause of Cindy's illness, show us how to treat her, or give us a prognosis, they finally released her three days after Christmas and twenty-one days after she had been admitted to L.A. Children's Hospital. What a happy day that was—that is, until we discovered how extensive her limitations really were and how difficult it was to care for her twenty-four hours a day. She no longer had any

*Lara and Michelle with Cindy
before she became disabled, 1972*

Cindy, about four years old, 1976

control of her head, trunk, legs, arms, hands, fingers, or tongue.
Consequently she couldn't sit, crawl, pull herself up to a stand-
ing position, hold her head up, hold a toy in her hands, or suck
from a bottle. In addition, her whole body was either very limp
or very stiff, and she still didn't recognize us.

Cindy's condition made life exceedingly difficult for our
family. First, she cried almost continually, which was extremely
nerve-racking and made each family member very irritable.
Second, because she could no longer suck, feeding her—which
took six to eight hours each day—was extraordinarily difficult
and frustrating. I had to squeeze her cheeks just to get her to
swallow any liquid, and it sometimes seemed that for every
spoonful of food I put into her mouth, two spoonfuls would
come back out. Then, if that weren't enough, Cindy slept only
about forty-five minutes each twenty-four hours. She didn't nap
at all during the day, and at night, if someone rocked her, she
dozed for a few minutes and then awakened and cried again.

This routine was so stressful and exhausting that after only five days we had Cindy admitted to the base hospital once again. Unfortunately, instead of it being a restful time for me, having her there was an emotionally draining experience. Each time I visited her she was dressed only in a diaper. She was cold and never had any blankets covering her. Even when the nurses had no other child to care for, they simply let her cry while they talked among themselves. When I asked them about their seeming disinterest, their response was simply, "She cries most of the time, and we can't pick up every crying baby."

It was almost unbearable for me to see Cindy that way. She looked so alone and so unloved. The last day she was there, I remember picking her up and walking across the large room to the window. Even the window was cold. As I held Cindy close to me, I looked heavenward, and with tears welling up in my eyes, I said aloud, "What are we going to do?" I paused, and as the tears flowed freely, I knew what we had to do. We had to take her home.

Bruce agreed. So, that day, we took Cindy home and committed ourselves to care for her there. We felt that even though she was nearly impossible to care for, at least at home she would know that we loved her and that someone cared.

In the days and weeks following Cindy's return from the hospital, the only time our family got any rest was when I kept her in the living room, away from the bedrooms. Nightly I would put her in her buggy, sit on the couch, lay my head on a pillow, and rock her back and forth with my foot. She didn't sleep very much and neither did I, but at least her crying quieted to a whimper as long as I rocked her back and forth. If I happened to fall asleep and quit rocking the buggy, however, she would immediately cry again. We couldn't believe she could survive with so little sleep.

The only real sleep I got was when Bruce, my visiting teachers, or other Relief Society sisters took turns pushing Cindy in her buggy outside the house while I slept inside during the day. How grateful I was for their compassionate service, as it helped me endure some very exhausting, discouraging, and stressful months.

Unexpected Relief

In addition to the help that others provided, I also received comfort from the Lord—comfort that came in a way I didn't expect.

It was a Sunday morning. Bruce had taken Michelle and Lara to Sunday School, and I was home alone with Cindy. I was tired—no, exhausted—and very discouraged. I just didn't know how I could go on much longer with so little sleep. So, almost in desperation, I decided to pray once again. Fortunately, Cindy was quiet, lying in her buggy, as I went into the living room and knelt by the couch. There, in a spirit of total submission to God, I pictured Him in my mind and poured out my soul to Him. There were no trite phrases, but a sincere conversation with Him. I told Him how tired and discouraged I was, that "if only I could get some sleep, that's all I want." I told Him how much time it took to care for Cindy, how much I loved her and wanted to keep her in our home. I told Him how much I loved Bruce and Michelle and Lara and that I just didn't seem to have any time or energy left for them after caring for Cindy. I explained to Him how Bruce did all the shopping and ran all the family errands, but I still didn't have enough time for everyone in the family. I told Him how frustrated I was. In short, I told Him how I really felt. I concluded my prayer with, "Heavenly Father, what do you expect of me? I need to know."

As I arose from my knees I felt consoled, but, for a reason I didn't recognize then, I also felt prompted to reread a chapter about prayer in the book *Spiritual Roots of Human Relations* by Stephen R. Covey. Without hesitation I randomly opened the book to page 157, where these words seemed to jump out at me: "I believe that *the Lord deals with his children largely in terms of their needs as he perceives them,* rather than their wants as they might perceive them. God's will is found in man's real needs, while man's will is generally embodied in man's wants." (Emphasis in original.) Never before had any words had the settling impact on me that those words did. I immediately felt a calming influence, but then I wondered, *What could our family need worse than I need sleep?* With that question, I began to list the things I thought we needed: More effective personal and family prayers, better family home evening planning and follow-through, better family cooperation, and daily scripture reading. I also listed skills I thought we needed to teach Michelle and Lara.

When Bruce came home from Sunday School, I told him about my experience and showed him my list of needs. He added the need to "properly fulfill Church assignments," and then we both agreed to commit ourselves to the things we had listed. For some reason, committing myself to doing the Lord's will had a calming influence on me, and I finally felt at peace about Cindy's illness. Although I didn't know how I was going to continually manage with so little sleep, I knew I could do whatever the Lord asked me to do. How grateful I am to have experienced that feeling of spiritual comfort, because it has helped me many times throughout my life.

At that point in time there were no immediate changes in Cindy, but there was a change in my devotion to the Lord. Although I had read the scriptures faithfully since my high school seminary days, I began reading them with much more purpose and intensity than ever before, and they began to have real meaning to me. One scripture that especially helped me was 1 Corinthians 10:13. As I read what living prophets said about that scripture, I realized that the Lord will never give people who are striving to be obedient any trial or temptation greater than their ability to withstand or overcome. That promise was very comforting to me. It gave me strength to know that even though what I was going through was difficult, the Lord would help me withstand the trial.

Another scripture that brought peace and understanding to my soul was Hebrews 5:8, where Paul, speaking of Christ, said: "Though he were a Son, yet learned he obedience by the things which he suffered." To me, that meant that even though Christ was the Son of God and obeyed His Father perfectly all the days of His life, even He had to taste the bitter and submit to Heavenly Father's will in order to be "made perfect." Even He had to learn personally that trials are given as opportunities for spiritual development and growth—growth that does not come with ease and comfort.

Besides reading the scriptures, I also began reading about how other people coped with difficult problems. I read about

Job, some of the early Saints, and several past prophets, but I was especially touched by Elder Spencer W. Kimball's account of the "anguish, terror, fear, and hopelessness" he felt as a twelve-year-old child. He recalled:

> There we were, eight of our mother's eleven, in our parents' bedroom. Our mother was dead. Our father was away. Our older brother Gordon sat in the chair holding our littlest sister while she died, with all of us youngsters around the chair frightened and praying and weeping. The doctor was miles away. His horse and buggy could not possibly have brought him there soon enough, and what could he do if he arrived? It seemed to be a combination of diphtheria and membraneous croup, and little Poche was literally choking to death. In terror, we watched the little body fight valiantly for air and life, then suddenly relax completely. The hard-fought battle was over. She had lost. Our older brother seemed to be reluctant to admit it was over. He held her for awhile, hoping hopelessly. And while we children convulsively held to each other in this traumatic experience, he tenderly carried the little lifeless body to the bed and covered it with a sheet, and there welled up in our hearts an almost uncontrollable anguish and a dark void and deep emptiness. ("Hope and Encouragement for Cancer Cure," pp. 244–45.)

In the same talk, Elder Kimball also related the heart-wrenching experience he and his wife had when their youngest child became paralyzed "with the dreaded infantile paralysis." He said:

> The family doctor did not recognize the symptoms, and our little three-year-old lay for days as we suffered with him. Finally, impatiently, we took little Eddie to another doctor who, on the second visit, got out his big book and compared the symptoms with the little fellow's aches and pains and fevers, and said: "You know, I am afraid this is poliomyelitis." . . .
>
>   In only hours, we were traveling through the night across the deserts of Arizona and California to take him to recog-

nized specialists. Our little one was taken from our arms, placed on a hospital truck, and whisked away to a fourth-story quarantine area. The suffering of our little fellow, his loneliness, his mother's telling him stories by the hour through the crack in the door, our huddling down under his window and agonizing as he cried in his fear and loneliness, is another story, as is also the many years of commuting to Los Angeles, the numerous operations, the therapy by his devoted mother, the metal braces from neck to toe, the casts, the crutches, the canes. (Ibid., p. 246.)

Knowing the heartache Spencer W. Kimball suffered throughout his life helped me understand that adversity comes to even the most righteous, which gave me strength to continue. Likewise, reading about the struggles of the Prophet Joseph Smith also gave me strength, and his afflictions began to take on a new personal meaning for me. For the first time in my life, I felt how desperately he wanted an answer when he pleaded with the Lord from Liberty Jail: "O God, where art thou?" (D&C 121:1.)

And then the Lord's answer meant more to me too (see D&C 121:7–46; 122). Those verses touched my inner soul and caused me to feel more love and compassion for the Prophet Joseph Smith than I had ever felt before. The fact that Joseph Smith was told that his afflictions would be "but a small moment" and that he later experienced all the adversities the Lord listed somehow gave me—with my comparatively small adversity—strength to continue. I finally understood what the Lord meant when He told the Prophet that trials and afflictions "give us experience" and are for our own good. Literally, our trials can be the motivation to help us rely on Jesus Christ—the only one to endure and overcome every possible adversity. They can help us see that no matter what we must endure, Christ endured even more. Then, as we humble ourselves and rely on Him, we discover that we can trust Him, that He loves us personally, and that He will comfort us and help us become more like Him.

Once I understood that process of humility-faith-comfort, I wanted to understand more fully other gospel principles. So I

began reading the scriptures and listening to general conference talks every day—and the more I read and listened, the
more I loved the Lord, His gospel, His prophets, and His children. Along with that there also came greater peace—a distinct
feeling that I was doing what the Lord wanted me to do and
that I would be able to accomplish whatever He required of
me. That peace and understanding gave me the strength to
cope with the adversities that were yet to come. Indeed, because of Cindy I had some important experiences that have
continued to affect me throughout my life.

Those experiences didn't remove or change any of the daily
struggles associated with caring for Cindy, however. She still
cried constantly, which annoyed everyone in the family, but it
was especially frustrating to me because I could never determine what made her cry. She was like a newborn baby who
couldn't communicate where she hurt. She still slept so poorly
that we hung blankets across the hallway to muffle any sounds
while she slept in her bedroom. Feeding her was still extremely
time-consuming. Every day was a struggle which tried everyone's patience.

After about six months Cindy finally recognized us and progressed to the point where she would quit crying if I held her.
So I held her in one arm while I cooked the meals, washed the
dishes, vacuumed or mopped the floors, sorted the clothes—
everything I could possibly do with one hand. It was tiring
carrying a fifteen-pound child who had no control of her head
or trunk, but it was certainly better than listening to her cry.

Heidi's Birth

When Cindy reached the point where she ate faster and was
a little less demanding, we decided to have another baby.
Consequently, Heidi was born in August 1974, and we were
overjoyed and thankful that she had a strong and healthy body.
After having Cindy, it no longer mattered to me that our fourth
child was not a boy. I was just grateful for a healthy baby.

I was anxious, however, about how I would be able to care

for her when Cindy demanded so much of my time. As it turned out, though, the Lord knew I needed a good baby, and that's exactly what Heidi was. She ate quickly and was satisfied in about a half hour. She napped well in the daytime and began sleeping through the night when she was six weeks old. When she wasn't eating or sleeping, she was content to watch me from her infant seat or from the floor. She even allowed a neighbor to hold her in church while I held Cindy and while Bruce sat on the stand. In short, Heidi demanded very little of my attention.

Although that was a blessing that I needed, I often worried about Heidi's lack of one-on-one attention from me. I knew I couldn't have done things differently, but I still worried about my relationship with her.

Moving to Camarillo

Early in 1976, because of the difficulties of caring for Cindy, and because of the reality that Bruce would need to spend two years on a remote assignment without the family, we decided to leave the Air Force. That decision caused us great concern because it meant we would have to find another job and another home.

Finding another job was hard, but the most frustrating part was finding an affordable home close to the new job Bruce accepted in Ventura, California. Though there didn't seem to be a home for us, we finally found one in Camarillo, a beautiful city near Ventura. Although we hadn't considered living there, I know that is where the Lord wanted us to live.

We had lived in Camarillo only two months when I learned I was pregnant. Unfortunately I developed complications that resulted in a miscarriage, a short hospital stay, and some seemingly insurmountable medical expenses. Although the medical expense concerned me, the most disconcerting part of the miscarriage was how I felt afterward. I was saddened and depressed for several weeks because I really wanted another baby. It was fun having Heidi—who ate, slept, ran, and played in normal ways—and I felt ready to have another one.

Heather's Birth

Almost a year after my miscarriage, and nearly six weeks before our fifth child was actually due, I found myself in the labor room of a local hospital. I was bleeding, but was fairly comfortable because there were no contractions. Suddenly my obstetrician took Bruce outside my room and said, "The only way to save the baby's life is to take it cesarean—immediately!"

Just moments before, Bruce and I had been talking about finding baby clothes, setting up the crib, and locating people to help us with our four children if indeed this baby were born early. Since our other children had normal deliveries, there was never any thought about this one being any different. We were aware that the doctor had been monitoring the baby's heartbeat, but we were unaware of his great concern.

When Bruce came back into the labor room, he told me what the doctor had just said. At first the word *cesarean* frightened me, but after being reassured by my doctor and Bruce, I quickly concluded that it must be done. Immediately I was given an anesthetic and wheeled off to the operating room. Within minutes we had a cute little four-pound fifteen-ounce baby girl.

Soon after Heather was born, my doctor told Bruce, "Seventy years ago we would have lost both mother and child under these circumstances." At that moment we were especially grateful, not only for the blessing of life, but also that Heather was strong and healthy for her size. Although she had a slight case of jaundice, she didn't have any problems that would cause undue concern.

During the week I stayed in the hospital, I had several worries. One, Heather had to remain in an incubator, and because I nursed her it was necessary to weigh her before and after each feeding to make sure she was getting enough milk. For me, all of the monitoring and worry about her growth took some of the enjoyment out of having a new baby. Another worry was that my obstetrician told me I shouldn't lift anything for one month. I wondered how I would be able to care for Cindy, since she needed to be held to be fed and had to be moved or lifted many times each day.

Other concerns came as I thought about the needs of each family member. I was especially apprehensive about Heidi's continuing lack of individual attention, but I was also troubled by the fact that she wasn't ready to be toilet-trained before Heather came. And perhaps the most urgent concern was that as Heidi began to talk, she seemed to imitate Cindy's guttural sounds. I had previously spoken to professionals about the problem, and they had counseled me to take her to a speech therapist if she didn't improve in the next few months. How would I ever find time to help Heidi now that I had to care for a premature baby, a severely handicapped child, Michelle and Lara, and a husband? Everything seemed so overwhelming and nearly impossible to do.

Going Home

When Heather was a week old, I was released from the hospital. However, because of Heather's size and jaundiced condition, she had to stay in the hospital incubator an additional week. That made it especially difficult for the family, as I had to travel back and forth to the hospital every three hours to feed her.

What a happy day when we finally took her home! Not only was it a homecoming for Heather, but it was also Michelle's ninth birthday. Everyone was excited and especially anxious to hold Heather, but no one could believe how tiny she was. A baby who weighs less than five pounds is so little and seems so fragile.

CHAPTER 2

Bearing One Another's Burdens

Shortly after Cindy became handicapped, I discovered two important truths. One, that regardless of the adversity, the ultimate source of peace and healing of troubled hearts is the Savior. And two, that a person occasionally feels the Savior's healing touch directly from Him, but most often it comes either through or because of another person. President Spencer W. Kimball expressed it this way: "God does notice us, and he watches over us. But it is usually through another person that he meets our needs." ("The Abundant Life," p. 4.)

That certainly was the case when we moved into the Camarillo Second Ward. There, I often felt the strength and support I needed from the Savior simply because members chose to obey the voice of the Spirit and "bear one another's burdens" (Mosiah 18:8). Actually, the help and caring began the day we moved into our new home when a sister in the ward stopped by our house and voluntarily took Michelle and Lara to Primary. That was meaningful to me, but it was just a small trickle in the flood of kindness and assistance we would yet receive from the wonderful people in that ward.

The first service of major proportions was rendered soon after Heather was born. Because I couldn't lift anything for a month, I needed assistance caring for Cindy every day. Although Bruce was able to arrange his work schedule so he could help me much of the time, he couldn't be home after school—a time when the lifting problem seemed insurmountable. The problem didn't remain for long, though. Two young women came to our home, lifted Cindy out of her school bus, pulled her up our nine front steps, and took her out of her wheelchair—each school day for a month. What an enormous burden was lifted from my shoulders, and what a blessing it was to our family! Each girl helped me feel the peace of the Savior through her service, and each one helped our family bear burdens that were impossible for us to overcome by ourselves.

Visiting Teachers Who Cared

Another event that helped me understand how important it is to "bear one another's burdens" occurred about five months later, around Christmastime. Heather had been developing normally and nearly on schedule—lifting her head, smiling, rolling over, and grasping things in her hands. Then, for no explainable reason, she stopped doing those things. First, she quit rolling over from her back to her stomach. Then, a couple of weeks later, she quit rolling over from her stomach to her back. After that it seemed as if she wasn't holding her head up as well as before, and I even thought she began posturing her hands like Cindy. I became concerned and took her to see our pediatrician.

Because the changes in Heather's muscle control were subtle, our pediatrician could see nothing wrong with her. Unconvinced, I made an appointment to see a physical therapist. Several days before the appointment, my visiting teachers came by, and during the course of our conversation they asked how my family was doing. Without any particular alarm, I mentioned that I was a little concerned about Heather's development and that I was taking her to see a physical therapist the following Friday. Little did I realize, but at that moment the "still small voice" whispered to those wonderful sisters that I would need help on Friday. So, acting on that prompting by the Spirit, one visiting teacher volunteered to watch Heidi, and the other one later secretly called Bruce and arranged to get a key to our house so she could clean our kitchen while I was gone.

Friday finally came. As I drove Heather to the clinic, I had a sick feeling in my stomach, a lump in my throat, and a prayer in my heart. I was trying to muster the courage to accept that which I had already suspected.

The therapist was still busy with another patient, so Heather and I waited for what seemed like an eternity. In reality, it was only about ten minutes. When the therapist was finally ready, I laid Heather down on a large mat on the floor and the therapist began a series of tests. After about five minutes of watching Heather fail to respond in normal ways with her head, trunk, and hands, the therapist confirmed my worst fears and said, "Heather is definitely developmentally delayed and appears to exhibit symptoms of cerebral palsy." I don't remember anything the therapist said after that. All I could think about was getting out of that place and finding "a little corner of the world" where I could go cry and pour out my soul to God. As I put Heather in our van, the thought came to me that I should go directly to Bruce's work and not wait until he came home that evening to tell him about Heather.

I really couldn't remember how to get to Bruce's office from where I was, but with a continuing sick feeling in my stomach and tears streaming down my face, I ventured out to find him. It seemed like a very long drive, and I could barely see the road through my tears, but I finally arrived at Bruce's office. Thankfully, he saw me drive up so I didn't have to get out of the van. He came directly out, and I told him the news. At first, neither one of us said very much. All we could do was cry—and we had a good one! Bruce finally broke the silence and said, "Heather is such a cute little girl, and she seemed so healthy. How can we care for two handicapped children? This just isn't fair. It isn't fair to Heather, and it isn't fair to the rest of us. What about Michelle, Lara, and Heidi? How will we ever give them the time, love, and attention they need?"

There were so many questions, but there were no answers. After about an hour, we had a heartfelt prayer together in the van, and I left for home. On the way, I cried, wondered, and pleaded with the Lord, "Why another handicapped child? Can't we learn everything we need to learn from just one? Cindy already takes so much time to feed; how am I going to be able to care for her and Heather and still have enough time and energy for my other children? Heavenly Father, please help me deal with this."

I finally arrived home, and what I experienced next I shall never forget. As I opened the front door, I was immediately hit by the aroma of freshly baked bread. Sure enough, in the kitchen on top of the stove were four loaves of bread. Then it suddenly dawned on me. The dishes were done, the kitchen counters were spotless, the floor was mopped and waxed, there was a new tablecloth (which was not mine) on the kitchen table, and the stove and refrigerator were clean. The kitchen was immaculate! Somehow my heart wasn't quite as heavy. Then I walked into the living room to set Heather's infant seat on the floor. There, the floor was vacuumed, the furniture was dusted, and on the television was a new vase containing a beautiful bouquet of freshly cut flowers.

With a less heavy heart, I went upstairs. There, I discovered the beds had been made, and the bedrooms and bathrooms were as spotless and shining as the living room and the kitchen were. The only thing that was out of place was all the folded laundry sitting on Michelle's bed. My entire house was clean and all my laundry was done—all at the same time!

As I entered my bedroom to pray, my previously heavy heart had now been filled with gratitude and love—gratitude for the gospel and an immense love for my visiting teachers, who had followed the promptings of the Spirit and asked five other sisters to help them! Although their cleaning my house didn't change anything about Heather's handicap, it helped me focus on something outside my immediate feelings of hurt and pain, and it helped me see that I really did have blessings to be thankful for. In a very real sense, it lightened my load and, in the process, taught me once again that the way we help each other is by serving and "bearing one another's burdens that they may be light." How grateful I am to have learned that lesson, for I believe it is central to the entire gospel plan.

Our New Car

During much of the time we lived in Camarillo, Bruce served as the priests quorum adviser in our ward. He was responsible for thirty-three priests, and he sincerely loved each one. Among other things, he went to their football games, coached their church basketball team, made cookies and special birthday cakes for them, helped them build road show props, visited the missionaries with them, and helped them collect and deliver food for the needy. In short, Bruce taught them how to serve by setting an example and by taking them through the process of serving.

As he helped them learn the sweet feeling that comes when we lovingly help our fellowmen, they demonstrated the things they learned by restoring our car. Shortly after we found out about Heather's handicap, Bruce hurt his back while lifting Cindy. During his recovery, as Jean Taylor described in a *New Era* article,

> The members of the priests quorum . . . carefully hoisted their adviser, Brother Bruce Erickson, onto a chair and carried him to the front door of his home. As he looked outside, Brother Erickson's eyes opened wide in surprise— there sat his 1966 Nova, a huge red ribbon draped across the hood. And that wasn't the only thing different about the car . . .
>
> In a specially called quorum meeting, 11 priests sat discussing a service project idea. It would be different—and better—than any they had undertaken before. Quorum leaders Jordan Allgood and Kevin Barker made the plans for a restoration of their adviser's decrepit '66 Chevy with the rest of the quorum. They all enthusiastically agreed that the project would be kept a secret from Brother Erickson.
>
> In order to obtain the keys to the car, the young men decided to take Sister Erickson into their confidence.
>
> "They told me that if I would give them the keys to the Nova, they would leave another car in its place so Bruce would have a way to get to work," she explained.
>
> After Church the next Sunday, Brother Erickson was startled to see that his battered old Nova had disappeared and in its place was an even more beat-up vehicle.
>
> "Just trust me," his wife told him. "Everything will be all right. Somebody needed to borrow the car."
>
> The following week was filled with action. The boys spent

over 50 man-hours preparing the car for painting. All the dents were filled in, the finish was sanded, and then the exterior was painted a metallic blue at a local body shop. The boys removed all chrome, trim, lights, etc., in preparation for the paint job (and later replaced them). One of the boys then pinstriped the car to give it a finished, professional look.

They added small chrome mud flaps to make sure their adviser's car had the "in look." The old radio antenna was removed and replaced with a new antenna, and one priest donated a radio and rear speakers. The boys also changed the air filter, painted the air cleaner, and changed the gas-line filter.

All chrome was cleaned and waxed, and the tires, floor mats, and dashboard were cleaned with a special cleaner to restore them to a like-new appearance. One ward member who owns a carpet store donated a piece of leftover carpet and showed the boys how to install it. A 10-inch dent in the rear bumper was almost totally straightened with a hydraulic jack.

The time and money for the project was donated entirely by the boys themselves. Jordan was the leader of the "restoration movement," having previously restored a 1968 Mustang.

After the car was ready, the boys went together to the Erickson home. Brother Erickson had injured his back a short time before and was lying flat in bed when the knock came at the door.

Sister Erickson told them he couldn't come to the door, so the young men went into his room, lifted him onto a chair, and carefully carried him to the front door.

In front of the house was the scarcely recognizable Nova.

"I couldn't believe it was my car," Brother Erickson said. "Those young men—I didn't know they cared that much about me. They thought up the project and carried it out entirely by themselves."

It isn't hard to care about an adviser like Brother Erickson, explained the quorum members, "because he cares about us." (Taylor, "The Case of the Missing Car," p. 45.)

Bruce really did care about "his" priests. Every day he thought about ways he could personally help them and teach them to serve their fellowmen. He was so involved in their lives that one day after I told someone that Bruce and I had five girls and no boys, Heidi said, "Yes you do, Mom. Daddy has his priests."

Other Gifts

As a result of my miscarriage and Heather's medical bills, we found ourselves in serious financial trouble. We lived off of our year's supply of food, and we lived as frugally as we possibly could, but it wasn't sufficient. We received financial support from our extended families, and Bruce got a second job cleaning offices every evening, but we were still unable to meet all of our financial obligations. Not only did that concern us, it also caused a great deal of stress in our marriage.

Although it appeared impossible for us to get out of debt, once again because of the wonderful people in the Camarillo Second Ward we were able to survive. Not only were we rescued from bankruptcy by a wonderful home teacher, but we were also the recipients of hundreds of individual acts of kindness and dozens of service projects involving many people. We were given money, food, clothing, furniture, gasoline, and new tires for our van. One sister made us a main dish for dinner each Monday evening for an entire year, "to lighten your load on family home evening night." Another sister brought us freshly baked bread every week for a year. Several other sisters made me and my five daughters skirts, blouses, dresses, and pants for Christmas, Easter, and Mother's Day. A brother gave Bruce two nice suits. The youth of the ward refinished some furniture, cleaned our house and yard, weeded our flower beds, and tilled our garden. In addition, when we moved, they moved furniture and painted our entire house. On another occasion, a married couple stayed with our children while Bruce and I spent thirty-six hours in Los Angeles together. It was the longest we had been together without the children in six years.

There are not words in our language to adequately describe the gratitude I feel toward the Lord for allowing our family the privilege of living in the Camarillo Second Ward. Because I was there, I learned how true charity and love fit into the gospel plan. I learned that, as President Kimball said, God does notice us, but it is usually through another person that He meets our needs. I learned that faith in Jesus Christ and genuine service to our fellowmen are necessary steps toward exaltation. I learned that even though it is difficult for proud people—as we were—to accept service, it is just as important to have receivers as it is givers. And finally, because of my experiences there I feel closer to heaven and have a better insight as to what heaven might be like, as I was able to feel the spirit of peace, love, unity, diligence, and strength from people who helped our family survive three very difficult years.

CHAPTER 3

Adversity Continues

Heather is definitely developmentally delayed and appears to exhibit symptoms of cerebral palsy." Those words continued to ring in my ears for many weeks after the therapist spoke them. My heart ached and I shed many tears as I agonized over those words. Knowing others cared gave me the strength to struggle on, but it didn't alleviate my grief and pain.

I prayed and read the scriptures almost continually, but there were so many unanswered questions: Why would the Lord send us a second handicapped child when one was so difficult and time-consuming to care for? Hadn't we already been tested to our limit when Cindy got sick? Hadn't we already learned about faith and trusting in the Lord? Hadn't we kept our covenants? How would we have enough time for Michelle, Lara, and Heidi?

Then, more than a month after Heather's problem was identified, there were the most nagging and puzzling questions of all: Why wouldn't peace and comfort come? It had come to me within two weeks after we brought Cindy home from the hospital. Why wouldn't solace come now? Why did the pain seem to intensify with the passage of time? Why did I feel abandoned by the Lord when I so desperately sought comfort from Him? Why did I have to hurt so deeply? Why was there no relief?

On one especially difficult day, in an attitude of prayer and meditation I tearfully pleaded with the Lord aloud, "What do you want me to learn from this experience? What more can we learn about faith and trusting in Jesus Christ? Please give me understanding and peace."

After my prayer I began reading a general conference talk about faith and how it operates. The speaker referred to Elder Matthew Cowley and how he was able to pronounce priesthood blessings of life and healing upon the Maori people because of their great faith. Upon reading Elder Cowley's name, there immediately flashed in my mind a picture of a fireside I attended while I was in high school, where I heard a recording of Elder Cowley's talk on miracles. I remembered how the Spirit bore witness to me as a teenager at that fireside that faith is real, that the priesthood is a powerful blessing in our lives, and that miracles really do happen.

As I contemplated the specific examples of healing given by Elder Cowley, I remembered his telling about blessing a man whose body was being prepared for burial, and the man arose! I remembered his blessing a young boy, who was in an iron lung dying of polio, to be made whole—and he was! I even remembered his telling about parents who took their child to Elder Cowley and asked him to give the child a name and a blessing—and at the same time to give the child his sight because he had been blind since birth—and the boy regained his sight.

Because those examples were so vivid to me, I decided to find and read a copy of Elder Cowley's talk. I soon discovered that my memory of the fireside talk was quite accurate. I also found the following pertinent words:

> Now, except ye believe as a child, you can't receive these blessings. We have to have the faith of a child in order to believe in these things, especially when you reach college age and your minds are so full of skepticism and doubt. I guess there are some things that you should doubt, but you can become as little children in these things. Miracles are commonplace, brothers and sisters. . . .
>
> . . . Sometimes I wonder if we do enough in our administration of the sick. . . .
>
> Sometimes we rush in, administer to a person, rush out

and say, "Well, he won't make it. I know he won't." . . . Sometimes I wonder, if we have a little time, if we shouldn't do a little fasting. "This kind cometh not out save by fasting and by prayer."

A little over a year ago a couple came into my office carrying a little boy. The father said to me, "My wife and I have been fasting for two days, and we've brought our little boy up for a blessing. You are the one we've been sent to." I said, "What's the matter with him?" They said he was born blind, deaf and dumb, no co-ordination of his muscles, couldn't even crawl at the age of five years. I said to myself, "This is it. 'This kind cometh not out save by fasting and by prayer.' " I had implicit faith in the fasting and the prayers of those parents. I blessed that child, and a few weeks later I received a letter: "Brother Cowley, we wish you could see our little boy now. He's crawling. When we throw a ball across the floor he races after it on his hands and knees. He can see. When we clap our hands over his head he jumps. He can hear." Medical science had laid the burden down. God had taken over. The little boy was rapidly recovering or really getting what he'd never had. ("Miracles," pp. 40, 42–43.)

As I pondered all the examples of faith and blessings found in Elder Cowley's talk, a distinct thought came into my mind and heart: *Bruce holds the same priesthood as Elder Cowley, and I know I have faith, so why can't I ask that Heather be healed? Surely the Lord could do it!* I knew it was a bold request, but since the thought had come the same way I had previously experienced inspiration come into my mind and heart, and since I felt I had been obedient and submissive to God's will, I believed it was a righteous desire. Consequently I sincerely concluded that the thought was not just wishful thinking but truly was inspired. So we decided Bruce would administer to Heather in six weeks.

During that time, while we watched Heather continue to lose muscle control, Bruce and I persisted with life in a normal way, except that we fasted more often than usual. We prayed for strength and understanding and for Heather to be made whole, always asking, "Thy will be done," but always knowing that nothing is impossible with the Lord. It was a time of great anxiety for me as I looked forward to the day when Heather would be blessed.

We approached that day in an attitude of much prayer and fasting—just as Elder Cowley had suggested. As our bishop and other priesthood brethren came to our home, I was anxious, but I remember thinking how grateful I was for the gospel and for the blessing of having the priesthood on the earth. I listened carefully to Bruce's words as he sealed the anointing and pronounced the blessing. It was beautiful. Bruce said that Heather would bring love and peace and joy into our home, but to my great disappointment, he said nothing about her being healed. I felt confused and even questioned Bruce's faith. Wasn't it the Spirit that had given me the thought that Heather could be healed? Why did I get that feeling if it wasn't to be?

Since Heather wasn't healed after much prayer and fasting, in the weeks following her blessing I began to question my own ability to recognize inspiration. I also began to ask many new questions: Why, when a person asks in faith and the request seems to have been inspired, is the request denied? Why doesn't He who raised the dead, healed the leper, the blind, and the crippled in His day do the same for Heather? Heather was a child of God just as those people were. If Matthew Cowley could use the priesthood to heal the faithful, why couldn't Bruce use the priesthood to heal Heather? And again, what new lessons could we learn from having another severely handicapped child in our home? A Book of Mormon prophet declared, "Ye receive no witness until after the trial of your faith" (Ether 12:6). Surely our faith had been tried with Cindy, and Heather came *after* Cindy. Didn't we deserve to have at least one of them healed?

As Heather entered her eleventh month of life, I continued to pray and to struggle with those same thoughts and questions. I also watched her continue to deteriorate in her development. She never rolled over again. She no longer grasped or held anything in her hands, and she had less head and body control than she had when she was born. In fact, the only way she could be held upright in our arms was if we steadied her head and back the same way one would hold a newborn baby.

Emotionally it was a most difficult time for me. I remembered how Heather, before her illness, had lain on her stomach in her buggy and lifted her head up so high that we could see her bright blue eyes peeking over the side. The realization that she would never do that again caused me great heartache. So did the realization that in this life Heather, like Cindy, probably would never crawl, walk, talk, or feed herself—or, for that matter, do anything for herself.

In addition to those heartaches there were many physical and emotional strains that I had to deal with every day. There were difficulties associated with caring for two handicapped children plus Michelle, Lara, and Heidi. I was trying to maintain a stable home and work on a shaky relationship with Bruce. There were the physical and emotional frustrations associated with Cindy's and Heather's eating and sleeping habits. Initially, because all of their food had to be specially prepared and because neither one of them could swallow properly, it took about seven to eight hours a day just to feed them, and neither one slept well at night. I was always tired, and Bruce and I never seemed to understand each other's frustrations. Besides that, I was still struggling to understand why Heather hadn't been healed. I spent considerable time reading the scriptures, listening to and reading general conference talks, and praying and then pondering about the things I had read and heard and felt. I often cried aloud as I poured out my soul to my Heavenly Father for understanding and peace.

In my heart I knew I needed to "trust in the Lord . . . and lean not unto [my] own understanding" (Proverbs 3:5). I knew that my adversity was "but a small moment" (D&C 121:7). I knew that the Lord doesn't give His children more than they can bear (see 1 Corinthians 10:13). I knew that even Christ "learned . . . obedience by the things which He suffered" (Hebrews 5:8), that even His request that the cup pass from Him didn't seem to be answered (see Matthew 26:39). I even knew that the Lord loved me. I understood adversity logically, but I still couldn't find peace and comfort.

Then one day, nearly eighteen months after Heather became ill, I finally felt what I sought so desperately. It came as I was reading a conference talk called "The Refiner's Fire" by Elder James E. Faust. He said:

Some years ago President David O. McKay told from this pulpit of the experience of some of those in the Martin handcart company. Many of these early converts had emigrated from Europe and were too poor to buy oxen or horses and a wagon. They were forced by their poverty to pull handcarts containing all of their belongings across the plains by their own brute strength. President McKay relates an occurrence which took place some years after the heroic exodus: "A teacher, conducting a class, said it was unwise ever to attempt, even to permit them [the Martin handcart company] to come across the plains under such conditions.

"[According to a class member,] some sharp criticism of the Church and its leaders was being indulged in for permitting any company of converts to venture across the plains with no more supplies or protection than a handcart caravan afforded.

"An old man in the corner . . . sat silent and listened as long as he could stand it, then he arose and said things that no person who heard him will ever forget. His face was white with emotion, yet he spoke calmly, deliberately, but with great earnestness and sincerity.

"In substance [he] said, 'I ask you to stop this criticism. You are discussing a matter you know nothing about. Cold historic facts mean nothing here, for they give no proper interpretation of the questions involved. Mistake to send the Handcart Company out so late in the season? Yes. But I was in that company and my wife was in it and Sister Nellie Unthank whom you have cited was there, too. We suffered beyond anything you can imagine and many died of exposure and starvation, but did you ever hear a survivor of that company utter a word of criticism? *Not one of that company ever apostatized or left the Church, because everyone of us came through with the absolute knowledge that God lives for we became acquainted with him in our extremities.*

" 'I have pulled my handcart when I was so weak and weary from illness and lack of food that I could hardly put one foot ahead of the other. I have looked ahead and seen a patch of sand or a hill slope and I have said, I can go only that far and there I must give up, for I cannot pull the load through it.' " He continues: " 'I have gone on to that sand and when I reached it, the cart began pushing me. I have looked back many times to see who was pushing my cart, but my eyes saw no one. I knew then that the angels of God were there.

" 'Was I sorry that I chose to come by handcart? No. Neither then nor any minute of my life since. *The price we paid to become acquainted with God was a privilege to pay, and I am thankful that I was privileged to come in the Martin Handcart Company.*' " (*Relief Society Magazine,* January 1948, p.8.) ("The Refiner's Fire, p. 53, emphasis in original.)

The words "the price we paid to become acquainted with God" sank deeply into my mind and heart, and the Spirit bore testimony to me that I had my answer. *Adversity, obedience, and sacrifice was the price I paid to become acquainted with God.* I was so overcome with the Spirit when I understood that. I needed Heather's illness to remain even after I received the testimony that she could be healed—so that I would sacrifice my pride and diligently strive to know the Lord. I finally realized there is a significant difference between "*could* be healed" and "*would* be healed," and I also realized that in order to progress spiritually, what I needed was to allow the Lord to do with my life as He wanted, not what I thought I wanted. In the words of King Benjamin, I needed to willingly "submit to all things which the Lord [saw] fit to inflict upon" me (see Mosiah 3:19).

As my thoughts raced back over the previous eighteen months of struggle, I remembered the times I had pleaded with the Lord to "please help me through this day"—and He did. I remembered the conference talks I had heard and read, the scriptures I had read, the prophets I had become acquainted with through the written word, the hours praying "continually," the days I had made it through with very little sleep, and the many people who had helped us bear our burdens, that they might be light (see Mosiah 18:8). All those months I was asking the Lord, "How can we take care of two severely handicapped children?"—and He was showing me each day. I was looking for a big miracle, and He was helping me live every hour of every day. That was the miracle! As I remembered all the ways the Lord had blessed my family and me, my soul was filled with love, peace, and gratitude. It was an indescribable feeling. It was also amazing how comforting it was for me to finally accept Heather's handicap completely and to find purpose in the priesthood blessing Bruce had given her many months earlier.

One passage of scripture that became especially meaningful to me during that time was Mark 14:37-41. Those words gave me a personal feel for an infinitesimal part of Christ's suffering. His pain was so intense that He asked His closest friends— Peter, James, and John—to "tarry ye here, and watch." He wanted their moral support. Then, "he went forward a little, and fell on the ground, and prayed that, if it were possible, the hour might pass from him. And he said, Abba, Father, all things are possible unto thee; take away this cup from me: nevertheless not what I will, but what thou wilt." Three times He asked His apostles to watch with Him, and three times they fell asleep. (See Mark 14:32–42.) As I read those verses, my heart ached for Christ. He was the only perfect being who ever lived on the earth, and yet He couldn't get His friends to help Him when He so desperately wanted it. I thought, *At least I have had great assistance from friends and loved ones during my hours of trial!*

When I considered those verses further, I saw two other personal applications. First, knowing that Christ asked that the cup might be removed, perhaps I was not such a bad person for asking Heavenly Father to remove my adversity by healing Heather when I knew how difficult it would be to care for her. And second, I somehow needed to submit my will to the Father's, even though it would be difficult—after all, submission to God's will is a requirement of all who wish to live with Him in His kingdom. It was even a requirement for Christ.

Moving to Salt Lake City

In 1979, due to serious financial problems, Bruce accepted a job offer from a firm in Salt Lake City. Although it meant we would receive an increase in pay, it was difficult for me to leave the wonderful people in Camarillo. They had helped our family survive three trying years, and I loved them dearly. In fact, my love was so deep that as we moved I felt as if my heart would break—as if I was going someplace but really belonged somewhere else. I literally cried all the way to Utah—and for many months afterward.

Moving meant not only separating from very dear friends, but also explaining Cindy's and Heather's "disease" all over again—not only to a new set of interested neighbors and ward members, but to a new set of doctors, nurses, and medical personnel too. I usually didn't mind doing that, but sometimes it was annoying, and occasionally it brought back painful feelings all over again.

Mark's Birth

Very early in 1981, when Heather was almost four years old, I learned I was expecting another baby. Everyone was excited—everyone, that is, except me. I was devastated. I had no idea how I would care for a new baby and two severely handicapped children and still give Michelle, Lara, Heidi, and Bruce the time and attention they needed. Although I knew the Lord would help me do what needed to be done, I didn't want to have another baby. Life already was difficult to cope with on a daily basis. Nevertheless, because of everyone else's excitement and because the whole family promised to help me, I soon accepted the reality of the pregnancy and actually became excited too. I remember that Heather was especially excited. She loved babies, she loved dolls, and she loved to listen to us talk about our new baby that was due in July.

Mark was born on July 25, 1981, while we were living in Ogden, Utah. What a day of rejoicing among our family and friends! Not only was he a beautiful, strong, and healthy baby, but everyone was thrilled about our having a boy after five girls. Our family loved him dearly, and each of our children loved to hold him. Even Heather and Cindy loved to have someone help them hold him.

Although it was wonderful having Mark in our home, it was a trying time for our family. Besides all the stresses that go along with having a new baby, about a week after Mark was born the car that the young men in Camarillo had restored was stolen and never found. In addition, Bruce was spending many hours after work each day building our new house in Centerville. It was especially hard for me to have him gone every evening.

Even though Mark was a good baby and Michelle, Lara, and Heidi helped me a lot, it was difficult caring for Cindy and Heather and a new baby too. Since I was the only one who could feed them, and since it took me more than eight hours to do that, about the only things I accomplished each day were feeding, bathing, and changing diapers. It seemed like someone was always crying and needed something only I could give. Indeed, it was a monotonous, frustrating, and emotionally draining routine.

Not only was that procedure stressful for me and Bruce, it was also trying for Michelle, Lara, and Heidi. Besides getting very little of their parents' undivided attention, they had to give up time children usually spend playing and doing things with friends in order to help us supply the basic necessities of life for the others. They also had to give up family outings, opportunities to develop their own talents, shopping with Mom, and many other normal family activities. It truly was a time of great sacrifice for them.

Michelle, who was thirteen when Mark was born, was especially helpful to me—so much so that I don't think I could have survived without her. She was big enough to hold any of the three helpless ones, and she was great at doing household chores. She also was sensitive to my personal needs, as she would often volunteer to watch all the children so I could take a nap or run a quick errand. She just seemed to sense how much I needed her help. Truly our all-knowing Heavenly Father knew what I would need when He sent us daughters first. What a blessing they have been!

When Mark was one month old we moved into our newly built home in Centerville. It was a time for enjoying an improved financial situation and our first unrented home, and for Bruce and me to celebrate our fourteenth wedding anniversary. It also was a time for making new friends, adjusting to new schools, and watching Mark grow and develop.

In fact, because of Cindy's and Heather's developmental problems, it was a time for all of us to enjoy every normal movement Mark made. With great satisfaction we watched him learn to smile and interact with people. It was fun having a baby who "worked," who we could hold in our arms without supporting his head and trunk. We watched him learn to grasp objects in each hand and then pass them from one hand to the other; we watched him learn to roll over and scoot around; and we watched him make his "jumper" that hung in the living-room doorway bounce high off the floor. It's amazing how it takes seeing a handicapped body like Cindy's and Heather's to fully appreciate the blessing of having a body that works correctly. We were so grateful Mark was developing normally!

For me, that gratitude turned to fear shortly before Christmas 1981. I first noticed that whenever I put Mark in his jumper, he didn't seem to be able to hold his head up as well as he had previously. I watched his every move, and a few days later it seemed that he wasn't jumping as high as before. Not knowing whether these changes were a reality or a figment of my imagination, I told Bruce about my concerns. I was hoping he would tell me that I was imagining things and not to worry. Unfortunately he couldn't tell me anything definite, so for the next month Bruce and I waited, watched, and wondered whether Mark's development would retrogress like Heather's and Cindy's had done years earlier at Christmastime. I remember that during the entire month of December I had a huge knot in my stomach, and I felt like crying most of the time. How could we have another handicapped child? How could our beautiful, robust, healthy-looking boy be handicapped too? I was heartsick.

Friends tried to be supportive by saying, "Oh, Heavenly Father wouldn't send you another handicapped child," or, "Mark's too big and strong to have the same problem as your girls." I appreciated their concern, but I didn't believe them. I *wanted* to believe them, but because I had watched every move Mark made for nearly a month and couldn't see any increase in normal development, I knew deep inside that he was retrogressing. Then, when he quit scooting around and when he stopped exchanging objects from one hand to another, I knew that he, too, like Cindy and Heather, would probably live his mortal life in a handicapped body. I took him to see our pediatrician, and he confirmed my worst fears.

This time, not only were Bruce and I devastated but so were Michelle, Lara, and Heidi. They were older now and had enough firsthand experience to know how much time, energy, and work would be involved in caring for another handicapped child. They just couldn't understand how this could happen again—and to our only boy. We as parents couldn't understand either.

I remember very clearly one particular Sunday afternoon shortly after our doctor diagnosed Mark's condition. Lara called me into her bedroom. It was evident she had been crying, so I sat down beside her and asked, "What is the matter, Lara?" With tears running down her face she said, "Mom, I have been praying every day since you told us you were pregnant that our baby wouldn't be handicapped, and now he is. I just don't understand." I put my arm around her, hugged her, and, with tears welling up in my eyes, replied, "I don't understand either, Lara." How do you answer a child when you, the parent, don't have an answer? All we could do was cry together.

Feeding, More Feeding, and Other Frustrations

The years after Mark became handicapped were filled with many new challenges. In addition to those that come with raising healthy children, Bruce and I now faced the challenge of caring for three severely handicapped children who were totally dependent on someone else for everything. Occasionally Bruce and I would discuss the possibility of putting them in a special home for the handicapped, but each discussion—and it was always brief—ended with the same conclusion: since none of the children was destructive, as long as we could physically care for them in our own home we would do that. It was a challenge that was emotionally and physically draining and that required the help, cooperation, and sacrifice of each family member in order to survive.

Even though there were many difficult situations to face,

most of our family's challenges were associated with having to feed Cindy, Heather, and Mark three or more meals every day. It was a difficult task, as it was time-consuming and required special equipment to prepare their food, as well as Herculean strength and energy to hold them. Since they were unable to chew, all of their food had to be either mashed or pureed. Then, because of their tongue thrust and inability to swallow properly, at least half of what was put into their mouths was spit out and needed to be put back into their mouths again and again and again. Sometimes they even choked on their food. Eventually I was able to reduce the food preparation and feeding time to about two-and-a-half hours every meal—or more than seven hours every day—but even that didn't leave much time to do much of anything with anyone else, which was something that worried me every day.

Another reason it was difficult to feed Heather and Cindy was that, because it was easier and less time-consuming for me, I held them on my lap while I fed them. That sapped my strength and energy, and it made my shoulders and back ache so severely that I was physically and emotionally drained at the end of every day.

It wasn't very enjoyable watching them eat either. Their mashed or pureed food never looked very appetizing to start with, and once I put the food in their mouths, it would always come back out. Besides that, Heather always "chewed" with her mouth open. This unpleasant sight meant that if someone outside of our immediate family was going to be at our home during mealtime, or if we were going to visit relatives, we would at least attempt to have Heather fed ahead of time, or we would feed her after everyone else was done eating. It also meant that it was nearly impossible for our whole family to go out and eat in a restaurant together. In addition, mealtimes were not very pleasant, because Cindy often cried or whimpered through the entire meal.

Needless to say, scheduling all the meals and feeding everyone created considerable stress in our family. It was especially disconcerting for me if I was in a hurry and needed to be somewhere at a specific time, because I would have to feed the handicapped ones before I could leave, and it just seemed to take forever. It was also frustrating to Bruce, Michelle, Lara, and Heidi if they wanted me to do something with them. There simply was never enough time for everyone! There was barely enough time to take care of basic needs.

That was the way it was—each and every day of the year. The routine was always the same. There was never any relief. I could never sleep in—even if I was sick—or leave home before 10:00 A.M. unless I got up very early and fed Cindy, Heather, and Mark first. And if Bruce and I wanted to go out in the evening, I had to begin feeding the children breakfast by 8:00 A.M. so I could begin feeding lunch by noon and supper by 4:30 or 5:00 P.M. The demands were never-ending.

Those weren't the only demands and frustrations either. We spent a lot of time changing the children's diapers, cleaning and changing their drooled-on clothes, bathing them, taking them to the doctor, mashing thousands of pills, spending time with them in the hospital, entertaining them, putting objects in their hands, playing guessing games, and moving them from room to room so they could be near the rest of us. It was especially frustrating to me whenever Cindy, Heather, or Mark cried and I couldn't figure out what was bothering them. Did something hurt? Was it their teeth, stomach, ears, head, or back? Did something itch? Was there a fly or some other bug on them or near them? In addition, there were many times that Bruce or I would stay home from our Sunday meetings so we could care for a handicapped child who wasn't feeling well.

Another challenge each person in the family faced was the self-consciousness associated with pushing three wheelchairs in public. Emotionally, pushing one wheelchair was difficult, pushing two was nearly unbearable, and pushing three was practically impossible. I remember Lara once said, "I hated 'lookie-looks.' It made it hard to want to go anywhere with Cindy, Heather, or Mark. I especially hated it when little kids said loudly, 'Mom, what's wrong with him or her?' Or if they said, 'Can she hear me? Does she know what I'm saying?' I also hated it when people talked about Cindy, Heather, or Mark like they weren't even there, or like they were deaf." For me, it was also irritating when people said, "You must be really blessed to have such special children in your home." I often felt like responding, "If you want to see how wonderful and special it is, you ought to come and live in our house for a week!"

A Difficult Marriage

As hard as it was caring for three handicapped children, for many years my biggest trial was that Bruce and I didn't get along very well. There were many contributing factors, but we thought most of them were associated with how little time we had to spend together. It was frustrating to both of us, but Bruce especially resented the fact that since no one could care for Cindy, Heather, and Mark except me or him, we could never get away together, even for a short period of time. The best we could hope for was to get away for a couple of hours once a week, which hardly seemed enough to smooth out the many problems we had in our marriage. And there were many.

Our relationship was so strained that it caused me anxiety and heartache every day. Because I never felt that I was living up to Bruce's expectations, I felt like a failure as a wife. I couldn't cook the way he liked; I couldn't keep his clothes cleaned, folded, pressed, and mended the way he liked; I couldn't keep the house clean and tidy enough for him; and—the thing that probably irritated him the very most—I had so little time and energy to give exclusively to him. I felt trapped and discouraged, and he never seemed to understand why. That really hurt! All I wanted was for him to understand my feelings, quit being so critical of me and the girls, and apologize at least occasionally.

I knew Bruce felt misunderstood and was frustrated with me and our family situation too, but I honestly didn't know what I could do differently. I was sincerely trying my best to make him happy, but it never seemed to work. I prayed every day that some way I could make him understand that I really loved him and that I desperately needed his emotional support.

As I look back on those times now, I believe I probably felt the same way women today feel when they claim they are emotionally abused. However, I now know the power that comes by forgiving, as Elder Richard G. Scott counseled in April 1992 general conference. I understand how difficult it is to forgive when criticism and censure continue day after day, but I also know the changes that can occur and the peace that comes when a person forgives without reservation.

Little Time for "Normal" Children

I knew Michelle, Lara, and Heidi must have often felt unloved because they had so little individual attention and because I often took my frustrations out on them. I always tried to apologize for my mistakes, but I'm sure apologies got old after a while. I also felt sorry that there was never time to do fun and frivolous things with them—like spending a whole afternoon shopping, going out to lunch, or even baking some yummy dessert. The only things I had time to help them with were those that were absolutely necessary, like homework and daily chores. Even things like mending and ironing got very little attention. I just prayed every day that Heavenly Father would bless them to know that I really loved them too.

I also felt bad that we seldom went anywhere as a whole family. Eating at church events and going to movies or sporting events were nearly impossible. Once we all went to a restaurant together, and occasionally we were able to go on a vacation. Disneyland was our favorite place because there are so many accommodations for the handicapped there. We also took a memorable vacation in a rented motor home in 1987, but for the most part our whole family was confined to home. Essentially we were somewhat like families with a child who has the measles or chicken pox—except that in our case, the ordeal wasn't over in two weeks. I'm sure Michelle, Lara, and Heidi felt very much like they had a ball and chain around their necks. I know Bruce and I often did.

The scripture that became my anchor during this time is found near the end of King Benjamin's great discourse. After teaching his people how they should live, he said, "And see that all these things are done in wisdom and order; for it is not requisite that a man should run faster than he has strength. And again, it is expedient that he should be diligent, that thereby he might win the prize; therefore, all things must be done in order." (Mosiah 4:27.) What that meant to me was that the Lord expected me to do only that which I was capable of doing—that with all the time I spent caring for our children, He didn't expect me to do community service, accept a demanding Church job, or see that my children had music lessons. And since I was unique (as we all are!) He didn't compare me to others, which meant I shouldn't compare myself to others either. All He expected of me was to diligently strive to know Him, keep His commandments, and love others—however I was capable of doing those things. What a comfort that was to me!

Heather's Operation

In 1982, when Heather was five years old, she, like Cindy and, later, Mark, had an "adductor tendonotomy." It was an operation whereby the doctor made two small incisions in her groin and cut the muscles that caused her legs to "scissor," or cross. The operation was done in order to keep her hips from dislocating and to facilitate changing her diapers. Although Cindy had to be in a full body cast for six weeks when the procedure was performed on her years earlier, Heather didn't have to be in a cast, but she did have to remain in the hospital for several days.

What a hectic three days those were! Michelle, Lara, and I took turns staying with Heather while Bruce stayed with whoever was at home. I fed Cindy breakfast as quickly as I could and then drove to the hospital and fed Heather. I then spent time with her, left Michelle or Lara, and returned home again to feed Cindy and prepare Heidi's lunch. That process continued all three meals for each of the three days Heather spent in the hospital, because it was impossible for the hospital personnel to feed her.

Although it was an extremely tiring time, I was especially grateful for our daughters' helpfulness and for their tenderness toward Heather. Seeing their sacrifice and service touched me deeply and gave me strength. And even though the days were difficult, I could see that this was a time for our children to "love one another, and to serve one another" (see Mosiah 4:15).

Breathing Problems

I was looking forward to all three handicapped children attending school in September 1986, as it meant I would finally have some free time. But, it just wasn't to be. For some unknown reason, about six weeks into the school year Cindy began to develop asthmatic-like reactions to many odors. She first developed breathing problems whenever the grass at school was mowed. Then pollens bothered her, then dust, then perfumes and other strong smells. Each time the attacks got worse, until finally I received a call from a school medical worker who said, "Cindy is having a really hard time breathing. You'd better come and get her immediately!"

When I arrived at the school Cindy was gasping for air, even though the medical people were giving her oxygen. The therapist and I quickly put her in our van and rushed her to the hospital, where a group of physicians and nurses were waiting for us. Upon our arrival, Cindy's heart rate was over 250 beats per minute and she was still gasping for air, so the medical staff immediately began searching for a vein in her arm so they could insert an IV. They must have poked her at least twenty times before they finally found an acceptable vein. It was almost more than I could bear to watch her struggle to breathe for more than three hours. What a relief when she was finally stabilized and moved into her own hospital room. I stayed and took care of her for the rest of the day and that night, and Bruce returned home to care for the other children.

After that experience, Cindy never attended school or church again. There were so many things that affected her breathing that we decided it would be easier on everyone if we kept her home. As a result of that decision, Cindy has been bedridden and homebound since 1986. So much for free time!

Out of Work

In early September 1986—about six weeks before Cindy developed her breathing problems—Bruce lost his job. Although he found another one and returned to work in October, the intermediate seven weeks was a most stressful time. Even though I felt strongly that Bruce would be able to find another job before his severance pay expired, my biggest concern was whether we would have to move. I didn't want to go through the whole process of uprooting the children and finding another house that was close to a hospital and a school for the handicapped and that accommodated wheelchairs. Besides, I had no idea how a move would affect Cindy's health.

Bruce shared my concerns, but his anxieties about his loss of employment ran much deeper than mine. Although I didn't fully understand it at the time, I now believe his extreme uneasiness was due to his overwhelming sense of responsibility to fulfill his eternal calling to provide for and protect his family. I discovered that responsibility weighs heavily on a righteous man (see D&C 83:2), and when he loses his job, he often feels very inadequate. Bruce's feelings of inadequacy and my feelings of uncertainty, along with my failure to understand his feelings, created a tense environment in our home. Thankfully, he finally found another job in Salt Lake City.

A Coma

Unexpectedly, in June 1989, Cindy began having grand mal seizures. At first they occurred once every two or three months, but by April 1990 they were happening four or five times each day. My heart ached for her once again as I wondered what she might have to endure next.

Nearly twenty-four hours after I had given Cindy a newly prescribed antiseizure medicine, I entered her bedroom to get her up for the day, but she wouldn't wake up. No matter what I did, she would open her eyes for a few seconds and then go back to sleep. At first, because she was relaxed and seemed to have a normal heart rate and breathing pattern, I was only slightly concerned. Consequently I decided to let her sleep a little longer.

When she didn't awaken by 11:00 A.M., I became very concerned and called the doctor. He came to our home, checked her, and concluded she probably was having a negative reaction to her medication. He told me to give her as many liquids as possible and to notify him immediately if there was any change in her condition.

For the next six days I sat by Cindy and gave her small squirts of liquid from a syringe, every minute wondering if her next breath would be her last. One moment she seemed a little better, and the next, a little worse. By Sunday I didn't know if I could take the emotional roller-coaster ride much longer and asked for a priesthood blessing. After Cindy and I both had one, I was resigned to the fact that she was going to die.

Thankfully, and much to our surprise, Monday morning Cindy awakened with a squeal and a smile. Evidently the negative effects of the medication had finally worn off, and Cindy was back to her normal self.

CHAPTER 4

Blessings Amid the Trials

As the years passed, even though there didn't seem to be an end to the daily struggles there were good things along the way that made life somewhat "normal" and, at times, even rewarding. There were ordinary blessings—like finding a medication that made Cindy more comfortable, and having the children eventually sleep through the night—but by far the most significant thing that happened was that Bruce and I finally began to see some improvement in our relationship. Through repentance and forgiveness and a subsequent change of heart (which Bruce will explain), we finally began to communicate and understand each other after nearly twenty years of marriage. That was a blessing that positively affected every other area of my life.

Another meaningful blessing was that as each of our children grew, I began to better appreciate the goodness and individual worth of each one. I saw that each child brought special gifts to our family, that each one contributed to the welfare of others, and that we all truly needed each other.

Gifts from Our Children

One of Michelle's many talents was that, from the time she was very young, she had a great desire to please her Heavenly

Father and her parents. As a result, her childhood was filled with years of service. She cleaned the house; helped dress Cindy, Heather, and Mark; and often held one handicapped child while I was feeding another. She was uncomplaining, patient, kind, and considerate of the feelings of others. She sacrificed her social life during her high school years to help us, as she sat with her brother and sisters so Bruce and I could go out for a couple of hours every Friday evening. She graduated from high school in 1986, served a mission from 1990-91, graduated from college in 1993, and subsequently married a wonderful young man in the Salt Lake Temple. She has a special spiritual sensitivity, and her testimony is a strength to our entire family.

Lara brought creativity and adventure into our home. From the time she was very young she was imaginative, neat and tidy, and willing to attempt new things. As a child she liked to draw, build Barbie doll houses and furniture, make unusual Halloween costumes and new desserts, and try new foods. As a youth she liked to be different. I remember one day while we were shopping, I said, "Lara, you don't want to buy those shoes. No one has shoes like that." She replied, "That's why I like them. No one else has them." Lara was especially sensitive to the needs of Cindy, Heather, and Mark. She always ran and rubbed their noses after they sneezed, saying, "Doesn't *your* nose tickle after you sneeze?" Lara also had an especially close relationship with Heather, as she was the one who took Heather sledding and "boating" in our front yard and usually held her whenever the whole family went somewhere. In late 1989 she married a fine young man in the Salt Lake Temple.

From the moment Cindy became handicapped in 1972, she has been unable to walk, crawl, roll over, sit, chew, scratch, swat a bug, hold anything in her hands, or talk. In short, she has been unable to do *anything*. Despite her limitations, however, she also has added much to our family. First, as the one with the spunky personality she was our pioneer in this journey of living with handicapped people. She was the one who blazed the trail for Heather and Mark, and yet, because of her inability to communicate, she was the one who received the least amount of recognition and attention from others. By preparing us for the worst, she taught us to be thankful for even the smallest of capabilities, and in the process paved the way for Heather and Mark to shine. For example, because of Cindy's inability to communicate in any consistent way, either verbally or nonverbally, we were grateful when we discovered that Heather and Mark had some communication skills. Being with Cindy, who could not communicate how she felt, what she needed, what she liked, or what she wanted, helped us appreciate someone who could communicate those things. Furthermore, she has shown us that a person can learn to be patient and happy despite a boring and often uncomfortable life. Today she is more mentally alert than she was five years ago, and she interacts with people better too. She now laughs whenever someone uses sarcasm, pulls a prank, does something silly, or trips and falls. She is also happy when someone else succeeds or excels, and she is very protective of everyone in the family, as she either cries or gets teary-eyed whenever she thinks a family member might be hurt. In short, although Cindy rarely goes anywhere and spends most of her time lying on a foam pad watching television, when she is feeling well she now is patient and pleasant to be around.

Heidi's special gift was that she was content and undemanding right from the beginning of her life. She was happy and uncomplaining even when our friends held her or cared for her. She also brought music into our home, as she could sing on key at a very young age. When she was three years old, every time I put her in bed she would sing an entire medley of Primary songs before she finally went to sleep. In her elementary years she was a great speller, good at putting jigsaw puzzles together, and especially adept at multiplying two-digit numbers in her head. She was such a huge help to me during her high school years that I don't know what I would have done without her. Today she is kind, considerate, friendly, conscientious, and a hard worker. She also has an understanding heart, a wonderful sense of humor, and a growing testimony of the gospel.

Heather was the handicapped child who required the most attention. It took considerable time, energy, and patience to care for her, to decipher her non-verbal communication, and to move her from place to place on her beanbag so she could be near the person she wanted to be with. But Heather also brought love and peace into our home. She gave everyone she met the opportunity to associate with one who possessed extraordinary faith, a purity of character, a joyful spirit, genuine love for others, and a devoted love of God.

Like each of our children, Mark has contributed so much to our family that I can't imagine what our lives would be without him. He has some verbal communication skills, which enable him to speak in short, choppy syllables. He is difficult to understand, but his limited speech is a great blessing to him and to us. He sits fairly comfortably in a special orthopedic wheelchair, and he is intelligent, handsome, and courageous. He has a great ability to be satisfied and thankful for even the simple things in life, and he has such a loving and fun personality that he naturally attracts other people to him. He loves all sports and knows the names, numbers, and positions of many college, NFL, and NBA players. He also knows all the referee's signals in both sports. He "bleeds BYU blue" and enjoys going to all the BYU home football games. He loves to win and hates to lose, and he is so competitive that he sweats profusely whenever he watches others play computer games or when he plays board games such as Monopoly or Life. He also loves to sing, especially his two favorite songs, "Battle Hymn of the Republic" and "I Am a Child of God." In fact, although his speech is labored and not very clear, he has sung solos in sacrament meetings and at his school. He also has sung with the Tabernacle Choir during a Choir rehearsal. Needless to say, he has brought a lot of fun and an immense amount of love into our home.

Indeed, I am grateful for all of our children. However, I feel especially thankful and blessed that each of our healthy girls has been willing to love, care for, sacrifice, and serve in our home, because that willingness to serve contributed not only to our welfare but also to their own character as well. On the other hand, I am also thankful that all three of them were able to attend the colleges of their choice, because it gave each of them an opportunity to experience a portion of life without their parents and handicapped siblings. Although it was hard on me when each left home, I felt it was important for their development.

It was a great blessing that Michelle won a scholarship before she entered college, but for me, even more important than the financial help was the essay she wrote when she entered the scholarship writing contest. Writing on the subject "How I Can Best Contribute to Even a Small Part of the World Around Me," she explained her family situation and then described her three handicapped siblings:

> Because Cindy, Heather, and Mark live in our home, I have seen that it usually takes sacrifice in order to improve someone's quality of life. My parents have set this example by choosing to keep Cindy, Heather, and Mark in our home, where I am sure they are much happier than they would be if they had to live in a nursing home. . . . A couple of years ago, I thought that it was unfair that I had to be in a family with three handicapped children, who require so much care and attention. It restricted my life greatly to live where I was needed so much. Now, I am very thankful for the many things I have learned living with handicapped people. I can see they have made me a better person. I am more responsible. I don't take as much for granted, and I think I understand others more. Because of them and the many experiences I have had, I feel that the best way in which I can contribute to the world is by helping others. If I follow Cindy's example of always smiling and trying to make others happy, Heather's attitude of helping others without desire for reward, Mark's example of a fun, loving outlook, my parents example of sacrifice and great care, and my friends' concern for others in need, I can accomplish this great task of making the world a better place.

Those comments were important to me because it was the first time one of our children indicated there was something positive about growing up in our family. It was something I had prayed for from the time Cindy became handicapped some fourteen years before.

Another monumental blessing for me was that despite all of our family trials and problems through the years, Michelle, Lara, and Heidi had chosen not to rebel but to remain active in the Church and obedient to their parents. Michelle chose to go on a mission, both she and Lara chose to be married in the temple to fine young men, and Heidi chose to participate in the Hill Cumorah Pageant. From an eternal perspective, I am grateful to have three children who are doing the things that have put them on the pathway leading to the celestial kingdom, and three other children who are assured of going to that kingdom (see D&C 137:10). What greater blessings could parents hope for?

Heather Could Communicate!

One of my most choice and far-reaching blessings actually began in 1980, on a memorable day when we discovered Heather could communicate. She was barely three years old, and I was holding her on my lap, feeding her at the kitchen table. Michelle was in the living room and called out, "Mom, what time is it?" The clock was high on the wall behind me, but before I could turn to determine the time Heather threw her head back, looked over her shoulder, and stared at the clock! I couldn't believe it. Heather not only associated the word *time* with a clock, but, unlike Cindy, she had the capability of turning her head and looking at a particular object! With that realization, I then proceeded to ask Heather, "Where's the refrigerator?" "Where's the toaster?" "Where's the carpet?" "Where's the door?" She looked at each item after each question. I was amazed!

Out of curiosity, to see if she could communicate "yes" and "no," I then asked her, "Do you like ice cream?" Her response was a smile and a direct stare at my eyes. Then I asked, "Heather, do you like bugs?" She responded with a slight shake of her head and a long blink. To my amazement, she had figured out how to communicate without speaking. What a discovery, and what a blessing to her and to us!

That discovery turned into a greater blessing in 1986, when Heather had a unique experience with her speech therapist, Jean Ernstrom. How grateful we are that Jean shared this experience, because it has had a profound spiritual effect not only on our family but on the lives of many others as well. In fact, it is a blessing that has made all of my struggles worthwhile. Jean's version of that experience follows:

Jesus, Listening, Can Hear

It has been two weeks and I am still deeply touched how in one fleeting moment, with great power, the Spirit was manifest to me through two bright blue eyes. The eyes belong to Heather, a nine-year-old-girl with a keen mind, infectious giggle, and a determined spirit housed in a very physically restricted frame. Due to the nature of her handicaps, the simplest of life's activities, if at all possible, are a major task. Unable to verbalize, Heather sends messages, quite efficiently, with her eyes; a direct gaze indicating "yes" and a blink meaning "no." So through a series of questions, gazes, blinks, giggles, facial expressions, more questions and more gazes and blinks, Heather has shared her vibrant spirit and brought incredible amounts of joy into the lives of those who know her and take the time to interact with her.

As Heather's therapist and teacher for the past four years, I have sensed on many occasions that for Heather, as with other handicapped children, the veil seems to be very thin. How often I have wondered what *she* could teach *me* about the things of the Spirit if only the expression were granted.

Heather is proud of her membership in The Church of Jesus Christ of Latter-day Saints and is a great little missionary in her own right as she struggles to share with others that which is of most value to her.

Summer school is a fun time for special students and teachers alike. The atmosphere is relaxed and the days are short. Its purpose is to maintain basic living skills during the long break between school years.

Monday morning, as usual, Heather arrived at school with a countenance as bright as the sun in the sky. As she was wheeled off the bus, we visited about the previous weekend. When we arrived at the classroom, Heather indicated to me that she had attended Primary so I began singing some of the Primary songs, looking for an indication of familiarity on Heather's face. A smile broke across her face in immediate recognition. Between songs I talked to Heather briefly and she responded in her usual manner. I asked Heather if I could sing my favorite Primary song "I

Wonder When He Comes Again." She responded positively and so I proceeded. At the conclusion of that song I asked Heather if she had a favorite song. Immediately her eyes focused on mine but then I faced the challenge of determining which song she loved above all others and to satisfy my own curiosity—why? Through a series of questions I discovered that it was a song she had heard in Primary. She wasn't sure which songbook it was in and most importantly, it was a song about Jesus. . . . I went through every possible song I could think of. To my dismay and Heather's disappointment, none of them were the right one. I didn't understand and concluded that Heather was confused. I had spent eight years collectively as Junior Primary Chorister and felt certain that I had not forgotten any of the songs about Jesus. But Heather refused to let the issue die. It was as if she needed for some reason for the two of us to share her favorite song. Finally I agreed that I would bring my Primary song books to school the following day and promised her that we would go through them together.

Tuesday morning Heather arrived and was wheeled into the classroom. Visually she was on the prowl for the songbooks. As her eyes fixed on the books across the room, she gave me a squeal and a look to let me know in no uncertain terms that she wanted to find the song—now! So we took a minute and went through the books, but to no avail. She liked all of the songs but none of them were *the* song.

Wednesday dawned a beautiful day. It was as if the day were created to reflect the beauty of what lay in store. Heather came to school more determined than ever that we find her song. Tucked in Heather's wheelchair was the new hymnbook. I took Heather out of her wheelchair and situated her comfortably on her stomach in a beanbag. I positioned myself on the floor at her side. Page by page we made our way through the hymnbook. With each page I sang the first phrase of the song and with each page Heather's eyes closed in a definite no. We were more than halfway through the book and I'm afraid I began to doubt the possibility of any success in the adventure but I continued. As a matter of routine I turned to the next page and began: "There is sunshine in my soul today . . ."

It was as if someone had stuck her with a pin. Heather jumped and smiled; her bright eyes looking directly my way. Together we laughed and reveled in the moment of completing a three day search. With the search ended it was time to get back to business. . . . Once she was situated in her chair with her head resting comfortably on my arm I said, "OK, now we can finally sing your favorite song." With a smile on her face she listened as I began:

> "There is sunshine in my soul today,
> More glorious and bright
> Than glows in any earthly sky,
> For Jesus is my light."

As I began the chorus Heather mustered all the effort she could and joined in with occasional sounds only slightly more audible than a sigh but booming with spirit to sing with me . . .

> "Oh, there's sunshine, blessed sunshine
> When the peaceful happy moments roll.
> When Jesus shows his smiling face,
> There is sunshine in the soul."

As I sang the words to the last line she looked at me steadily, as if to say, "I like that part." I felt so grateful that we had found the song. Heather was so happy that it was worth the effort and then some. Little did I realize that the real message was yet to be discovered. I asked if she wanted the rest of the verses. She, of course, responded with a firm, "Yes." . . . So I continued:

> "There is music in my soul today,
> A carol to my King,
> And Jesus listening can hear
> The songs I cannot sing . . ."

And Jesus, listening, can hear the songs I cannot sing. Heather seemed to really come to life at that line in the song. Her reaction was so strong that I stopped. I looked at her as the reality and significance of the moment pressed on my mind. I queried, "Heather, is that it? Is that what you like about the song? Is it what you want me to know? That Jesus is listening and He can hear the songs *you* cannot sing?" She lifted her head and looked me straight in the eyes with excitement and yet almost relief evident on her face. The testimony had been borne.

I felt a great reverence at what was taking place. Feeling guided by the Spirit myself I ventured on to ask, "Heather, does Jesus talk to you in your mind and in your heart?" Immediately her little head again came up and her look was penetrating.

Knowing her close relationship with the Savior and feeling surely an answer awaited, there was one more thing I wanted to know. So with reverent anticipation I whispered, "Heather, what does He say?" My heart pounded as I viewed the clear look in her eyes as she awaited my questions so she could in fact share with me her insight. I feel that the Lord gave me the right questions to ask as I took a deep breath and proceeded. "Does He say, 'Heather, I *love* you?'" Her eyes were simply radiant as she confirmed that statement. I paused, swallowed and continued, "Does He say, 'Heather, you're *special'?*" With a newfound energy source her arms began to wave with excitement and her eyes were as big as quarters as she looked into my face. I paused again with a lump in my throat and then followed with, "Does He say, 'Heather, be patient, I have *great* things in store for you'?"

What I next witnessed, I will never forget. Heather's head became erect; every fiber of her being seemed to be electrified as her eyes penetrated my own soul. She *knew* she was loved. She *knew* she was special. She *knew* she needed only be patient, for great things are in store.

The moment was too sacred for further words. I leaned forward and pressed her cheek against my own. Without any words, but with bright blue eyes as windows to a valiant soul, the truth was made known.

Yes, Heather, Jesus, listening, *can* hear.

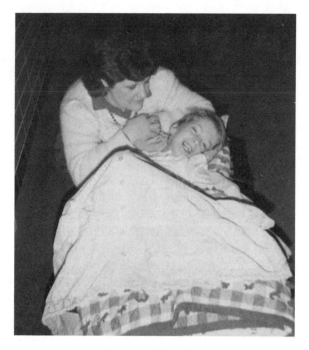

Jean and Heather

My Reaction to the Story

I remember clearly my own reaction when I first read Heather's story. Jean had already told me that she was going to send me a written account of a special experience she had shared with Heather, so I was prepared to read something—but I certainly was not expecting to read something with that kind of impact!

As I began reading the story for the first time, and particularly as I read Jean's description of Heather in the first paragraph, I thought, *Jean certainly has captured the essence of Heather.* At that point it was obvious that Jean really did love our little girl. Then as I continued I was touched by Jean's words, by Heather's sweet testimony, and by the realization that now someone else also knew that Jesus was Heather's light. However, what I read next I was not prepared for:

There is music in my soul today,
A carol to my King,
And Jesus listening can hear
The songs I cannot sing.

By the time I finished reading those words, my heart was full and tears were running down my cheeks. In fact, the tears were flowing so freely I could no longer see the words clearly, and I was unable to continue. At that point I remember thinking to myself, *What incredible faith and trust!*

After a few moments I finally composed myself enough so I could once again decipher the words on the page. Again the tears came freely, but I finally was able to finish the story. As I did so my heart was filled with an overwhelming amount of love and gratitude not only for Heather, but also for a kind and loving teacher who helped make it happen. I loved her not only for helping Heather bear her testimony, but also for helping me understand why "There is Sunshine in My Soul Today" was Heather's favorite song. Up until that day I knew "Sunshine" was Heather's favorite song—because we had to sing it every week in family home evening—but my perception was that it was because the first verse so typified Heather's personality. I always knew "Jesus was her light," but I just didn't realize to what extent.

I also felt extreme gratitude and love for a kind and loving Heavenly Father who allowed a special little girl to live in our home—a little girl who was beginning to bless us in very unexpected ways, a little girl who seemed to be one of the people described by Elder Neal A. Maxwell: "Some who are very young, chronologically, can be Methuselah's as to their maturity in spiritual things" ("If Thou Endure Well," p. 6).

Two weeks after I read Heather's story, Jean asked for my permission to send it to the *Ensign* magazine. Of course, I consented, and more than one year later Jean received a letter from the Church Magazine Department indicating that an edited version of "Jesus, Listening, Can Hear" would appear in the June 1988 *Ensign.*

A Surprise Blessing

One December day in 1988, as I retrieved our mail, my attention was drawn to the return address on a large manila envelope: "Janice Kapp Perry"! I was surprised and curious and quickly opened the envelope. Inside I found a cover letter, along with the music and lyrics of a song written by Sister Perry. With great anticipation I sat down and read the letter:

Dear Sister Erickson:

In April 1988, I received a letter from your sister Karen, which was a touching tribute to you for your selfless service to your handicapped children. Then in June, I read about Heather in the *Ensign* in the article entitled, 'Jesus, Listening, Can Hear.' I was deeply touched by the story, and in a quiet moment one evening, I wrote this song for Heather. I know that she will not be able to sing it except in her mind and heart, but I hope it will mean something to her.

May the Lord bless you as you continue to teach, love, and care for your sweet children. Merry Christmas and much love—

Janice Perry

As I finished reading the letter, there was a lump in my throat and tears in my eyes. Then I looked at the music. Up in the corner of the first page was a handwritten note which read, "With love, to Heather—Janice Kapp Perry." I then read the words to the song:

God did not give me voice to speak,
And yet my faith is quite complete.
When I pray I have no fear,
For in my mind the words are clear.
And Jesus listening can hear.

He did not give me voice to sing,
But in my heart sweet music rings.

Melodies that no one hears,
Rise from my soul to heav'nly spheres
And Jesus listening can hear.

I cannot speak to testify,
But faith shines brightly in my eyes.
In my heart it's very clear
The testimony I would bear,
And Jesus listening can hear.

When I need to have Him near,
I think His name through silent tears,
And Jesus, listening, can hear.*
(Music in back of book.)

Once again, my heart was filled with love and gratitude. This time it was also appreciation for my dear sister, and for Sister Perry, who had responded to the Spirit and shared her talents with us.

The next order of business was to share the letter and music with the rest of my family. They were all thrilled, but no one was more excited than Heather. Her face lit up, her eyes opened widely, and she could hardly wait to hear the song sung by someone who could sing well, which coincidentally turned out to be Jean Ernstrom.

I will never forget the day Heather came home from school with a tape recording of Jean singing the song. Heather was so excited as she anxiously waited for me to hear it. I did—and then Heather must have listened to it at least fifty more times that evening. She loved that tape and never got tired of hearing it.

Actually, she never grew weary of hearing her testimony borne, either through the written word or through music. Either way, Heather seemed thrilled and almost relieved that her testimony finally had been borne. We too were awestruck by the happenings, and several months later I discovered that many other people were also touched by Heather's testimony.

---

* "Jesus, Listening, Can Hear," copyright 1988 by Janice Kapp Perry. Reprinted by permission.

Continued Help

Even though Heather's testimony and song became a major source of many subsequent blessings, today we are blessed in many other ways too. For example, since Cindy has been bedridden members of the Relief Society and Young Women organizations come to our home each Sunday and tend her while our family attends church meetings together. I am especially grateful that it is a situation where both giver and receiver are blessed. A sixteen-year-old girl who sat with Cindy wrote:

> I'm so thankful for the opportunity I have had of tending Cindy. She helped me realize how grateful I am for my ability to walk, sit up, and respond to others. She helped me see that a person's physical appearance doesn't make her/him less loved by God. In fact, she made me realize that Christ isn't really that far away and if I really need him, he will be there for me. I have felt Cindy's love for Christ as I have watched her listen to the Church songs. I truly believe that she is singing them loud and clear in her heart. I will always love and cherish the things she taught me.

I am also grateful for the many blessings that have come through Mark. People have arranged for him to meet football and basketball players at BYU, to meet a local TV weatherman, to sing with the Tabernacle Choir, to tour the U.S.S. *Nimitz* and meet its captain, and to tour the Kennedy Space Center. These things have meant a great deal to him and to us, but so has the daily service rendered by his teachers and aides at school and church, as well as the concern and patience which his friends have continually shown him.

How grateful I am for people's prolonged thoughtfulness and generosity! Their help continues to bring a great deal of peace and comfort to my soul.

CHAPTER 5

Heather's Death

In January 1989, Michelle was a student at BYU, Lara was a student at Ricks College, and Heidi was a ninth-grader who spent considerable time helping Bruce and me care for Cindy, Heather, and Mark. It was difficult for me to care for the three handicapped children with both Michelle and Lara away from home, but with Heidi's help we somehow managed.

January was also the month I shared with my stake Relief Society president Jean and Heather's story "Jesus, Listening, Can Hear" and the song by Janice Kapp Perry. My Relief Society president was touched by the message of the story and song, and several weeks later she asked Jean and me to speak at an upcoming stake leadership women's conference to be held April 22. The theme of the conference was to be "Jesus, Listening, Can Hear," and the Relief Society president wanted us to talk about Heather and share our testimonies.

Jean and I gladly accepted, and from that moment on I began pondering and praying about how to fulfill the assignment so that what I said would be edifying and meaningful to those in attendance. After consulting with Jean, we decided that the way to approach the talks would be to relate some eternal truths we had learned from Heather. That seemed to be the best way to capture Heather's spirit and testimony and to share our testimonies as well.

On Tuesday, April 4, around noon, I received a telephone call from one of Heather's teachers at Monte Vista School who said Heather was complaining of a little sore throat and wanted to come home. Even though Heather didn't have a fever I went and picked her up, since she wouldn't ask to leave school for an insignificant reason.

She didn't seem to be ill at all until about ten o'clock that night, at which time I treated her for a cold and put her to bed. She awakened five times during the night but slept well in the early morning hours. Then, at about 10:30 A.M., she seemed to be struggling to breathe, so I picked her up and held her on my lap. As she became more relaxed, I thought she might go back to sleep. All of a sudden she took four successive deep breaths, with a big sigh after each one. My first thought was, *Finally she got some really good breaths of air.* That thought quickly turned to great concern, however. After the fourth deep breath it didn't look as though her chest was moving anymore! I called her name a couple of times and gently patted her cheeks, but there was no response.

Sensing a real need for help, I dialed 911 and explained to the lady what had just happened. Upon hearing my words, Mark, who didn't feel well and was lying on the floor beside Cindy, started to cry. At that same time, the dispatcher on the telephone—in a very reassuring manner—first determined my address and then that I did not know how to administer CPR. Very clearly and methodically the lady helped me perform each step of CPR. I went through that whole process four times without seeing any response from Heather, at which time the lady then directed me to go quickly and unlock the front door. As I did so, surprisingly the paramedics were on our front porch. I quickly let them in, returned to the telephone, and thanked the lady for her help. Even at that very hectic moment I couldn't help but think, *What a nice, helpful lady. She really had a calming influence on me at a time I would have normally panicked.*

While the paramedics worked on Heather in the family room, Cindy lay on the floor with a sad and concerned look on her face, and I called Bruce at work. As I explained to him what was happening, I saw through the living room window several emergency vehicles and many concerned neighbors outside. I felt somewhat relieved because I saw that one kind friend was holding Mark and consoling him. Apparently she had come inside while I was talking to the paramedics.

Then, as I again turned my attention to the paramedics working on Heather in the family room, I saw them pick up her crooked little body, place it on a low stretcher, and wheel her into the living room. As they passed by me through the kitchen I could see her lifeless little body was *still* lifeless, and I started to cry. Up until that time I had been extremely calm.

I walked back into the family room, sat down on the couch, and, with tears running down my face, started thinking about the events that had led up to that moment. I was nervous and wanted to go into the living room and see what was happening there, but I stayed in the family room, as I was trying to muster enough courage to accept what, in my heart, I was afraid I would see. Finally, however, with a heavy heart I slowly walked to the living room doorway. As I stood there, the first thing I saw was Heather's motionless body. Then I noticed that there was a straight line on the machine that monitored her heartbeat. Knowing what that meant, I asked the paramedic, "Have you gotten any heartbeat since you arrived?"

He answered, "No, I'm sorry, ma'am."

Knowing that severe brain damage can occur when a person goes several minutes without oxygen, I said, "Please, just let her go. I want to always remember her the way she was, not some other way."

"I'm sorry, but once we begin this procedure we must continue it until we get an order from a doctor telling us to do something else," he replied.

At that moment I had very mixed emotions. On the one hand it was hard to accept the fact that she might be gone, but, for me, it would have been even harder to accept Heather's condition if they had revived her and she had suffered severe brain damage. In my heart I prayed that whatever was best for Heather would happen.

After what seemed like an eternity, the paramedics finally decided to move Heather outside to the ambulance and transport her to the hospital. I traveled with them and was met by Heather's pediatrician, who was waiting for me outside the emergency room entrance. It was comforting to see him. As I climbed out of the ambulance, he gave me a hug and said he was sorry. I thanked him for being there and asked him if the paramedics had ever gotten a heartbeat. He quietly and gently said, "No."

As we reached the doorway to the emergency room where Heather's body lay, I noticed the paramedics were beginning to attach electrodes to her little chest. I said to our doctor, "Please, don't let them try to revive her now. Just let her go in peace."

Just then, Bruce arrived. Our doctor quietly asked the paramedics to leave, and suddenly Bruce and I were alone with Heather's body. She looked so cold and lifeless, but struggled no longer. For the first time, I really cried.

It was hard to leave, but before we did, Bruce and I had a prayer. We thanked Heavenly Father for Heather's sweet life and for allowing us the privilege of having her in our home for a few short years. What a special spirit she had! Our only request of the Lord was to "please help us to live our lives so that our whole family will be worthy to live with her again."

Plans for Heather's "Graduation" Ceremony

Thankfully, the plans for the funeral services came together quickly. It was easy deciding the songs we wanted sung, the people we wanted to provide the music, and the people we wanted to speak. The hard part was contacting them. There were so many concerned people who stopped by our home or called on the telephone, who shared their love and kindness with us, that it was extremely difficult to even make a telephone call. The doorbell and the telephone rang almost constantly. At one point it was so steady that Lara, somewhat humorously, asked if she could make an appointment to talk to me in my bedroom.

In all sincerity, despite how hectic it seemed at times, it was all worth it. By the end of the day we had been able to accomplish everything that needed to be done, and we had felt love and support from many, many people. Each accomplishment and each person had helped to lift my spirits. It was especially gratifying that we were able to contact everyone we wanted to have on the program, and each person had agreed to come and participate—even my close friend from California. I not only felt grateful that all could participate, but I also felt strengthened by the fact that they felt honored to do so.

Although I was exhausted that night, I couldn't sleep. When it was quiet, I really missed Heather. So, rather than keep Bruce awake with my tossing and turning, I decided to sit in the family room for a while. As I entered that room, a feeling of loneliness overwhelmed me. The family room was Heather's bedroom, and she really was gone. Now, without her there, the room felt so empty. I sat on the couch, where I last held her, and cried again.

I thought, *I am this sweet little girl's mother. I was supposed to teach her about spiritual things, but she was the one who taught me. She taught me about faith, about trusting in the Lord, about enduring affliction well, about loving one another.* I knew in my heart that Heather was now free from sickness and pain—but I missed her terribly.

After a good cry, I actually felt relaxed. I returned to bed and went right to sleep.

About that day, Michelle wrote:

> I was a student at BYU the day Heather died. And, of course, it was an important test week. When I got home from taking my biology midterm, I saw a note my roommate wrote which said, "Call home after your test."
>
> I wondered why my parents would call in the middle of the day. And, finally, when I was able to get through, Mom told me Heather died. I was speechless. If anything, I thought Cindy would die first because she had been in and out of hospitals and much more sick than Heather.
>
> I couldn't go home until after my two other midterms. So the funeral was set for Saturday so I could take my tests and Heather's teachers and friends could come.
>
> My roommates were great. I cried and they listened and comforted me. But, that night, I couldn't sleep. I was wearing the yellow sweat pants that Heather gave me for Christmas. I remember how excited she was to *give* during the holidays, and any day for that matter.

I got up in the night after tossing and turning, and for some unknown reason, I went straight to my roommate's stereo. I pushed the "play" button on the tape recorder, and I couldn't believe what I heard. The song, "Together Forever," began. Who knows how that tape got in the recorder, and who knows how it was put in the right place, but it was.

It was as if Heather was singing to me, "We can be together forever someday." I cried, but I was comforted. And ever since that day, it hasn't been a bad thing she died, but a sad thing. We all miss her, but we know she is happy and doing what the Lord wants her to do. She did the Lord's will during her life, something that we all should try to do.

Busy Days

The day after Heather died was very difficult. Although the funeral preparations went smoothly, Cindy developed breathing problems, and Bruce and I ended up caring for her until about 1:00 A.M. At that time we took her to the hospital, where we found ourselves assigned to the same private room where Heather was the day before. Worried that we might lose Cindy too, Bruce and I nervously watched the medical personnel work on her until she finally began breathing easier. Relieved, we took her home shortly after 4:00 A.M.

Although we were tired that day, we spent most of Friday preparing for the viewing to be held that evening. Once again, many people assisted us, but the two who were especially helpful were Lara and Jereck, Lara's fiancé. They spent most of that afternoon finding snapshots of Heather and making two large photo collages, which we put on display for people to enjoy while they stood in line at the viewing.

The viewing had a profound spiritual effect on me. I will never forget the indescribable sweet feeling of love and reverence I experienced as I walked into the mortuary room where Heather's mortal body lay. Although her body looked so lifeless and older than her mortal years, Heather's peaceful, loving spirit permeated the room. It brought tears to my eyes as I contemplated her sweet life and wonderful spirit that she brought into our home. I was truly grateful that God had allowed her to live with us for as long as she did, and that there were no feelings of fear or regret—only love, faith, peace, and true joy.

I was especially thankful for those feelings because they brought great comfort to my soul. They also served as a confirmation to me that the viewing and funeral were going to be spiritually uplifting, and would be true reflections of Heather's life. More than anything else, that was what I desired, because I knew that if those two occasions were spiritually uplifting, Heather and the Lord both would be pleased with the proceedings. That realization gave me the strength I needed to make it through the evening.

As I stood by the opened casket with my family and greeted the wonderful people who came, I felt strengthened by their presence and their outpouring of love. I was uplifted by the people who shared their personal thoughts and feelings about Heather and how she had touched their lives in so many different ways. It was amazing to me to learn how one little girl who could not walk and could not talk could have such a profound effect on so many people.

"Graduation" Day

One of the hardest things to deal with after Heather's death was Mark's reaction to it. He was seven years old at the time, and while we were preparing for the funeral he was unusually quiet and subdued. We thought it would be good for him if he would talk about his feelings, but about all he would say was, "No go viewing; no go funeral," and "I miss Heather." He was insistent about not going to the viewing or the funeral, which concerned us, but at least he cried whenever he said, "I miss Heather." He knew she wouldn't be back with us, and at least he was dealing with his grief by crying.

I don't know exactly why he didn't want to go to the viewing or the funeral, but Bruce and I knew we needed to respect his wishes. Nevertheless, I kept hoping he would agree to attend the funeral on Saturday morning. No matter what words of encouragement we used, however, when we put him to bed Friday night, he still insisted he would stay home the next day.

Mark's Dream

Saturday dawned a beautiful, spring day. The sun was shining, the sky was blue. Weather-wise, it was a perfect day for people in this world to honor "our sunshine." But it also turned out to be a nice day for Mark. It began when Bruce awakened him and said, "Good morning, Mark. How are you this morning?"

Very unexpectedly, considering Mark's demeanor during the previous three days, he cheerfully replied, "Happy!"

Surprised, Bruce asked, "Why are you so happy, Mark?"

"I dream," said Mark.

"What did you dream about?"

"Heather."

"Where was she?" asked Bruce.

"Heavenly Father."

"What was she doing?"

"Singing and walking."

"What was she singing?" Bruce asked.

"Sunshine in My Soul Today."

"Did she say anything to you, Mark?" asked Bruce.

"She say, 'Don't cry. Be happy. Sing my song!' "

"Did she say anything else, Mark?"

"No, but I go funeral. Okay, Dad?"

After Mark related the dream to me exactly as he had related it to Bruce, I gave him a big hug and thought to myself, "*And a little child shall lead them*" (2 Nephi 21:6). Evidently, for a brief moment in time Mark had seen the whole picture. How reassuring to know that a kind and loving Heavenly Father knew and fulfilled the needs of a valiant little soul that day! For Mark, and our family, that dream has been a continual source of comfort and peace.

Understanding a Gospel Truth

For me, Heather's funeral was exactly what Elder Packer said a funeral ought to be: a meeting that combines the "doctrines of the gospel, the spirit of inspiration, and [the family] gathered in tender regard for one another" ("Funerals—A Time for Reverence," p. 21). I truly felt the Spirit of the Lord there.

One of the most significant things that helped me feel at peace after Heather died was my understanding of a precious gospel truth regarding the eternal destination of people who die before they become accountable—which includes some who are physically handicapped and mentally deficient. First, regarding little children who die, the Prophet Joseph Smith beheld in vision "that all children who die before they arrive at the years of accountability are saved in the celestial kingdom of heaven" (D&C 137:10). And second, on the status of people who are mentally deficient, Elder Bruce R. McConkie said: "It is with them as it is with little children. They never arrive at the years of accountability and are considered as though they were little children. If because of some physical deficiency, or for some other reason unknown to us, they never mature in the spiritual and moral sense, then they never become accountable for sins. They need no baptism; they are alive in Christ; and they will receive, inherit, and possess in eternity on the same basis as do all children." ("The Salvation of Little Children," p. 6.)

What solace to know that Cindy's, Heather's, and Mark's eternal destinations are celestial!

Gifts of Love

Another thing that brought comfort to me after Heather died was the compassion expressed by many concerned people. There were those who helped by writing the obituary, cleaning and altering clothing, bringing meals to our home, giving us money, and sending cards, flowers, and gifts. Each act of kindness lifted my spirits, as knowing others cared made difficulties easier to bear.

One gift that I was especially grateful for was actually given to Lara the day after the funeral. That day was Lara's nineteenth birthday, and with all the activities of the previous four days, I had completely forgotten it. I was reminded of her special day, however, when her former Young Women adviser gave her a present. As soon as I saw the gift, many feelings rushed through me. I felt sorry for Lara and terrible that I had forgotten her birthday, but I also felt grateful that a dear lady had remembered. I apologized to Lara, and she said that she understood.

Although she said it was okay, I knew it must have hurt her feelings deeply. It certainly wasn't the first time she had sacrificed something because of a handicapped child. She and Michelle and Heidi have grown up having to sacrifice a lot.

On that same day, another gift was delivered to our home by our bishop and his wife. After the usual greetings, the bishop said, "Heather continues to inspire people to be their best. This is a gift that two young boys wanted you to have." He then handed me a sealed envelope that had "For Heather" written on the outside. The bishop explained that before the funeral Saturday morning, the young boys, ages seven and eight, approached him and asked if they might make an appointment to see him. He made one for the next day, at which time they gave him the envelope and asked him to give it to us anonymously. Inside the envelope was eight dollars, which they had earned collecting aluminum cans and doing odd jobs. Bruce and I hope that somehow those boys understand that their thoughtfulness and service was a real blessing to our family.

A most cherished gift that was presented to us after Heather died was a journal entitled *Memories of Heather.* It was the idea and creation of two good friends, and it was placed outside the viewing rooms for people to write in as they waited in line. The book was a 9-by-7-inch three-ring binder that held pages of journal-type lined paper. Printed on the top of each page was a drawing of a wreath of flowers with the words "Memories of Heather" inside. The first page had these words typed in bold letters:

> As a beautiful melody stirs the spirit
> So Heather touched the hearts of all who knew her!
> Please share a memory of her with her parents!

How grateful I am for all the things written in this book! People wrote on more than 120 pages, and their comments are indeed cherished memories. Knowing others are touched by her testimony buoys me up and brings peace to my soul. I now know that when people are faithful and their hearts are turned to Christ, they can have a positive influence in the lives of others—even if they have severe limitations.

Keeping a Commitment

Another thing that brought me peace after Heather's death—and continues to bring me peace even today—came as a result of Jean's and my deciding to keep our commitment to speak at the stake leadership women's conference on April 22. Personally, it was therapeutic for me to share my testimony and innermost feelings about Heather that soon after she died. It was a great spiritual boost for me to feel the spirit that was present in that meeting and to see the effect that Heather's faith-promoting experiences had on those in attendance. Thankfully, I have never really lost that feeling, as Jean and I have shared Heather's story and our testimonies regarding faith and the Savior's touch many times. What a joy it is to do that!

CHAPTER 6

Reflecting on Heather's Life

W hat a joyous experience to reflect on Heather's life! She taught me so much about life and spiritual things, and I felt peace whenever I thought or talked about her. She taught me about love, faith, service, devotion to God, and, through her example, showed me the keys to finding peace in adversity. Hopefully, learning some details about her life will help others (particularly those who deal with handicapped children) feel comfort and peace too.

Physical Development

After Heather was diagnosed as being developmentally de-layed, she continued to have poor head and trunk control. She also continued to be shorter than normal and extremely skinny. In fact, she was so skinny that when she was ten years old, we could slip an adult-size bracelet over her thigh. No matter what we fed her, it never significantly increased her weight.

As Heather grew, her spasticity changed. At first she was quite floppy, but as time passed her spasticity increased. We first noticed a major change when her leg would involuntarily inter-nally rotate and fly up when she sat in her wheelchair. Placing a heavy bag of buckshot on her leg seemed to help a little, but when she lay on her back her legs began to "scissor" so badly that it became difficult to change her diapers. That was when she had her adductor tendonotomy, an operation that was painful and caused her a great deal of anxiety.

The adductor tendonotomy stabilized the "scissoring" tendency in Heather's legs for a short time, but eventually all of her muscles became tighter and tighter, especially in her back and neck. In addition, her muscles, like Cindy's and Mark's, pulled more on one side of her body than on the other, and her scoliosis, or lateral curvature of the spine, continually worsened. Muscle relaxant medication provided little relief, and even orthopedic surgeons felt that nothing could be done. In fact, most doctors believed that because the muscles in her back pulled so tightly, if they were to insert a rod in her spine the tension probably would break her vertebrae.

As Heather's discomfort grew into outright pain, we took her to another pediatric orthopedic surgeon, who immediately took X-rays of her back and hips. As he reviewed the finished X-rays he exclaimed, "Wow! It's no wonder this little girl is in pain. She has two ninety-degree curves in her spine!" Unfortunately, only a complicated surgical procedure was suggested as a possible short-term solution, and even that was accompanied by serious doubts that Heather would survive such a long operation. Additionally, the doctor felt that even if she did survive, she probably would require the use of a respirator for the rest of her life because her lungs were weak.

After Bruce and I discussed the pros and cons of having Heather operated on, we talked to Heather about it, and we all decided it wasn't worth the risks. Consequently Heather continued to live with ever-increasing pain. In fact, there were times when she hurt so badly that tears would roll down her cheeks. There would be no sound, only tears. The only relief she would get was when a therapist from her school would come to our house and massage her back. Heather loved that, but each time the therapist came she would whisper to me, "Heather is in incredible pain!" My heart ached for her then, but as I look back on those times now, I am amazed at the courage she exhibited as she endured to the end. Indeed, she showed everyone who knew her what the term "long-suffering" means.

When Heather finally died, she did not have a beautiful physical body. Because of her disease and the way her muscles pulled, she had a crooked torso, a distorted face, buck teeth, and very skinny arms and legs. Although she was almost twelve she was less than four feet tall and weighed less than thirty-five pounds. Truthfully, except for her eyes and her smile there was nothing attractive about her body. What I remember most, however, is not her deformed body but her radiant countenance, her personality and character, and what she taught me about life and spiritual things.

Personality Development

As I mentioned earlier, when Heather was barely three years old we discovered she had nonverbal communication skills. To some that might not seem too significant, but it was extremely important to us. Because her initial development had retrogressed like Cindy's, we assumed that Heather's limitations would be just like her sister's. What a blessing it was that one of them could tell us what she needed, what she wanted, and where she hurt! Besides, Heather's ability to communicate was the key to unlocking her personality. It opened up the world to her and, later, many eternal truths to us.

Expressing the joy of discovering Heather could communicate, Heather's aunt wrote:

> Christmas of 1982, I had been married just a few months when we gathered with the family to celebrate the season. Heather was there, consumed with excitement over her Christmas gift—a Barbie doll! It soon became clear that there was something Heather wanted to communicate. As unaccustomed as I was to understanding Heather's "language," even *I* could read the intense concentration in her eyes as she struggled to help us know what she wanted to say.
>
> Lara and Michelle finally pinpointed Heather's request. She had chosen a name for her Barbie doll and insisted that we know what that name was. Now came the arduous task of trying to second guess this bright and active mind. Where

to begin? Heather was not about to let the issue drop. Persistence was one of her strengths, to be sure!

The game of "twenty questions" began. I watched in bemused amazement to see Heather's sisters, mother, grandmother, aunts, cousins, etc., all joining in the game. These people *really* cared about a little girl and her Barbie doll. However, one after another, all the names they tossed out were rejected. None of them was *the* one. Finally, a good half hour later, the name "Joanie" was suggested and Heather wriggled in delight. SUCCESS! The smiles in Heather's eyes seemed ample thanks to all.

Besides answering "yes" and "no" and "maybe" and "sort of" with her eyes and facial expressions, Heather was good at leading us to the idea she wanted to communicate. For example, one morning I spent an hour trying to figure out what she wanted to take to school that day. All I knew at first was that it had something to do with "lips" because she kept looking at my lips. I asked Heather if she wanted to kiss someone. "No!" she laughed. I finally figured out it had something to do with "blowing"—then "blowing out candles"—and then "it is someone's birthday." From there I finally determined that Heather wanted to take a birthday card to a friend.

On another occasion, as Heather was wheeled off the school bus I noticed she had a candy bar in her lap. That wasn't unusual, because kind people at Monte Vista were always giving her something she liked. Thinking it was probably easy to guess who gave her the candy bar, I asked her, "Who gave it to you—a teacher?" She blinked her eyes no. "An aide?" I asked. No, she answered again. "A student?" It wasn't a student. "A man?" Yes, it was a man. "The custodian?" I asked. No again. I finally determined it was a man who didn't even work at the school and whose name I didn't even know! I then said, "Heather, you'll have to think of a way to tell me the man's name."

She did. As soon as I took her in the house, she looked toward the drawer where we keep the county telephone directory, a directory that lists both the husband's and wife's names. I opened the directory and, after a series of questions, determined she wanted me to find the name of a specific female aide at her school. I then turned to the page and read the aide's first name and her husband's first name. That was it! The first name of her aide's husband was the same first name of the man who had given her the candy bar!

Having Fun

Along with Heather's ability to communicate, the things she did for fun told a lot about her personality. She loved going to Disneyland and to Lagoon, a local amusement park, plus all the field trips with the people at her school. She enjoyed the annual trips to the zoo and the Festival of Trees, and she loved to dress up and go trick-or-treating every Halloween. Some of her favorite Halloween costumes, which she always decided on herself, were a princess, mummy, ghost, and witch. Her excitement always made it fun for everyone.

Heather also loved to invite girlfriends over to play and spend time with her. She especially loved slumber/birthday parties, but even simple things excited her. A younger friend wrote: "I remember when I took Heather for a walk in her wheelchair, and we walked and walked and I found out that her head was tipped and I didn't know how to put it back and we started to laugh and laugh! I also remember when I went to play dolls with her. She was always happy when I came over, and she always loved me to play with her!"

And Heidi wrote: "I remember whenever the neighbor girls came down and played, Heather always wanted to be near us. She liked us to put on little shows for her. She and Mark would watch the shows, and they would laugh and laugh and want us to do more. She liked socializing with me and my friends."

Another fun incident took place before our lawn was planted. There was just dirt and one big low spot that had collected water after a hard rainstorm. Lara asked Heather if she would like to ride on a raft in a lake. Of course, Heather was thrilled! Lara then got a plastic air mattress, blew it up, lay Heather on it, and proceeded to push her around on the "lake" in our front yard. What a rewarding scene to watch! Lara was helping Heather do something she couldn't do for herself, and

Heather was having a great time doing something so very simple—and to her, every bit as fun as riding in a real boat.

When Heather was about ten years old, one of her favorite pastimes was for *her* to tell jokes. Think about that. How does a person who can't talk tell a joke? Our family would pause for a couple of minutes, allow her to think of the joke she wanted to tell, and then everyone "listening" would try to guess which joke she was thinking about. As soon as we guessed the correct one, someone would tell the joke and we would all laugh.

That process worked well until one particular occasion when everyone guessed and guessed and no one could guess the correct joke. Finally, after quite a few minutes I asked, almost exasperated, "Heather, have we ever heard this joke before?" After a slight pause, and with a mischievous grin on her face, she shook her head and blinked her eyes, "No!" Then she laughed and laughed—and so did we!

Another of Heather's favorite things to do was to sit on her beanbag in the kitchen and watch someone cook. She called it "cooking class." She always wanted to help stir, but since she couldn't she loved to watch because, she said, "it is necessary that I learn how to cook."

If Heather couldn't actually participate in an activity, the next best thing for her was to pretend. Often she would be sitting in her beanbag and would give a quick look up toward the ceiling. That meant, "Let's pretend." She could play "pretend" for hours, and she would pretend for as long as someone would play with her. If she pretended "going to Hawaii" or "going to Disneyland," or anywhere else, we would have to think about packing our bags, buying our plane tickets, boarding the plane, taking off, eating on the plane—even the kind of food served—landing, going to the hotel, and sunbathing on the beach. Whatever a person would do on such a trip, Heather thought about it and imagined doing it. If Heather pretended "going to the hospital," she might be the doctor or sometimes the patient. She would pretend that a kidney, a heart, a brain, or other body part would be operated on, a broken leg would be fixed, a baby would be born. Just about anything that might happen in a hospital Heather could imagine. She also liked to pretend "cops and robbers" with Mark. She would usually be the cop and Mark the robber. He would usually "rob" a bank or a store, and then she would chase him in her police car along the freeway to the Utah border. At the border they would each get out of their cars and get in their own helicopters, and Heather would chase Mark for a while longer. Sometimes she would catch him and put him in jail, and sometimes he would get away, only to rob another bank or store. It was always fun to watch them "argue" about who was going to do what.

I will never forget the time it took me several days to figure out what Heather wanted to pretend. All I could piece together was that she needed a towel and a belt, and she needed to go to California. I guessed every logical thing I could think of. Did it have to do with taking a bath, a shower, sunbathing, or tightening some pants because they keep falling down?

No, Heather blinked, laughing.

After exhausting all my logical guesses, I then resorted to guessing some pretty weird ideas. I guessed and guessed and guessed and it got pretty silly after a while, but Heather still wanted me to know what she wanted to pretend. I finally told her I would keep thinking but that I would have to think about something else for a while.

Three days later—of course, Heather wouldn't let it die—I was walking down the hallway, and all of a sudden it dawned on me what Heather wanted to pretend. I ran into the family room where Heather was and I said excitedly, "Heather, I know what you wanted to pretend the other day!"

She looked at me with her big blue eyes and stared at me in anticipation, as if to say, "Tell me what you think, Mom! Tell me!"

"Heather, you wanted to pretend you were a magician. You wanted to put the belt under the towel and make it disappear!" That was it! She had seen a magician from California on TV, and she wanted to pretend she was a magician too.

I got a towel and a belt, and Heather pretended to make the belt disappear. However, it didn't end there. She then wanted to make other things disappear. First it was the couch, then the TV, then the bookshelf, then the refrigerator, and then the overstuffed chair. With each object she would have me say, "Abracadabra, couch [or whatever], disappear." I would look surprised, as if the object was really gone, and then after a few seconds she would have me say, "Abracadabra, couch, reappear." After the couch reappeared, she then would move her eyes to another object. She proceeded in that manner with each object—first making it disappear and then making it reappear—until she got to the overstuffed chair. Oh, she made it disappear, all right, but since the chair was old and worn out, she decided not to make it reappear. We laughed a long time about that one.

Heather also enjoyed watching others work and play. Even though she couldn't actually participate with those she was watching, she pretended she could. She would pretend to help someone cook, hoe weeds, or clean the house, and although she couldn't physically play a softball game with the girls, she pretended she was playing with them.

It would be impossible to get a true picture of Heather's personality without listing some of her favorite movies and TV shows. First, her favorite movies were *Annie, King Kong, The Slipper and the Rose,* and *The Black Stallion.* Some of her favorite TV programs were *Wonder Woman, Beauty and the Beast, The Frugal Gourmet,* and *The Greatest American Hero.* She also liked to watch anything that had to do with Kermit the Frog and Miss Piggy. A special TV spot she loved was "Wednesday's Child," a short segment on the news every Wednesday evening that highlighted a handicapped child who needed adoptive parents. She wanted us to adopt every child on the show. She also loved to watch every beauty pageant on TV. She especially loved the Miss USA Pageant, and she always cheered for Miss Texas to win.

Heather also enjoyed going to school. Even the "work" there was fun for her—which was what was most important to me. I felt that because she was already assured of going to the celestial kingdom, and because there was no possibility of her ever having a job, as long as the people at her school were kind to her and she was happy there it really didn't matter what she learned. I believed that her happiness was far more important than her intellectual development.

Regarding the fun Heather had at school, an aide at Monte Vista wrote:

One of my favorite memories of Heather is the time that I stopped by Jean Ernstrom's office to talk a minute. Little did I know that inside the door, Heather and Jean were engaged in a tea party, complete with make-believe tea, crumpets, and British accents. Of course, they lost no time in inviting me to join them, and we three giggled as we tasted, munched, and even spilled our imaginary goodies. Each time that Jean or I would start talking with a British accent, Heather would laugh and wiggle. She seemed to think that we were the most entertaining act she had ever seen.

Surely Heather proved that even a severely handicapped person can have fun. How grateful I am that the people at her school were always kind to her and made her life so enjoyable. They certainly had a profound positive effect on her life.

Fears and Hurt Feelings

Despite everything Heather did for fun, there were things that frightened her and hurt her feelings. For example, I clearly remember a beautiful summer day when Heather wanted to go outside to watch other children play and ride their bicycles in the cul-de-sac. I put her on her beanbag on our front lawn and then went back in the house. Soon I heard her crying and screaming. I quickly ran outside and discovered that no one was near her, but big tears were running down her face. I asked her if someone or something had hit her or if an animal or bug had bothered her. She indicated no.

Relieved that she hadn't been physically hurt, I picked her up, consoled her, and then proceeded to find out what happened. "Did your feelings get hurt? Was it a girl? Was it a boy?" I finally determined that a group of boys on bicycles had ridden by and called her "a little retard." As soon as I figured it out, she began to cry again. She hurt so deeply that my heart ached for her. I held her close again and said, "You know you aren't 'a retard.' I know it, and Heavenly Father knows it. Those boys just don't understand, do they?"

She blinked her eyes no, and soon she quit crying.

That experience was a traumatic one for her, but the entire episode ended in a funny way—with her trying to find a solution to the problem. The next day when she wanted to go outside and watch children play again, she insisted that she take the tape recorder so she might record the boys' voices if they called her names again. That way she could catch them. Much to her disappointment, however, the boys never returned.

Besides feeling normal kinds of hurt, Heather also had normal fears. For example, she loved to participate in the school programs, but she truly was nervous before each one. Even though her part was to simply dress up in a costume and be pushed around on stage, she was always a little afraid. She was nervous too about going to Young Women because it would be new and different, and she didn't know if she would fit in. She also was deathly afraid of animals and bugs. I think it was because she felt so defenseless and helpless whenever they came near.

Her True Character

We began to see Heather's true character and spirituality when she was seven years old as she communicated her understanding of her divine heritage and mission. Bruce and I had just given her a bath, our house was quiet, and we were alone with her. Bruce, holding her, asked, "Heather, do you remember anything about your life before you came to live on this earth?"

To our surprise—and yet, knowing Heather, it really shouldn't have been—she answered with an unmistakable yes and looked as if she wanted to tell us more. So, with a series of questions, gazes, and blinks, Bruce and I learned what Heather had known all along: that she knew before she entered mortality she would come in a handicapped body; that in premortality she made an agreement with Heavenly Father that if she would spend her mortal life in a handicapped body, she would be assured of living with Him again.

I am convinced that this knowledge was the stabilizing factor in her life, the basis of her Christlike character, the reason she loved the Lord and her fellowmen, and the reason she could endure to the end. She truly knew who she was, why she was here, and that her Heavenly Father loved her!

She Loved the Lord

One evidence that Heather loved the Lord was that she loved to attend church meetings. Even if she didn't feel well, she hated to miss sacrament meeting or Primary. Another evidence was that she loved to "read" the scriptures and take them to church. Even though there was no indication that she could actually read, she would ask me to put her opened Book of Mormon on the floor so she could lay on her beanbag and "read" the scriptures. Periodically she would ask me to turn the page for her. She always remembered to take her scriptures to Primary—because that's what Heavenly Father and her teacher wanted her to do.

Heather also showed her love for the Lord by being a peacemaker. She hated contention so much that if ever there were quarreling or arguing in our home, she wanted it stopped, or she would cry to be taken into another room where she couldn't hear it. She was never content until the quarreling ceased and proper apologies were made.

Her Baptism

Bruce and I thought that since the Church teaches that baptism is not necessary for people with severe physical or mental handicaps, Heather, like Cindy, would not be baptized. However, one evening as I talked to Heather about that idea, she communicated to me in no uncertain terms, "Oh, yes, I do want to be baptized, Mom!" She then looked up toward the ceiling, meaning, "Heavenly Father wants me to be baptized!" She obviously had heard that everyone needs to be baptized to enter the kingdom of heaven (see John 3:5), and she wanted to fulfill every commandment.

Heather was baptized and confirmed a member of The Church of Jesus Christ of Latter-day Saints on June 1, 1985—a day that I believe was one of the happiest of her life. She was elated that members of her immediate and extended family were there, and that teachers and aides from her school and teachers and friends from Primary were there, but she was ecstatic that her non-LDS friend from Monte Vista School was there. I truly believe she wanted him to somehow feel the same joy she felt on that special occasion as she became a member of the Church.

I will never forget all that was associated with her baptism. First, she was so excited and wiggly while I was putting her white clothes on that it was extra hard to dress her. Then, as I held her up so she might see herself in the mirror in her pretty white dress and white socks, she was so happy she could hardly contain herself. She was ready at last, and her heart was beating faster than I had ever felt it before.

When the time for her baptism arrived, I handed her to Bruce and he took her down into the water. Because she was prepared, and because she trusted her father, Heather felt happy and secure, and her face beamed with excitement. Bruce held her by wrapping his left arm around her chest and under her arms. After the prayer he covered her mouth and nose with his left hand and immersed her in the water face first.

What I next witnessed is indelibly imprinted on my mind and heart. When Heather came up out of the water she had a huge smile on her face, and her whole being was simply radiant. She truly looked like an angel.

Bearing Her Testimony

Heather also showed her love for her Heavenly Father by sharing her testimony, which she would do whenever someone would help her. The first time it happened I was holding her during a fast and testimony sacrament meeting, and about halfway through the meeting she communicated to me that *she* wanted to go up to the pulpit and bear her testimony. Talk about panic on my part! I thought of every possible excuse and tried to talk her out of it, but she insisted.

I soon became convinced that she sincerely wanted to bear her testimony, so I reluctantly gave in and asked her what she wanted me to say for her. She communicated to me that she wanted to tell the congregation that she knew her Heavenly Father loved her, and she knew she would be resurrected with a perfect body. So, with *my* heart pounding, I carried Heather up to the pulpit and held her in my arms so that she could face the congregation. I told the people about Heather's and my "conversation" in the back of the chapel and then what she told me to say. I told them some details about Heather's feelings about the Resurrection, and that it was so clear to her that she had already planned what she wanted to do when that day arrived. I explained that one of the first things she wanted to do after she was resurrected was to ski.

As I said the word *ski,* Heather began blinking her eyes and slightly shaking her head, meaning, "No!"

Puzzled, I said to the congregation, "That's what she told us she wanted to do first after she was resurrected. She must have changed her mind."

Heather gave me a direct gaze, meaning, "Yes, I did change my mind."

I then told the congregation, "As soon as I find out what she wants to do first, I'll tell you, if you would like to know." I then concluded by bearing my testimony.

As I walked back down the aisle carrying Heather, I noticed many people wiping away tears. Heather's testimony truly had touched their hearts. Later, I discovered that Heather actually wanted to *walk* before she skied. It seems that a teacher at school had asked her, "Don't you think it would be a good idea to walk before you ski?" Obviously Heather agreed.

One person who was touched by Heather's testimony on another occasion was her Primary teacher. She wrote: "One Sunday during Primary class, I was bearing my testimony to the girls. I looked at Heather and her sweet spirit touched mine in such a way that said, 'Yes, you're right.' Chills went up and down my spine as I looked into her sweet eyes. I felt so strongly that she was bearing her testimony to me."

Heather also loved to give talks. When she was seven years old she volunteered to give a talk in Primary. Since it could be on any topic she chose, I had to determine the subject she wanted before I could begin helping her prepare. As I began discussing the talk with her I discovered that she already had a subject in mind, so I began by asking, "Do you want to talk about families? On choosing the right? On being kind to others?" I proposed a number of topics I thought would be relevant to her, but for every topic I suggested she gave me a definite no. Finally I asked, "Do you want to give a talk about Jesus?" She gave me a "kind-of" look, so I proceeded to ask about topics such as Jesus blessing little children, Jesus healing people, and then, the Resurrection. Yes, that was it! Heather wanted to give a talk on the Resurrection. I really should have guessed that topic earlier, because that frequently seemed to be a favorite one of hers. With Heather's help and approval I wrote the following talk, which she gave in Primary the following week: "Everyone will be resurrected because Jesus was resurrected. When we are resurrected, our spirits and bodies will come back together, and our bodies will be perfect. We will have no handicaps. I will be able to walk, run, ski, roller-skate, play hopscotch, cook, and do all kinds of things. I am thankful that Jesus made it possible for us to be resurrected. In the name of Jesus Christ, amen."

Many people felt her testimony that day. One Primary teacher wrote: "I'll never forget the beautiful talk Heather gave in Primary. I knew that even though she didn't speak the words, they came from Heather. She wanted to be a part of the Primary and participate in the best way she could. She was a great example to all of us. I appreciated her valiant spirit."

Her testimony of the reality of the resurrection was evident many times at home too. Often she would indicate that she could hardly wait to be resurrected so *she* could cook dinner for *us*. What a testimony, and what a giving, thoughtful child she was!

The Little Missionary

Heather's testimony and great love for the Lord was also shown by her desire to be a missionary and to get others to live the principles of the gospel—even when they weren't members of the Church. I think she sincerely believed that if everyone could feel the joy she felt, everyone would want to conform to the Savior's teachings and join His Church, and that if they would do that they would all be happier. I also think Heather recognized each individual for what he or she was—a spirit offspring of a loving Heavenly Father—and as a result, she wanted each person to reach his or her spiritual potential.

There was one schoolteacher in particular who became the recipient of much of her missionary zeal. This teacher had a habit of taking the Lord's name in vain—not in anger, but just in the course of normal conversation, and Heather thought that behavior should change. So after much discussion, Heather came up with the idea that every time her teacher swore, she would be required to put a quarter in a jar. Everyone involved— the teacher, her aides, and Heather—agreed to those terms. From that time on, whenever Heather heard her teacher swear she would look at her teacher and then at the jar, as if to say, "If you're going to swear, you have to pay!"

It ended up being a humorous way to solve a problem, but I think it also was a means for Heather to feel that she was doing missionary work by making the world a better place in which to live. As parents, we are grateful for that teacher for being so kind and unoffended by Heather's insistence that she conform to Heather's values.

Confirming the idea that Heather never was ashamed of her testimony but only anxious to share it with everyone, an assistant at Monte Vista School wrote: "Although Heather's body was unable to give her the use she needed, I do believe she was the greatest missionary and influenced more people than anyone I know. What an example for all!"

Heather's Love and Concern for Others

The Prophet Joseph Smith once said, "Love is one of the chief characteristics of Deity, and ought to be manifested by those who aspire to be the sons [and daughters] of God. A man filled with the love of God, is not content with blessing his family alone, but ranges through the whole world, anxious to bless the whole human race." (*Teachings of the Prophet Joseph Smith,* p. 174.) That certainly seemed to be what Heather was anxious to do, because one of her most predominant characteristics was her love for all people. It was manifested by her kindness, thoughtfulness, patience, and sensitivity, and by the fact that it was reciprocated by those whom she loved. For example, her patience was evident as she voluntarily agreed to be the last of the three handicapped children to eat each meal. It was demonstrated as she waited for someone to play with her or to help her do something, and it was manifested as she tried to communicate with us. She never became angry, even if we couldn't understand what she was trying to tell us.

Michelle wrote about Heather's ultimate display of patience: "Heather literally did all she could to prepare herself for the future, even though it was impossible for her at the time to make it come to pass. She was content to prepare and wait. For example, she wanted to be a wife and mother and never let up on that, even though it was impossible in this life."

Heather's love and concern was also shown by her selflessness and sensitivity to the feelings of others. She was always more interested in what she was giving for Christmas than in what she was receiving. She always wanted to console the person who was sad or hurting, and she always wanted to take flowers or candy to someone at school. Her sister Heidi wrote: "Heather always wanted to come in our room with us when we felt sad about something, so that she could make us feel better. And when we wanted to talk to someone about our problems or felt like we were being ignored, Heather would be there."

Heather also showed her selflessness toward the end of her life when she was in such severe pain that she needed me to move her five or six times a night. She would insist that I go back to bed each time after I moved her so I wouldn't get too tired. Her keen sensitivity to my feelings, as well as her expression of gratitude and love to me for helping her, often brought tears to my eyes as I desperately tried to make her more comfortable.

Heather's love also was demonstrated by her great desire to be helpful. She wanted to help do everything that needed to be done. Although she was unable to do anything by herself, she loved to have someone lay her on her beanbag in the yard so she could "pull" weeds. She especially loved to have someone hold her and move her from room to room while she "dusted" around the house.

In a different vein, Heather's love and sensitivity was demonstrated one evening when she was watching the movie *King Kong* on television. At the beginning of the movie she was afraid of King Kong because he was a big monster. As the movie progressed, however, Heather's feelings toward him changed. As soon as King Kong showed kind feelings toward the heroine, Heather was no longer afraid. In fact, her feelings for King Kong became so strong as the movie progressed that in the end, she cried when he was attacked and finally killed.

Heather's life truly was an example of love and concern for others, as well as an example of unwavering faith and trust in the Lord. Surely, the way I show my faithfulness is by doing as Heather did: trusting that "Jesus, listening, can hear" me too, being obedient, choosing to be happy despite my circumstances, loving God with all my heart, loving my fellowmen by serving them and being patient with them, and enduring to the end of my mortal life. It is my testimony that that is the way we all may find peace.

CHAPTER 7

Heidi, Lara, and Michelle
Share Their Feelings

As much as I enjoyed receiving telephone calls, letters, and even heartrending poetry about the effect Heather had in people's lives, the words that brought me the most comfort after Heather died were those written by our three healthy daughters. Knowing that growing up in our family was not easy for them, I asked them to share their feelings about their personal efforts to find peace.

Heidi's Comments

I think Michelle, Lara, and I had to sacrifice a lot while growing up in a family with handicapped siblings. We had to sacrifice interaction time between parent and child and time to communicate with each other. There were not many times when one of our parents (or both) were able to do something with any of us on a one-on-one basis. And if they were able to go somewhere with us, we were always resigned to the fact that Mom would eventually say, "I need to get home so I can feed Cindy, Heather and Mark." And that would end the fun time we had together. Sometimes when that happened, it made me feel like I was not an important member of the family, and I really resented it. We also had to sacrifice such things as long family vacations and picnics with the entire family. Stated simply, because we had three people in wheelchairs, I felt cheated out of a normal family life, and it was very hard to accept.

Another thing that was hard to accept was the feeling that my needs weren't considered. I remember a Christmas Day a few years ago, when Cindy was very sick. I had awakened early, excited for the day, but the excitement soon ended when my parents had to call the doctor, order some oxygen, care for Cindy, and call someone to help Dad give her a blessing. I was waiting for the day to be a happy one, but it wasn't. Mark was laying on the floor, not even stressed out about the situation, and a visitor came in and said to him, "Oh, are you all right?" I was sitting there too, but no one seemed to care how I felt. Needless to say, it was a terrible day.

Growing up, I wondered if I would ever find *my* place in the family, and not feel like I was just "Heather's sister, Mark's sister, or Cindy's sister." I wondered if I would ever feel important for just being me. Then, when I became a teenager, I often wondered why I didn't rebel. Maybe I was somehow hoping that things would get better, or else I was waiting for the time when I could be out on my own and become the person *I* wanted to be—to get the chance to experience life.

The thing that helped me the very most, and probably kept me from rebelling, happened the summer after my junior year in high school. My parents paid my way back to New York so I could be a cast member in the Hill Cumorah Pageant, and that was one of the *greatest* experience of my life! I felt *totally* loved and accepted. I also gained an appreciation of the Book of Mormon, and a knowledge that Christ loves me. I still did not know why God gave me this challenge, but one day as I was in the Sacred Grove with my study group, I prayed earnestly and asked if Joseph Smith *had* the vision there. I also asked God to help me find the reason for my family challenge. I found out that Joseph *did* have the vision, but my prayer to know the reason for my family challenge went unanswered. Time will tell, I guess. But, regardless of that, I still felt the love of Christ with me.

I found that the feeling I had at the Pageant was the best feeling I could ever have, and after that, I knew that I did not want to rebel—there is no point in it. The thing that counts is having the Spirit, and being kind to everyone. What would we have to show for our life if we only felt love for a bottle of beer and a pack of cigarettes? That is not what God wants. He wants us to be happy and return to Him, to have His Spirit with us, so we can find help with our problems.

Just because I am now trying to love Him and have Him help me with my problems, however, doesn't mean that I now know why He gave me this family challenge. I may never know, but there *has* to be a reason. I hope that I someday find that reason and find complete peace. Even though it's hard, I just can't give up. Right now, I am trying to get a smile on my face, look for the positive, and help other people.

One thing I think I have learned from this challenge is that we all are important—even if we're in a wheelchair or look different. Also, I have learned that it is hurtful when people stare at someone who may be different. Those who look different are people too. Essentially, I have learned to be kind to all people. Compassion is a good word, I guess.

Heidi wrote those words when she was seventeen, right after she attended the Hill Cumorah Pageant. Showing the growth that can come when one takes personal responsibility and continually humbles herself, she wrote the following two years later:

These last 2 years at Ricks College have opened many new avenues of thought and new friendships to me. Consequently, I have many more feelings in my heart at this time.

Although the Pageant opened my eyes to many new thoughts, and I felt the Spirit deeply there, I now realize that my *heart* still held a lot of anger because of my family situation. The Pageant was not the "cure-all" for that anger; rather, it was a way of speeding up the process of recognizing the need for change. But the need for change, and the desire *to* change, did not come until I went to Ricks College.

I think that there is no better way to explain my feelings now than to share a final exam I wrote for my communications class at Ricks. It begins: One thing I want to remember is the scripture, "In due season we shall reap, if we faint not." (Galatians 6:9) This scripture has a very strong application with me. I am not referring to exercising, and reaping benefits of exercise, or of studying and reaping benefits of good grades. I am talking about this from a spiritual standpoint.

It seems that sometimes, when challenges and trials come into our lives that we don't understand we have a tendency to question God and wonder "why me?" We wonder what we can possibly learn from the experiences we have been given. "In due season we shall reap, if we faint not," means that if we continue to sow, to put our "shoulder to the wheel" and give things *time,* we will reap the blessings and better be able to understand the will of God in our lives.

I'm sure that many college freshmen are excited to get to college, be out on their own, and to experience the world by *themselves.* I was no exception. I was looking forward to being away from my parents and my family. I was especially ready to get away from living with 3 handicapped siblings. Eighteen years had been enough for me.

Well, God obviously didn't think the same way I did. The day before my freshman year began, I found out that I had a handicapped roommate. She said "hi" to us, and right away I knew what was wrong.

"Oh no," I thought, "not *again.*" My world, and my whole freshman year had just turned upside down. All the justice and the love that I thought God had for me just went out the window. "Why would He do this to me *again?*" I thought to myself.

I struggled with the question for months. I didn't understand it. I had gone away to school to get away from it, but it just followed me. I was angry and frustrated.

As the year went on I accepted it a bit more, but I still had problems and challenges with accepting other things. I looked harshly at my parents; the love for them or a relationship, was not there. I did not love myself and thought that other people "had it in for me." The whole world was just a big disappointment for me.

I say again: "In due season we shall reap, if we faint not." My thoughts and my behavior was what I sowed, and I reaped anger and hate in my heart. I was not able to understand; many things were cloudy to me.

The school year ended for me, and was I excited!! No more of my handicapped roommate. I didn't have to deal with it anymore—just run away and leave the whole situation. "Never again," I thought, excitedly.

The summer was a time of working and learning for me. My conscience finally caught up with me for how I had treated my roommate(s). I began to feel sorry for my behavior. I began to see that it was *my* problem; my behavior was because I had not taken care of feelings in my heart that had built up inside of me. I did not love her because I did not love *me* and was unsure of a lot of things in my heart.

The new school year began; I returned with a summer's experiences and a greater desire to love others. I also had been blessed with more forgiveness from the year before. My old roommates soon were not my enemies, but my friends. Maybe it was because we no longer lived together, but I don't think so. We had all grown up and become older, and each of us better understood our mistakes and weaknesses.

Now what does all of this have to do with the saying, "In due season we shall reap, if we faint not?" I believe that, as the last few years of my life have unfolded at Ricks College, this has been a reaping period of my life. Many questions were always in the back of my mind. I fainted not and endured to the end. It just took me a while to keep in mind that I needed to continue reaping, to realize that what I put in, I got out.

My handicapped roommate has given me some very profound statements that I will always remember. She also has helped me see that *I* needed the experience with her to seek forgiveness, to learn humility, to learn to trust God. If I had *not* been her roommate, many of the feelings I'd carried around with me my whole life would not have surfaced so quickly.

I have continued to be friends with my handicapped roommate, and I have been greatly blessed to know her. She has taught me a lot about life, about loving, and about God. He sometimes will hand us things that are hard to see the meaning; we only see a part of the picture while God sees the whole thing. But if we faint not, and keep the faith, we shall reap. We shall reap the blessings and better understand the love that God *does* have for us.

I have also reaped many other blessings: love for my other roommates, appreciation for their vital friendships, and the ability to *love myself* and see challenges as *learning* experiences rather than a reason to curse God.

I am grateful for the things I have learned. I am grateful to reap the blessings of what I sowed because I "fainted not." I am so grateful that I did indeed have a handicapped roommate. It did not look like something I would reap from, but I was wrong.

Lara began by expressing some feelings about our family's inability to go places together.

Lara's Comments

Something that was hard was not being able to go a lot of places as a family. Although I looked forward to going to Disneyland whenever we could go, I sometimes felt angry about not being able to go to simple, meaningless places, just for fun. It was so difficult to go to the mall, ward activities, out for ice cream, to see a movie, or even just a drive, that we very seldom enjoyed such activities.

Sometimes, I felt angry about my circumstances. Occasionally, I felt bitter toward Mom and Dad for not always supporting me, or giving me all of the attention that I wanted. I felt like I had to compete for attention and take a back seat to the handicapped people in our family. While other parents were doing things with their children, my parents were at home taking care of the handicapped children. Sometimes I even felt upset towards Cindy, Heather, and Mark for not letting Mom and Dad spend more time with Michelle, Heidi, and me. Then I would feel guilty, because I knew it wasn't the handicapped children's fault, and I knew it wasn't Mom's and Dad's fault either. I still often wished that I could do more things with my parents, though. I especially wished I could go to the store with Mom without having to wonder when we would have to "go home and feed Cindy, Heather, and Mark."

As I got older, I think I became more understanding and definitely less embarrassed about the family. I still don't like telling people about my situation though—not because I'm embarrassed but because I don't feel like explaining everything. I always wonder if people will treat me differently or feel sorry for me.

Now, since I have been married, I can see positive and negative effects of living in a home with three handicapped siblings. One advantage is that the "normal" children are very independent or self-reliant. In a sense, we had to "raise ourselves." We had to learn to handle a lot of things by ourselves. This is good—it makes me a stronger person, I think. I am able to handle situations well because I have had to stand up for myself. This has also made me a very hard worker and determined person. Jereck, my husband, has noticed this in our marriage. I work very hard in school and will "get the project done" no matter what.

Another advantage of being in the Erickson family was that sometimes we got special privileges that normal families didn't get. For example, we always got a parking space close to the entrance at Disneyland, and we got to meet a lot of people (even famous ones). When Heather and Mark got to meet special people, I always thought that was pretty neat, and I was proud to be their sister. I even felt kind of special.

One negative effect of growing up in a home with three handicapped siblings is that now, in certain situations, I don't always know how to do routine household tasks. Mom simply didn't have the time to teach us how to do such things as ironing a shirt, shopping for groceries, cleaning a bathroom, or cooking. Some of these things might have been taught once or twice, but without a lot of repetition, they were hard to remember. This has caused some stress in our marriage. Jereck has been frustrated with me for not knowing how to do certain tasks, and I have felt inadequate. We both have a better understanding now of how to deal with this, because of many hours of expressing our feelings. This is still a sore spot for me, but knowing that Jereck knows why I am like this and being patient with me has helped a lot.

I realize more now how difficult it was for my parents to give me the support and attention that I wanted. The demands and tremendous amount of time that Cindy, Heather and Mark required were incredible. One example that shows the support of Mom and Dad was when I had my sophomore review at Utah State University. Mom, Mark and Heidi came up to see it. I was so happy, and it really meant a lot to me. Jereck even noticed that I was really happy about my family coming to see my review.

Something that Jereck brought to my attention was that Mom and Dad really made holidays important and special. They made a big deal of Christmas, Thanksgiving, Easter, etc., and they were always lots of fun. Dad always overdid it on the food and goodies, but we loved it (and still do). Christmas was always a lot of fun—and I loved the traditions—12 days of Christmas, tons of presents, notes in the tree, the order we opened presents. It was also fun to see Cindy's, Heather's, and Mark's reaction when they opened the present that I had given them.

Michelle expressed her feelings by sharing some essays she wrote for a college class.

Michelle's Comments

Whether it's Dad's big ears, Mom's obnoxious laugh, or your little sister's irritating habit, all of us must learn to accept our families. True, sometimes it might be nice to go to the local Families-R-Us store and exchange what we have for what we want, or at least take it back. But we can't.

Take my family for example. Not exactly your typical, normal family. And it's not because we're all a bunch of sweet spirits either. In fact, the joke in our house is that three of us are handicapped and three are normal, but you have to figure out which three.

I would be lying if I said that I have always felt that having Cindy, Heather and Mark in our home has been the choice, special experience that some say Deity has blessed us with. Because, in all honesty, it is an understatement to say that accepting my family was, by far, the biggest challenge of my life.

When I was growing up, we moved 11 times in my first 18 years. How I hated having to tell the "unknown disease" story to every new church ward we went to. How I hated being told we were "special sweet spirits." Adults seemed to flock toward the situation, while my peers shunned it. I didn't want attention. I just wanted friends. In fact, it was amazing that I would invite a "friend" to my house to play, and she would avoid me from then on, as if she thought the disease was contagious or something.

So, then I began to avoid my family. I remember walking past my home when the school bus dropped us off, just because the special education bus was in our driveway.

How I hated being seen with my family. Going into stores or other public places was sheer torture for me, especially when other people stopped and stared at the three wheelchairs. How I hated to be noticed.

Feeding the three handicapped people, changing them, and entertaining them required what I thought was too much time, and deprived me of my own life, my own happiness. How I envied people in healthy families. They could all jump in a car and go to a movie or go out to dinner as a family, while we had to have a minimum of 20 minutes to get everyone in their wheelchairs, up the ramp, in the van, and clamped in. And, of course, we couldn't let everyone around us feel uncomfortable in a restaurant as Cindy, Heather, and Mark drooled and struggled to keep food in their mouths. So we always ate at home.

Then a funny thing happened. I can't justly describe the significance it had for me in words. But several incidents made me realize a couple of things. First, I realized I was lucky because our family problems were keeping us close together. They weren't depriving me of a social life, but they were keeping me from temptation. And, most importantly, it finally became obvious that we can't necessarily change the situation, but we can change our reaction. There are two possibilities to every action—one positive or one negative. Happiness depends on us.

A positive attitude hasn't healed Cindy, Heather, or Mark, but it sure has made all those incidents that I shunned before bearable, even enjoyable. So much so, dare I say, that those who know me now and didn't know me before, would find this a shocking revelation into my dark side.

Now, if anything, I'm accused of speaking too much about my great family. And even being away at school makes me miss the challenges and benefits of being with them, not to mention the handicapped parking privileges. For example, we now go to the malls and have wheelchair races. We are a circus side show with our own little wheelchair train when we go to Disneyland and wave to everyone, and we never have to grow up. We play ring-around-the-rosy, London Bridges, house, and lots of 20 questions. And I can't forget how great it is when Mark hugs me as he struggles to jerkily place his arms around my neck, and grunts out an "I uv oo," for "I love you." It's great.

Sure, it takes a long time to care for them. But look at what they have taught me—how to love, smile, be sincere, not take even small abilities for granted, and most importantly, you can be happy with what you've got.

Then there is the experience Michelle shared at her missionary farewell. She calls this experience "Thankful for Blessings."

I had just finished a semester at BYU and was home from college. Mom was gone and asked me to get Heather off her school bus. As I did, Heather proceeded to tell me she wanted me to make a chocolate creme pie for a family in the neighborhood. I didn't want to make the pie, so I asked her about her day, about school, and told her Mom would be home soon. I was trying to get out of making the pie. But, it didn't work. She just kept insisting that I make a chocolate creme pie.

I finally gave in and, reluctantly, took her out of her wheelchair, put her on her beanbag, brought Cindy and Mark to the kitchen and found the ingredients to make the pie.

In our house, when we make chocolate creme pie, we make it from "scratch." We have to stir it constantly while it cooks. As I was mixing the ingredients and telling her how much to put in, I said everything I could think of in cooking terms. Heather was all smiles. But, after about 20 minutes of stirring, and the pudding still didn't come to a boil, I was getting impatient and irritated. You know how it is when you stand in one place for a long time stirring? I got a cramp in my hand. The steam was rising up in my face, I was hot, and I said, "Heather, this is *not* fun."

She just smiled and wiggled as if to say, "Yes, yes it is!"

"No, it's not," I said. "If you could do it you would know that *it is not fun*."

But she still insisted that it was.

I guess it was just because of the mood I was in that I said, "Heather, if you think it is so fun, why don't you do it yourself."

Heather's reaction was something I will never forget. She stared at me; then she looked up at the ceiling; and then she looked right back at me. That was her way of saying, "I can't now Michelle, but I will when I am resurrected."

Her answer to my stupidity hit me at the heart. You see, she always looked at the ceiling when she talked about her resurrection. But, even more, it taught me not to take my abilities for granted. It made me realize that my burdens may be another person's greatest blessings and desires, and I should be thankful for what I have and can do. Here I was complaining about something that Heather was anxiously waiting over a lifetime to do.

I've thought about that experience many times. It has helped me while walking up steep hills or hundreds of stairs in the snow to campus, while reading 450 pages of a boring book, and while writing 20 page reports. I should be thankful I can walk, and read and write, rather than complain about what I must do.

I hope, if I remember nothing else while I am on my mission in Barcelona, Spain, I will remember that. I hope I will remember that I shouldn't complain about wearing nylons, tracting all day, or knocking on doors and getting turned down. I shouldn't complain about doing any of those things, because there are people who would very much like to do them but can't. We all should be very thankful for the things we can do.

We are grateful that Michelle shared these thoughts and feelings, which she titled "Think as She Would Think."

From Heather's direct gaze in the eyes for "yes," and blinks and shakes of the head for "no," I got to play a lot of 20 questions. I learned that in order to really communicate with someone, words aren't necessary, only consideration for the other person.

Heather could never verbalize a word, but I learned that if I thought as she thought, it would cut down on the time it took to figure out what she wanted and we both would be happier. For example, when she got home from school, she would want to eat something. By knowing her, I knew she didn't like hot dogs, she didn't like orange juice, but she did like milk and peanut butter and honey. So, I didn't have to bother asking her dislikes, but only had to concentrate on her likes.

I realized that if we take time to place ourselves in the other person's shoes, then we can communicate and get along better, whether or not we can speak. This has helped me in my life to better relate to other people and attempt to understand how they are feeling and what they really like.

Michelle also shared with us an incident that occurred two weeks before Heather died:

It was Easter. I came home that weekend from college and was kind of disappointed I was there. I wanted to be with some friends that were going to St. George, Utah, for the holiday. But now, I know I was where I was supposed to be. Mom was teaching Relief Society and her lesson was on the atonement and resurrection. About half way through the lesson, I was informed I had to get Heather from Primary.

As I held her during the rest of the lesson, I was amazed at how bad her scoliosis had become. She had become so much more difficult to hold. All the usual positions didn't work. I was appreciative of how much my mom did. Mark was there with us. They loved it as I would draw little faces on their fingernails with a pen.

My mom bore her testimony and left the rest of the time for our testimonies. The Spirit was strong. My heart was pounding. As I stood up with Heather, she had the biggest smile on her face. We both, together, bore testimony of the reality of the resurrection. We talked about how Heather would fix dinner for us; how we would all be able to go to Disneyland together and ride on all of the rides; and how she would be a mom someday. We both thanked Christ for what He had done. I sat down and felt good. Little did I know that was to be the last time she attended church because the last Sunday of her life was General Conference. It was a perfect way to celebrate Easter.

Finally, I love this expression of faith by Michelle:

One day during dinner, I remember Heather wanted
more milk, and it always seemed that I had to get more milk
for her. As I did, I asked her, "Heather, when are you going
to get *me* some milk?"

She looked up at the ceiling, meaning, "in the next life."
She then also looked at her plate, meaning that she wanted
to make dinner for the family in the next life.

Heather's faith in the resurrection gave me the comfort
I needed to realize that life will be fair, that someday
Heather will sing, Cindy will walk, and Mark will play football. Without that, I don't know if I would have been able to
overcome the trial of having three handicapped siblings.

On the day of her funeral, I kept remembering
Heather's desire to feed us and thinking what food she
would make and how happy a day it would be. At that moment, I realized that I must live so I can make that dinner
appointment. The words came to me, "Michelle, whatever
you do, live so you can attend that feast." This has been a
motto for me. I have a card with that on it pinned up in my
room. Every time I look in the mirror, I think of that. And
thanks to Heather, it has become a life goal for me.

Bruce and I are extremely grateful that Michelle, Lara, and
Heidi chose to help us care for Cindy, Heather, and Mark, that
they didn't rebel against us or the teachings found in the gospel
of Jesus Christ, that they actually learned worthwhile lessons
while living in our home, and that at least to some degree each
one has found peace and comfort.

PART II

"After the Trial . . ."

Joyce J. Erickson

CHAPTER 8

Personal Lessons

Concerning the matter of faith, the prophet Moroni wrote, "Wherefore, dispute not because ye see not, for ye receive no witness until after the trial of your faith" (Ether 12:6). Now, after more than twenty years of struggling with adversity, I can say without reservation that Moroni's testimony is my testimony—that in matters of faith, most lessons and witnesses come *after* we prove our devotion and unwavering faithfulness to God. Some of the lessons I learned from my experiences follow.

The Worth of a Soul

Today we hear many voices regarding the worth of a soul. One loud chorus says, "Only the fit should survive," "Quality of life is of utmost concern," "Do whatever feels best for you" (see Alma 30:17), and "Abortion on demand." A much quieter set of voices says, "The worth of souls is great in the sight of God" (D&C 18:10); "*Every* spirit that comes to this earth to take upon it a tabernacle is a son or a daughter of God, and possesses all the intelligence and all the attributes that any son or daughter can enjoy" (Joseph F. Smith, *Gospel Doctrine,* p. 453, emphasis added).

How grateful I am for the many important lessons each of our handicapped children has taught me regarding the worth of a soul. Together they have helped me answer the questions posed by Elder James E. Faust: "Is life not worth living if it is not perfect? Do not the people with handicaps also bring their own gifts to life—and to others who are free of those handicaps—in a manner that cannot come in any other way?" ("The Works of God," p. 54.) They have taught me that "many of the special ones are superior in many ways. They, too, are in a life of progression, and new things unfold for them each day as with us all." (Ibid. p. 59.) And they have taught me that "every quarter of an inch of physical and mental improvement is worth striving for" (Packer, "The Moving of the Water," p. 9) and that "all the minds and spirits that God ever sent into the world are susceptible of enlargement" (*Teachings of the Prophet Joseph Smith,* p. 354).

They also have helped me learn that the works of God are manifest (John 9:1–3) in handicapped children. Since the handicapped are natural-born receivers, they give those who interact with them an opportunity to perform the works of God. Elder Boyd K. Packer said: "In Mendoza, Argentina, we attended a seminary graduation. In the class was a young man who had great difficulty climbing ordinary steps. As the class marched in, two strong young classmates gracefully lifted him up the steps. . . . In *them* the works of God *were being* manifest." ("The Moving of the Water," pp. 7, 8, emphasis in original.)

Like the young man in Elder Packer's example, our handicapped children have given their parents, sisters, teachers, friends, and aides at school, church, and home an opportunity to perform the works of God. For that reason I have often thought it would be appropriate to place a sign over the doors of schools for the handicapped—a sign which reads, "The works of God are manifest here." Surely that would be a fitting tribute to the people who lovingly care for the disabled.

I love Elder Packer's comforting words regarding all the time and effort required of those who care for the handicapped:

You parents and you families whose lives must be reordered because of a handicapped one, whose resources and time must be devoted to them, are special heroes. . . . Never mind the tears nor the hours of regret and discouragement; never mind the times when you feel you cannot stand another day of what is required. You are living the principles of the gospel of Jesus Christ in exceptional purity. *And you perfect yourselves in the process. . . .*

I bear witness of the restoration which will come. Each body and mind will be restored in perfect frame. However long and unfair mortality may seem, however long the suffering and the waiting may be, he has said:

"After that cometh the day of my power; then shall the poor, the lame, and the blind, and the deaf, come in unto the marriage of the Lamb, and partake of the supper of the Lord, prepared for the great day to come" (D & C 58:11). (Ibid., p. 9, emphasis in original.)

How much more worthy could a soul be to "partake of the supper of the Lord," than the many who are handicapped in mortality? Surely Cindy, Heather, and Mark will be there. My daily hope and prayer is that every other member of our family will be there too.

Accepting Our Circumstances

I am convinced that one of the most important things we can do to find peace during our trials is to pray that somehow we can accept the unchangeable circumstances that accompany our adversity. Great comfort comes when we finally accept our allotment from the Lord. To illustrate this concept, Michelle shares a college essay titled "Truth Really Does Make You Free."

I haven't always thought it was a blessing or advantage to have handicapped siblings. In fact, I hated it until high school. I thought God wasn't fair. I couldn't figure out what more we could learn from two handicapped (and later with my brother Mark, three) children, that we couldn't learn from one. It seemed very unfair.

The following is the incident that was a big step in helping me feel more open in sharing my story with others. It is more about Cindy, but I later told the same class about Heather.

I have told myself again and again that I must stop lying about my family. But it's one thing to say it and another to actually do what you say. Maybe this move from South Salt Lake City to Centerville will help because no one here knows of my past.

Today is the second day of class for me at Viewmont High School. Just my luck, I have the most meticulous English teacher. Her name is Miss Davis and she is the English department chairman and girls' volleyball coach.

She wears a hideous key chain attached to her belt loop. As she lectures, she slides her thumbs through the belt loops, as if to keep her large pants from falling off her lanky body. It is an irritating habit. She stresses punctuality, neatness, and exactness on everything from attendance to where we write our names on our papers.

Our assignment for today is to give a five minute oral report on a tragedy in our lives. I am terrified. Speaking in public is as hard for me as digesting my mom's spinach. I'm still not sure what I will say. Cindy's illness would be the best story, but I don't dare. That is too close to me. Last night I decided I would speak about our car that was stolen three years ago.

It is almost my turn. I feel my heart pounding against my desk. My hands are clammy, and I shouldn't have worn this sweater because I am too hot. Oh, no, she called my name.

I stood up and walked to the front of the long, narrow room with no windows. I coughed and put my hands in my pockets to hide my shaking fingers, and looked at the floor. I hesitated. My mind went numb. Before I realized what I was saying, I began telling strangers the story I didn't want to tell.

"Um . . . my tragedy happened when I was four years old. I had a favorite red toy telephone that I played with all of the time."

What am I saying? Just three months ago, I would rather have died then tell this story. Reluctantly, I continued.

"One Saturday evening after I had taken my bath, I placed my phone on a chair in our living room."

As I spoke, I raised my head and stared at the clock on the back wall. I didn't dare look down at my classmates. I noticed how the fluorescent lights brightened the ugly, gray paneled walls.

"While I was playing, my eight-month-old sister, Cindy, crawled over to me. She stood up against the chair and knocked the telephone off with her hand, and laughed. I said, "Cindy, no, no, don't touch.""

I heard a snicker in the front corner of the classroom. I looked towards it; a blonde girl smiled. I was relieved.

"I moved her away and placed the toy back on the chair. Cindy did it again. She laughed and laughed. Finally my mom took her away to give her a bath. And the next thing I heard was my mom screaming."

This is too difficult, but I have to continue now. I looked up. All eyes were on me. The class was actually listening to me. I took a deep breath and continued the story I didn't want to tell.

"I went in to see what was wrong. Cindy was lying on the floor like a dead person. In fact, the only way we knew she was alive was because her heart was beating. Her eyes were glazed over. She didn't react to anything we did. We tried waving a hand in front of her, slapping her, tickling her, and talking to her, but she did nothing.

"My parents then rushed Cindy to the March Air Force Base hospital. The doctors didn't know what was wrong with Cindy so they sent her to Los Angeles Children's Hospital, where she stayed for three weeks. There they ran hundreds of tests on her. They put needles in the bottom of her feet, took X-rays, brain scans, and electrocardiograms, but she still did nothing. "

I hate this part. My mouth is dry and my eyes are slightly moist. I notice the blonde girl rub her eyes.

"After three weeks, Cindy finally came home. During this time, she lost 3 pounds and all muscle control. Cindy has been crippled with an unknown disease since then. And that was my tragedy."

"Thanks," Miss Davis uttered, and I sat down.

What exactly did I tell them? My heart is pounding harder than before. I can't believe I actually admitted to myself and my classmates the truth. This is a big step for me. It is the first time I have ever openly revealed my family situation. And the class accepted me despite Cindy's handicap.

Maybe it really is okay if people know about my sister. Even though telling that story was painful, I have an overwhelming feeling that I cannot describe. I did it! I finally spoke the truth to my peers! The chains have been removed. Truth really does make you free!

As I look back on this experience, I can see that it was the first step in making me who I am today. Sometimes I am unsure of my major, my abilities, and my mission in life. But today I am no longer chained to my past lies. I am a free person. I am a person who loves my family and I am not ashamed of them.

I am convinced that we each can find a degree of peace and comfort when we understand and accept the unchangeable circumstances in our lives, just as Michelle did.

Self-Esteem

Although Heather was totally dependent and had no visible talents, I sensed that she had very healthy self-esteem. Because of that, and because self-esteem is a topic that is discussed often today, I became curious as to what really contributes to a person's feeling of self-worth. Most discussions on this subject seemed to be centered around learning techniques for improving relationships with others; helping children get good grades in school; providing them with music lessons, dancing lessons, swimming lessons, or ice skating lessons; helping them learn baseball skills, basketball skills, or soccer skills; helping them develop their artistic talents—helping them learn how to do something that would make them feel good about themselves.

I am not sure about all the factors that contribute to self-esteem, but because Heather could not do any of the usual things that supposedly contribute to a child's self-esteem, I am convinced that true self-esteem comes not from learning skills and participating in activities alone. Instead, it seems to me that true self-esteem comes from those things that were so much a part of Heather's character—knowing you are a child of God and that your Heavenly Father loves you, knowing you are becoming what He wants you to become, keeping His commandments, and knowing you are genuinely loved by your parents and family.

With those ideas in mind, I began reading and listening carefully to what latter-day prophets and Apostles said about self-esteem. First I read what President Ezra Taft Benson said: "The proud depend upon the world to tell them whether they have value or not. Their self-esteem is determined by where they are judged to be on the ladders of worldly success. They feel worthwhile as individuals if the numbers beneath them in achievement, talent, beauty, or intellect are large enough. . . . If we love God, do His will, and fear His judgment more than men's, we will have self-esteem." ("Beware of Pride," p. 6.) Then, I discovered that Elder Marvin J. Ashton stated: "To gain exaltation and happy daily life, we must follow a pattern of righteousness. Our self-esteem and success can best be measured by how we follow the patterns of life which prevent deceit, haughtiness, pride, or pessimism." ("A Pattern in All Things," p. 22.) And finally, I read that Elder M. Russell Ballard said, "The youth told me that a clean conscience improves their self-esteem" ("Purity Precedes Power," p. 36; see also D&C 121:45).

As I reread President Benson's talk "Cleansing the Inner Vessel," I became even further convinced that true self-esteem is tied more to what we are and what our hearts are set on than to what we can do. President Benson said, "A wholesome view of self-worth . . . is best established by a close relationship with God" (p. 6).

As I continued to read what prophets and apostles said, I began to wonder what Bruce and I could do specifically to help our children develop healthy self-esteem. I found statements by President Harold B. Lee and Elder M. Russell Ballard which

provided the answer for me. President Lee said healthy self-esteem is "a righteous self-respect that might be defined as 'belief
in one's own worth, worth to God, and worth to man' "
("Understanding Who We Are Brings Self-Respect," p. 4).
Elder Ballard said, "Transgression of any kind is always accompanied by a loss of self-esteem" ("Be an Example of the
Believers," p. 97).

Those two statements, together with the words of Elder
Ashton and President Benson, helped me reach the conclusion
that the best things I can do for my children's self-esteem are to
genuinely love and cherish them for who they are (children of
God), to treat them kindly, and to teach them that Heavenly
Father loves them—because they are His children also. I should
teach them about God's commandments, the importance of
obeying them, and the consequences of disobeying them. I
should teach them to obey their parents, to pray, and to repent
when they offend another person or God, and I should teach
them the principle of forgiveness. Essentially, if I want my children to develop healthy self-esteem I should teach them the
principles of the gospel of Jesus Christ.

I emphasize the word *principles* as opposed to *practices* because it was the principles that Heather lived, not the practices.
She lived such eternal principles as faith, repentance, obedience, forgiveness, keeping the Sabbath day holy, and service to
God and fellowmen, but she never danced, participated in ath-
letics, received straight As in school, or played a musical instru-
ment. For that reason, although there are probably a number of
factors that contribute to a person's self-esteem, I believe the
most important and absolutely necessary ingredients are knowing we are literal offspring of heavenly parents who love us,
obeying God's commandments, knowing we are doing what the
Lord wants us to do, and loving and serving our fellowmen.

Hectically Engaged

One of the consequences of caring for Cindy, Heather, and
Mark is that instead of being a participant in many of life's hec-

tic activities, I have simply been an observer, watching life from the sidelines. Initially I felt bad about the situation, but as time passed I could see that there were actually advantages to being a nonparticipant. One was that it allowed me time to observe and empathize with other mothers whose daily routines were complicated by many choices outside the home. Not only were other moms short-order cooks, laundry maids, nurses, tutors, and counselors, but they also were chauffeurs. I actually felt sorry for them as I witnessed their never-ending trips to sports activities, practices, amusement parks, stores, PTA meetings, Cub Scouts, Girl Scouts, school field trips, music lessons, and a host of other activities.

As I ponder those dedicated mothers' expressions of frustration at being unable to keep up with all the demands on their time, I am so thankful for a new perspective given by Elder Neal A. Maxwell:

> A few in the Church are needlessly laden with programmed hyperactivity. They unwisely and unnecessarily exceed their strength and means, running faster than they are able (see D&C 10:4; Mosiah 4:27). Their fatiguing, Martha-like anxiety should yield more often to a Mary-like sense of proportion about what matters most. . . .
>
> . . . While we should be "anxiously engaged," we need not be hectically engaged. We can be diligent and still do things in "wisdom and order"—without going faster than we "have strength and means" (Mosiah 4:27; D&C 10:4). (*Men and Women of Christ,* pp. 3, 24.)
>
> Each of us has different strengths and faces different circumstances that call for calibrations that are highly individual. Happily, the Lord really does increase the capacity of the diligent. . . .
>
> Many things in life act upon us over which we have no control, but there is a zone—of differing size for each of us—in which we can act for ourselves, rather than merely be acted upon (see 2 Nephi 2:26). . . . What we do within that zone is especially up to us to determine. ("Wisdom and Order," p. 41.)

In a very real sense I am grateful that I have been compelled to remain at home where I actually have few choices and where, unlike most mothers, I know exactly what I have to do on a daily basis.

The Blending of Opposites

During all the years we were going through our adversities, one of the things that frustrated me most was that Bruce and I seemed to live in two different worlds. We never seemed to see eye to eye on much of anything. From my perspective, he always seemed to be more concerned about things that had to do with work and money than about the people in our family.

An example of this frustrating situation occurred during a recent Christmas season when Michelle and Heidi were involved in an automobile accident. It was snowing and Michelle was driving our car, when it was hit from the rear. She called me soon afterward and said, in a very shaky voice, "Mom, we've been in a car accident. Heidi and I are okay, but the car is totaled, and the police officer wants to know where you want it towed." At that moment all I cared about was Michelle and Heidi, and I replied, "Are you sure you're okay?" Michelle said, "We're shaken up, but we're okay, Mom." I said a silent prayer of gratitude and walked into the other room to tell Bruce. He could tell I was upset, but as soon as he found out why, and learned that Michelle and Heidi were not hurt, his immediate concern was for the status of our car. All he seemed to care about was whether it was repairable, how much damage was done, and how we would be able to pay to replace it. I thought to myself, *How insensitive. Who cares about the car as long as the children are all right!*

Later that afternoon, as I saw how badly the car was damaged and realized how blessed we were that Michelle and Heidi were not badly hurt, I wondered why Bruce and I responded so differently to the accident. Then the thought came to me that it had something to do with our eternal natures and callings. I feel it really is part of a woman's nature to be sensitive and compassionate and to feel a responsibility to nurture children, whereas it is part of a man's nature and calling to feel a responsibility to finance the family operation and to see that each family member has the things that he or she needs. In our case, Michelle needed a car in order to do her seminary student-teaching in a few weeks. Surely I was responding to my feeling of responsibility and Bruce was responding to his.

Shortly after that incident, Elder Boyd K. Packer not only confirmed my conclusion but also enlightened my understanding about how a husband and wife become one. In a BYU devotional talk he spoke of a "catalytic process where two seemingly antagonistic influences can merge and each give strength to the other":

> The blending of opposites is everywhere present in life. A base metal, fused with a precious one, can produce an alloy stronger and more resilient than either component ·alone. . . .
>
> Marriage is the wedding of opposites, the union of the man (who faces the world) with woman (who is often the more refined in spirit). When neither seeks to replace the other, the complementing differences in their nature are fostered. Then, in expressions of love, life itself is conceived, and together they receive a fullness of joy. (See D&C 93: 33–34.) ("'I Say Unto You, Be One,'" p. 90.)

Now, after years of struggling and of trying to understand our marital challenges, I realize that it was meant to be that husbands and wives feel responsible for different aspects of life so that they might fulfill their eternal roles, complement each other, and finally become one by learning to see with an eye single to the glory of God. How grateful I am to have learned that lesson, for it has made an enormous difference in my relationship with Bruce.

The Father's Role

I have always known that fathers have a sacred responsibility to provide spiritual leadership in the family, but it wasn't until I watched Bruce's struggle with the loss of his job and his reaction to our car being wrecked that I really began to understand the far-reaching implications of the father providing for his family.

Additional insight came as I reread a talk by President Benson, who declared to priesthood bearers: "In the beginning, Adam, not Eve, was instructed to earn the bread by the sweat of his brow. . . . I continue to emphasize the importance of mothers staying home to nurture, care for, and train their children in the principles of righteousness." ("To the Fathers in Israel," pp. 48, 49.) President Benson added this prophetic observation and counsel:

> As I travel throughout the Church, I feel that the great majority of Latter-day Saint mothers earnestly want to follow this counsel. But we know that sometimes the mother works outside of the home at the encouragement, or even insistence, of her husband. It is he who wants the items of convenience that the extra income can buy. Not only will the family suffer in such instances, brethren, but your own spiritual growth and progression will be hampered. I say to all of you, the Lord has charged men with the responsibility to provide for their families in such a way that the wife is allowed to fulfill her role as mother in the home. (Ibid., p. 49.)

I have since read this counsel from President Howard W. Hunter: "You who hold the priesthood have the responsibility, unless disabled, to provide temporal support for your wife and children. No man can shift the burden of responsibility to another, not even his wife. The Lord has commanded that women and children have claim on their husbands and fathers for their maintenance (see D&C 83; 1 Timothy 5:8)." ("Being a Righteous Husband and Father," p. 51.).

In spite of Bruce's weaknesses, he truly understood his responsibility to provide for me and the children. Not only has his acceptance of that responsibility helped me fulfill my role, but because of its eternal relevance it has contributed to his self-esteem as well.

CHAPTER 9

Understanding
Adversity and Faith

Adversity and faith are so closely related that it is difficult to explain the one without discussing the other. My experience has shown that without adversity, faith usually doesn't grow very rapidly, and without faith, adversity becomes almost impossible to endure.

What Is Adversity?

One of the most revealing and helpful things I learned during the year after Heather died came during Relief Society as I listened to the lesson entitled "Unfulfilled Expectations" (see *Follow Me,* pp. 283–88). We talked about unmarried women who long for an eternal companion but have no worthy opportunity for marriage, about wanting children but being childless, about having spouses who are inactive in the Church, about having a handicap that keeps us from doing the things we want to do, about having rebellious children. We discussed how everyone has unfulfilled expectations which "tear at our fondest hopes and deepest desires [and] leave us feeling bewildered and alone" (Ibid., p. 283). We talked about how differently people react to their pain and about how our unfulfilled expectations sometimes leave us bitter and even angry with the Lord. As stated in the manual, "We are full of questions: Am I not righteous enough? Do I lack sufficient faith? Does the Lord truly keep his promises? Why am I denied these blessings when I so greatly desire them and strive to live worthy of them?" (Ibid., p. 283.)

As I pondered the lesson later I thought, *Can't any personal unfulfilled expectation be considered adversity?* I was surprised at the thought, because I had never really thought of adversity exactly like that before. But I like this definition: Adversity is any unfulfilled expectation we have. I like it because everything from the most major event to the very mundane fits the definition. For example, having a loved one die, having a marriage that is different than you imagined, having a child born with a handicap, having no children, being divorced, losing your job, and going bankrupt are all situations that fit the definition. But, not being asked to the dance, not receiving the grade you thought you deserved, having parents who make mistakes, growing up in a family that is different than what you expect, and having the hair dryer break are also experiences that fit the definition. In short, using "unfulfilled expectations" as a definition for adversity is easily understood, because surely we all have unfulfilled expectations.

With that newly discovered understanding, I reread the Relief Society lesson. In part, it said, "Most of us have a certain vision of what our life should be—a vision that includes receiving certain opportunities and blessings. Sister Ardeth G. Kapp, for example, as a young girl 'envisioned living in a small white house with a picket fence. I thought I would just take care of the flowers, be active in the Church, friendly with my neighbors—and have lots of children.' For Sister Kapp the blessing of children never came." (*Follow Me,* pp. 283-84.) That expectation was never fulfilled, and it became her adversity.

For me, my adversity was having Cindy, Heather, and Mark become handicapped and then watching other people's children sit up, stand, walk, hold things in their hands, and feed themselves; not having enough time for Michelle, Lara, and Heidi individually; never getting enough sleep; not being able to participate in activities that I liked; having a demanding routine every day of the year with no relief in sight; and having a real struggle with my relationship with Bruce. And today it is being unable to alleviate Cindy's and Mark's daily pains and struggles. It is lifting and caring for them as I get older and they get heavier and more difficult to handle. And it is wondering every morning if Cindy will still be breathing when I get her up for the day.

Why Adversity?

For centuries philosophers have pondered and written about the question, "If there is a God, how do you explain all the pain and suffering in the world?" In more modern times people have asked, "If God is kind and loving and responsible, how can He allow all the horrible things to happen in this world? Why do bad things happen to good people? Why must the righteous suffer? Why do we have adversity in our lives?"

Those are indeed difficult questions—questions that are impossible to answer adequately without the perspective of the gospel of Jesus Christ. Even with the gospel they are perplexing questions, but without the gospel they seem very obscure and impossible to answer. As Elder Boyd K. Packer said: "If our view is limited to mortal life, some things become unbearable because they seem so unfair and so permanent. There are doctrines which, if understood, will bring a perspective toward and a composure regarding problems which otherwise have no satisfactory explanation." ("The Moving of the Water," p. 9.)

Indeed, if this mortal life were all there is, there would be no satisfying answer to the question, Why adversity, pain, sorrow, and suffering? Early death truly would be a calamity. But because life is eternal and stretches "far into the premortal past and on into the eternal post-death future" (Kimball, *Faith Precedes the Miracle,* p. 97), it is possible to find at least some satisfying answers to the question, Why adversity?

From the prophets we learn that we lived in a premortal state as spirit offspring of heavenly parents who love us and whose "work and glory [is] to bring to pass the immortality and eternal life of man" (Moses 1:39). In other words, we lived with heavenly parents who wanted us to become like them and to enjoy the life that they enjoy—something that couldn't happen as long as we remained with them in the premortal existence. We needed to leave their presence, receive a mortal body, exercise faith, choose between good and evil, and prove our faithfulness to them in order to progress. That necessitated a mortal, earth-life experience (see Abraham 3:24-25), which then would become our laboratory of learning. As President Spencer W. Kimball stated:

> We knew before we were born that we were coming to the earth for bodies and experience and that we would have joys and sorrows, ease and pain, comforts and hardships, health and sickness, successes and disappointments, and we knew also that after a period of life we would die. We accepted all these eventualities with a glad heart, eager to accept both the favorable and unfavorable. We eagerly accepted the chance to come earthward even though it might be for only a day or a year. Perhaps we were not so much concerned whether we should die of disease, of accident, or of senility. We were willing to take life as it came and as we might organize and control it, and this without murmur, complaint, or unreasonable demands. (*Faith Precedes the Miracle,* p. 106.)

Thus, we understood before we came to earth that adversity and suffering would be a part of our experience here, since the mortal body we would receive would be subject to pain, disease, deterioration, and death—and each of those things would cause suffering of some kind. Yet we chose to come to earth anyway. We even "shouted for joy" when the earth, our mortal home, was created (see Job 38:7). Concerning what we knew in the premortal existence, Elder Henry D. Moyle said:

> We might well be assured that we had something to do with our "allotment" in our pre-existent state. This would be an additional reason for us to accept our present condition and make the best of it. It is what we agreed to do. . . .

We unquestionably knew before we elected to come to this earth the conditions under which we would here exist, and live, and work. . . .

. . . I have a conviction deep down in my heart that we are exactly what we should be, each one of us, except as we may have altered that pattern by deviating from the laws of God here in mortality. I have convinced myself that we all have those peculiar attributes, characteristics, and abilities which are essential for us to possess in order that we may fulfill the full purpose of our creation here upon this earth. (In Conference Report, October 1952, pp. 71–72.)

Another thing we knew before we came here was that Satan would tempt us, and we would use our God-given agency to choose good or evil, light or darkness, and liberty and eternal life or captivity and death (see 2 Nephi 2:27). I now know that so much of the pain and suffering in this mortal world is the result of people using their agency to choose sin and Satan's evil ways. When a person chooses sin, not only does he bring misery and suffering upon himself, but he often brings pain and adversity to innocent victims as well. For example, not only do the adulterer and the alcoholic bring misery upon themselves, but they bring suffering upon innocent family members too. The same is true of murderers and child abusers. When they commit their despicable acts, they cause the innocent to suffer pain and adversity that sometimes lasts a lifetime.

As I wondered why a loving and kind God would allow innocent victims to be brutalized, I learned that the answer lies in the eternal truth that God will not take away the agency of anyone—even someone who would choose to do the vilest of acts. God allows each of us to use our agency so that we each will receive the eternal reward we deserve. For example, if God were to stop the murderer before he committed his evil act, He would be interfering with the moral agency of that person, mercy would rob justice, and "God would cease to be God" (Alma 42:25). In the words of President Kimball: "[Can] the Lord [prevent] these tragedies? The answer is, Yes. The Lord is omnipotent, with all power to control our lives, save us pain, prevent all accidents, drive all planes and cars, feed us, protect us, save us from labor, effort, sickness, even from death, if he will. But he will not." (*Faith Precedes the Miracle,* p. 96.)

Concerning innocent people suffering from adversity, Elder James E. Talmage wrote: "No pang that is suffered by man or woman upon the earth will be without its compensating effect . . . if it be met with patience" (as quoted in ibid., p. 98). And Orson F. Whitney said:

> No pain that we suffer, no trial that we experience is wasted. It ministers to our education, to the development of such qualities as patience, faith, fortitude and humility. All that we suffer and all that we endure, especially when we endure it patiently, builds up our characters, purifies our hearts, expands our souls, and makes us more tender and charitable, more worthy to be called the children of God . . . and it is through sorrow and suffering, toil and tribulation, that we gain the education that we come here to acquire and which will make us more like our Father and Mother in heaven. (As quoted in ibid., p. 98.)

As to the value of adversity, while President Brigham Young was at Winter Quarters in January 1847, the Lord revealed to him: "My people must be tried in all things, that they may be prepared to receive the glory that I have for them, even the glory of Zion; and he that will not bear chastisement is not worthy of my kingdom" (D&C 136:31). And President Kimball said: "Being human, we would expel from our lives physical pain and mental anguish and assure ourselves of continual ease and comfort, but if we were to close the doors upon sorrow and distress, we might be excluding our greatest friends and benefactors. Suffering can make saints of people as they learn patience, long-suffering, and self-mastery." (*Faith Precedes the Miracle,* p. 98.)

As I understood that "suffering can make saints of people" and that "the basic gospel law is free agency and eternal development" (ibid., p. 96), I came to know that the Lord uses our pain and afflictions to teach us obedience. That was the Lord's message to the Prophet Joseph Smith at Zion's Camp. Speaking of the Saints collectively, the Lord said: "But behold, they have not learned to be obedient to the things which I required at their hands, but are full of all manner of evil, and do not impart of their substance, as becometh saints, to the poor and afflicted among them. . . . And my people must needs be chastened until they learn obedience, if it must needs be, by the things which they suffer." (D&C 105:3, 6.)

Similarly, the Lord told the Prophet that He was not pleased with many of the Saints in Kirtland because "they do not forsake their sins, and their wicked ways, the pride of their hearts, and their covetousness, and all their detestable things, and observe the words of wisdom and eternal life which I have given unto them. Verily I say unto you, that I, the Lord, will chasten them and will do whatsoever I list, if they do not repent and observe all things whatsoever I have said unto them. (D&C 98:20–21.)

Even those in the school of the prophets were chastened and called to repentance: "Nevertheless, my servants sinned a very grievous sin; and contentions arose in the school of the prophets; which was very grievous unto me, saith your Lord; therefore I sent them forth to be chastened" (D&C 95:10).

From those scriptures it became obvious to me that the Lord requires all who want to attain the celestial kingdom to repent of *all* their sins and transgressions and to keep *all* the covenants they have made with Him. He requires them to rid themselves of all pride and selfishness and to consecrate their all to the building of His kingdom. Furthermore, He often uses an individual's suffering to motivate him to repent of his sins, such as unkindness toward others, rebellion against God and His servants (see D&C 121:16–18), sacrilege (see D&C 63:61–64), idolatry (see Exodus 20:3–5), deceitfulness, high-mindedness, bitterness toward God, ingratitude (see D&C 59:21), impatience—or whatever unholy and impure practice that calls for repentance.

Another reason God allows people to suffer pain and afflictions may be related to our coming to know the Lord (see John 17:3) and to our need to "always remember him" (see D&C 20:77, 79). As stated in Helaman 12:3, "And thus we see that except the Lord doth chasten his people with many afflictions . . . they will not remember him."

In my case, I didn't diligently strive to know God and to

remember Him when life was easy for me. Before Cindy became ill I remembered the Lord by attending my meetings, fulfilling my church assignments, having personal and family prayers, having family home evenings, and attending the temple, but not with the diligence or intensity that I did afterward. Similarly, after Heather's handicap was identified, as I struggled to understand why Heather had become handicapped and then why I felt so strongly that she would be healed when it wasn't to be, I yearned for answers. In my desperation I learned what it means to pray continually and to plead with the Lord for comfort and understanding. I certainly remembered Him much more during those trying times than I did when life was easier. As the Lord Himself told the Prophet Joseph Smith: "In the day of [the Saints'] peace they esteemed lightly my counsel; but, in the day of their trouble, of necessity they feel after me" (D&C 101:8).

It is my testimony that as we "feel after Him" we begin to know Him better. We begin to learn that God, in our best interest, isn't satisfied with what we are now—He knows what our potential is and wants us to reach that potential. We learn that He is a tutorial Father who uses adversity to teach us, because He knows it is through adversity that we grow. He knows the only way to perfection and to become like Him is through soul-stretching work, which, unfortunately, usually requires suffering. As Elder Neal A. Maxwell said:

> So much of life's curriculum consists of efforts by the Lord to get and keep our attention. Ironically, the stimuli He uses are often that which is seen by us as something to endure. Sometimes what we are being asked to endure is His "help"! Help to draw us away from the cares of the world; help to draw us away from self-centeredness; attention-getting help when the still, small voice has been ignored by us; help in the shaping of our souls; and help to keep the promises we made so long ago to Him and to ourselves. ("If Thou Endure Well," p. 6.)

In answer to the question, Why is adversity necessary? President Kimball said: "Is there not wisdom in his giving us trials that we might rise above them, responsibilities that we might achieve, work to harden our muscles, sorrows to try our souls? Are we not exposed to temptations to test our strength, sickness that we might learn patience, death that we might be immortalized and glorified?" (*Faith Precedes the Miracle,* p. 97.) And finally, in the words of Sister Kapp, "It's the soul-rending experiences that bring us to God. Trials lead you into a diligent search; they make you ask questions that only the Lord can answer. You have to turn to him and one day the peace comes that compensates for all the yearning." (As quoted in *Follow Me,* p. 284.) What a glorious day that is!

Finding Peace and Overcoming Adversity

In the Book of Mormon, when Alma was teaching the people in Gideon, he spoke of Christ: "And he shall go forth, suffering pains and afflictions and temptations of every kind; and this that the word might be fulfilled which saith he will take upon him the pains and the sicknesses of his people." (Alma 7: 11.) From that scripture and many others I learned that because of the atonement of Jesus Christ, no matter what the trial is or how difficult it is to endure, the Lord has personally shown us the way and has given us a formula for a way to escape (see D&C 95:1). Furthermore, He has promised to lead us through the struggle: "Trust in the Lord with all thine heart; and lean not unto thine own understanding. In all thy ways acknowledge him, and he shall direct thy paths." (Proverbs 3:5–6.)

I now know, however, that in order for Him to help us through our struggles, there are certain things we must do if we are to feel the comfort that is available through His atonement. "It is evident that He intends that we do our part," said Elder Richard G. Scott ("Obtaining Help from the Lord," p. 84). Referring specifically to priesthood blessings, which often heal troubled hearts, Elder Scott said:

The blessing resolves those things which are beyond our own capacity to influence either personally or with the help of others. Yet we must do our part for the blessing to be realized. We must strive to be worthy and to exercise the requisite faith to do what we are able. Where it is intended that others help, we must use that help also. It is through the combination of our doing what is within our power to accomplish and the power of the Lord that the blessing is realized. (Ibid., p. 85.)

As I pondered Elder Scott's words, the thought occurred to me that our trial might be likened to our being on a ship during a storm. If we are to keep from sinking, we must do the part we are capable of doing—manning the rudder, bailing out water, and making repairs as needed. Likewise, when we work to overcome our adversity by doing the part we are capable of doing—which may include allowing others to help—the Lord has promised that He will carry us through our personal storms and give us the blessing of peace and calmness. "And after their temptations, and much tribulation, behold, I, the Lord, will feel after them, and if they harden not their hearts, and stiffen not their necks against me, they shall be converted, and I will heal them" (D&C 112:13).

It is my testimony that the feeling of peace, comfort, and understanding that finally comes is a gift from God, and it comes as a result of our keeping the commandments, diligently striving to know Him, and turning our hearts to Him. It comes after we have done our part, shown our unwavering faithfulness to Him, and gained from the experience what He wants us to learn. It might come in a day, a week, a month, a year, a decade, or a lifetime. It eventually will come if we are faithful, but only according to the Lord's timetable for us. We must wait on Him, because He knows what's best for us, and "[we] cannot force spiritual things" (Packer, "Prayers and Answers," p. 21).

A Summary of How I Found Peace

As I tried to analyze the way I found peace and comfort during my trials so that I might know how to help my children and others, I settled on the following ideas—ideas which are numbered but are not necessarily sequential.

1. *I committed myself to do the Lord's will.* I believe with all my heart that a major key to my finding peace when Cindy was nine months old was that I committed myself to doing the Lord's will even though I was exhausted and wanted more sleep. My commitment to have more meaningful personal and family prayers, better family home evenings, and more effective scripture study seemed to give purpose to my adversity, which, in turn, brought peace to my soul.

I now realize that in order to continually feel at peace, it is necessary for me to do whatever I can. I need to continue to obey God's commandments, read the scriptures and other good books, treat others kindly, attend weekly church meetings, partake of the sacrament weekly, attend the temple, and serve whenever and wherever possible. President Kimball quoted one General Authority who noted, "If we are not careful, we can be injured by the frostbite of frustration; we can be frozen in place by the chill of unmet expectations. To avoid this we must—just as we would with arctic coldness—keep moving, keep serving, and keep reaching out, so that our own immobility does not become our chief danger." (In "Small Acts of Service," p. 4.)

Along with those basic responsibilities, I also need to refrain from watching tasteless TV shows and movies. I need to be obedient to the voice of the Spirit as well as to the voices of my priesthood leaders. Some of the most helpful counsel I ever received came from a priesthood leader. He said, "Don't pile up all of the problems and difficulties you see coming in the next five years, the next year, month, or even a week, and try to solve them all today. Just take one day at a time, and the Lord will help you solve your problems as they come." What a help those words have been!

I am convinced that one of the reasons my children didn't rebel, Bruce didn't leave me, I didn't leave Bruce, and our marriage finally became a happy one was that we all kept doing what we knew was right and didn't give in to the temptation to give up, even though giving up would have been much easier in the short run. In scriptural terms, we tried to be steadfast.

2. *I tried to understand God's eternal perspective.* One thing that became evident as I sought to do the Lord's will was that truly God's ways are not man's ways (see Isaiah 55:8–9). My limited

perspective saw one thing, and God saw something much greater. For example, after Heather's handicap was identified my limited perspective was evident when I prayed for her to be healed and couldn't understand why she wasn't. I didn't understand the Lord's perspective, which in looking back seems to have been that Heather would touch the lives of many more people, including my own, in a more profound way with a handicapped body than she probably could have without a handicapped body. God knew the best thing for all concerned was for her not to be healed. I certainly didn't have that perspective when she was eight months old, but I surely do now. In fact, now, after Heather's passing, I honestly can say that I am grateful that Heavenly Father did not heal her as I wanted Him to, but that He gave me the strength to turn my heart to Him, accept His will, and develop stronger faith. I am grateful, too, that I now can see that the priesthood blessing Bruce gave Heather when she was nine months old really did come to pass, for truly Heather did bring love and peace and joy into our home.

Although I now have a clearer view, it is obvious that even with the scriptures and words of living prophets, we get only a glimpse of God's eternal perspective—we still don't know and understand His perspective completely. Our perspective is narrow and shortsighted because we simply aren't given the whole picture.

Because that is the case, I now realize that when I undergo trials and suffering I must seek to know that God sees the whole picture—"the end from the beginning" (Abraham 2:8)— that He knows what's best for me and that "all things shall work together for [my] good" (D&C 90:24) if I am obedient. Then I can put implicit faith in Him.

One of the best explanations that helped me understand God's perspective and why we need adversity is a quote by C. S. Lewis, paraphrasing George MacDonald, who compared the human soul to a living house:

> Imagine yourself as a living house. God comes in to rebuild that house. At first, perhaps, you can understand what He is doing. He is getting the drains right and stopping the

leaks in the roof and so on: you knew that those jobs needed doing and so you are not surprised. But presently He starts knocking the house about in a way that hurts abominably and does not seem to make sense. What on earth is He up to? The explanation is that He is building quite a different house from the one you thought of— throwing out a new wing here, putting on an extra floor there, running up towers, making courtyards. You thought you were going to be made into a decent little cottage: but He is building a palace. (*Mere Christianity*, p. 160.)

My limited perspective was of a "decent little cottage," and God's perspective was of a palace. I am convinced that the plan of salvation was intended to be that way so that we might learn to trust the Lord and walk by faith.

3. *I diligently searched the scriptures.* As I read the scriptures and diligently strived to understand them, I came to know the Lord better and even began to see the whole picture more clearly. Besides the scriptures already mentioned, others that helped me cope with my trials follow.

- "Verily, thus saith the Lord unto you whom I love, and whom I love I also chasten that their sins may be forgiven, for with the chastisement I prepare a way for their deliverance in all things out of temptation, and I have loved you" (D&C 95:1). After dealing with adversity in our home for more than twenty years, I truly believe that God is a tutorial Father—that one of the main reasons He chastens us is to encourage us to repent of *all* of our sins. Even though I had not committed grievous sins, I did have a need to repent of my pride and selfishness. I also needed to treat others better, be more obedient and devoted to the Lord, and understand the Lord's will more fully.
- "For all those who will not endure chastening, but deny me, cannot be sanctified" (D&C 101:5). Obviously, I need to taste the bitter and endure suffering in order to someday be sanctified. Enduring trials and being sanctified seem to go hand in hand.

- "Peace be unto thy soul; thine adversity and thine afflictions shall be but a small moment; and then, if thou endure it well, God shall exalt thee on high; thou shalt tri-
umph over all thy foes" (D&C 121:7–8). While I was
going through the most difficult times of my trials, it
didn't seem that they lasted "but a small moment." At
those times, the long nights and the painful and discouraging days seemed as though they would last forever. But
they really didn't. There really did come a day when I
found the peace and saw the blessing.

4. *I read inspirational talks and stories.* I read and pondered
hundreds of talks given by General Authorities, which not only
helped me understand many eternal truths but also helped me
feel the Spirit at times when I really needed it. I also read inspirational stories of other people who endured trials and overcame adversity, which in turn gave me the encouragement, motivation, and strength to say, "If they made it through their
afflictions, I can make it through mine!"

It is my testimony that power comes when we read of others'
trials, because we can always find someone who endured even
greater adversities than our own. From my own experience,
when I read about the trials of others I began to see my own
blessings better and was even thankful for them. I found that
when I was thankful, I was less likely to murmur and complain.

Some of my favorite inspirational talks and writings that
deal with the subject of adversity follow.

Brown, Hugh B. "The Currant Bush." *The New Era* (January
    1973): 14–15.

Chidester, C. Richard. "No Place for Pride." *Ensign* 20
    (March 1990): 16–21.

Faust, James E. "The Refiner's Fire." *Ensign* 9 (May 1979):
    53–59.

Kapp, Ardeth G. "You're Like a Mother." *Ensign* 5 (October
    1975): 57–59.

Kimball, Spencer W. "Tragedy or Destiny," *Improvement Era*
    (March 1966): 178–180; 210–217; Also in *Faith Precedes
    the Miracle.* Salt Lake City: Deseret Book Co., 1972.

Maxwell, Neal A. *All These Things Shall Give Thee Experience.* Salt Lake City: Deseret Book Co., 1979.

———. "If Thou Endure Well." Address given at Brigham Young University, December 2, 1984; typescript, Church Historical Department, Salt Lake City.

Moyle, Henry D. "Allotment." In Conference Report, October 1952, pp. 71–72.

Packer, Boyd K. "The Balm of Gilead." *Ensign* 17 (November 1987): 16–18.

———. "The Moving of the Water." *Ensign* 21 (May 1991): 7–9.

Robinson, Stephen E. *Believing Christ.* Salt Lake City: Deseret Book Co., 1992.

Scott, Richard G. "Healing the Tragic Scars of Abuse." *Ensign* 22 (May 1992): 31–33.

———. "Obtaining Help From the Lord." *Ensign* 21 (November 1991): 84–86.

5. *I learned to pray in a meaningful way.* As I searched for divine help and endeavored to know God's will for me, I found myself praying continually (see Alma 34:27). As Elder Packer said, "If you need a transfusion of spiritual strength, then just ask for it. We call that prayer. Prayer is a powerful spiritual medicine." ("Balm of Gilead," p. 18.) It is my testimony that, indeed, prayer is powerful spiritual medicine. It was the way I made connections with my main source of comfort, and it was also the hourly "shot in the arm" that got me through my afflictions on a daily basis.

Three questions I often asked myself as I prayed continually were: "What course does God want me to take? What does He want me to repent of? What does He want me to learn?" In the words of Elder Richard G. Scott, "When there is suffering or pain, we ask ourselves a lot of questions. Some of them ought to be: What does the Lord want me to learn from this experience? What do I need to do? What do I need to change? Whom do I need to serve? Or what characteristic must I improve? Pondering and prayer will help us understand what we are to learn from the challenges we are asked to overcome." ("Obtaining Help from the Lord," p. 85.)

I know that if people ask the right questions, praying can help them understand their true needs and God's will because, as Stephen R. Covey explained, the Lord answers our prayers in terms of our real needs, rather than our wants as we perceive them. Knowing my needs was a great source of comfort to me.

Elder H. Burke Peterson's counsel helped me improve my personal prayers. He said:

> As you feel the need to confide in the Lord or to improve the quality of your visits with him—to pray, if you please—may I suggest a process to follow: go where you can be alone, go where you can think, go where you can kneel, go where you can speak out loud to him. The bedroom, the bathroom, or the closet will do. Now, picture him in your mind's eye. Think to whom you are speaking, control your thoughts—don't let them wander, address him as your Father and your friend. Now tell him things you really feel to tell him—not trite phrases that have little meaning, but have a sincere, heartfelt conversation with him. Confide in him, ask him for forgiveness, plead with him, enjoy him, thank him, express your love to him, and then listen for his answers. Listening is an essential part of praying. Answers from the Lord come quietly—ever so quietly. ("Adversity and Prayer," p. 19.)

Unfortunately (or perhaps fortunately), very sincere prayers often are not answered immediately. Sometimes it takes a long time for them to be answered, and sometimes they don't seem to get answered at all. I believe all of our sincere and heartfelt prayers are answered, but just not always in the way or in the time frame we think they ought to be.

6. *I found it essential to repent and forgive.* Now, after dealing with adversity for nearly twenty-five years, I can see that the most significant key to my finding peace after Cindy became ill was my repentance and commitment to do the Lord's will even when I was exhausted and wanted sleep so desperately. Likewise, when Heather developed her handicap, it wasn't until after I repented of my pride and then submitted myself to God's will that I finally felt peace. In a very similar way, it wasn't

until I sought to forgive Bruce for hurting my feelings that I felt better in our relationship. It wasn't until I quit praying, "Help him to understand me," and began praying, "Help *me* to forgive him, for he doesn't know how he has offended me," that our relationship began to improve. Ironically, it seemed that when I began to change my approach and repent, the Lord also began to bless Bruce with a changing heart.

Although I didn't fully understand the correlation between repentance and peace until Bruce and I began writing this book, I now recognize the significance of an event that occurred a few months after Cindy became ill. The setting was a sacrament meeting, and our bishop was talking about repentance and forgiveness. As I listened, I remembered very clearly a time in college when I had been dishonest and cheated on a test, an act which I hadn't tried to repent of until after I left school. I had previously prayed to Heavenly Father and asked for His forgiveness many times, but I never felt completely forgiven for my act of deception—that is, until after I followed a prompting and confessed to our bishop privately. As I did so, I received an undeniable testimony that Christ suffered because of *my* sins while He was in Gethsemane, and that His atonement was for me personally. It was an indescribable feeling as a heavy burden was lifted and the repentance process for that sin was completed. What a comfort to feel I was forgiven!

Because of my experiences and because of the testimony of both ancient and modern prophets, I firmly believe that if a person is wronged, offended, or even abused, the way for him to receive comfort is to repent of his own sins, turn his own heart to God, and forgive his fellowmen of their trespasses against him. Elder Spencer W. Kimball wrote: "But if each of us keeps his own heart pure and his own mind free from bitterness, and serves the Lord with all his might, mind, strength, and heart, he can be at peace" (*Miracle of Forgiveness*, p. 272). The reason that process works is that the way we make connections with the Savior, His atonement, and the peace that He brings is to sincerely repent.

This concept is explained very clearly in the Book of Mormon. When Alma and his people were in bondage and persecuted by Amulon, they "did pour out their hearts" to God and begged Him to help them. Because they were repentant and humble, the Lord said:

> Lift up your heads and be of good comfort, for I know of the covenant which ye have made unto me; . . .
>
> And I will also ease the burdens which are put upon your shoulders, that even you cannot feel them upon your backs, even while you are in bondage . . . that ye may know of a surety that I, the Lord God, do visit my people in their afflictions.
>
> And now it came to pass that the burdens which were laid upon Alma and his brethren were made light; yea, the Lord did strengthen them that they could bear up their burdens with ease, and they did submit cheerfully and with patience to all the will of the Lord. (Mosiah 24:13–15.)

It is my testimony that during tribulation or affliction, people must repent of their own unkindnesses toward others and their hostility toward God or man, and must forgive those who have offended them, if they are to receive peace and comfort from God. By doing those things, Bruce and I finally resolved our marriage problems and found peace in our adversity.

I believe the reason this formula works is that somewhere in the process of complete and sincere repentance, a person realizes his own dependence on God, that Christ's suffering in Gethsemane was for him personally, and that he cannot be saved without Him. When that happens, the person then makes himself eligible for the permanent peace and comfort that comes only from the Lord.

Concerning the importance of forgiveness, Elder Kimball indicates in *The Miracle of Forgiveness,* that a primary key to determining whether a person will suffer bitterness and misery or peace and comfort during his trials lies in whether he is forgiving or unforgiving. "He who wishes to revenge injuries by reciprocal hatred will live in misery" (p. 267), for "retaliation certainly is not repentance" (p. 266). On the other hand, Elder Kimball also quotes this pertinent message: "One of the glorious aspects of the principles of forgiveness is the purifying and ennobling effects its application has upon the personality and character of the forgiver. Someone wisely said, 'He who has not forgiven a wrong or an injury has not yet tasted one of the sublime enjoyments of life.' The human soul seldom rises to such heights of strength and nobility as when it removes all resentments and forgives errors and malice." (In ibid., p. 266.)

Elder Kimball then explains the joy which comes to those who truly forgive: "Let us each look back over his own life, and recall the time when he has forgiven someone. Has any other joy been more uplifting? The destructive feelings of smallness, pettiness, and hate, or longing for revenge, are crowded out by the attitude to forgive." (Ibid., p. 277.) He then cites examples of forgiveness as demonstrated by people in the scriptures (Paul, Stephen, and Jesus), people in our day, and characters in the book *Les Miserables*.

The modern-day experience Elder Kimball cites is the Glenn Kempton story. In 1918, when Glenn Kempton was a child, his father was brutally murdered in cold blood by outlaws. As an adult Glenn Kempton wrote a long letter to Elder Kimball about the effects of that incident and included the following testimony:

A few years ago, just shortly before Christmas, a season when the love of Christ abounds and the spirit of giving and forgiving gets inside of us, my wife and I were in Phoenix on a short trip. . . . As we rode along, I expressed the desire to detour and return home via Florence, for that is where the state prison is located. My wife readily assented. . . .

[After Tom Powers and I were introduced, we were] led into the parole room where we had a long talk. We went back to that cold, gray February morning thirty years before, re-enacting that whole terrible tragedy. We talked for perhaps an hour and a half. Finally, I said, "Tom, you made a mistake for which you owe a debt to society for which I feel you must continue to pay, just the same as I must continue to pay the price for having been reared without a father."

Then I stood and extended my hand. He stood and took it. I continued, "With all my heart, I forgive you for this awful thing that has come into our lives."

He bowed his head and I left him there. I don't know how he felt then, and I don't know how he feels now, but my witness to you is that it is a glorious thing when bitterness and hatred go out of your heart and forgiveness comes in.

I thanked the warden for his kindness, and as I walked out the door and down that long flight of steps I knew that forgiveness was better than revenge, for I had experienced it.

As we drove toward home in the gathering twilight, a sweet and peaceful calm came over me. Out of pure gratitude I placed my arm around my wife, who understood, for I know that we had now found a broader, richer and more abundant life. (Ibid., pp. 292–93.)

Elder Scott bore a similar testimony regarding the effects of forgiveness when he said: "You cannot erase what has been done, but you can forgive. Forgiveness heals terrible, tragic wounds, for it allows the love of God to purge your heart and mind of the poison of hate. It cleanses your consciousness of the desire for revenge. It makes place for the purifying, healing, restoring love of the Lord." ("Healing the Tragic Scars of Abuse," p. 33.) What comfort to know that we can find peace if we forgive!

Incidentally, I have found that in order to truly forgive, a person needs to quit blaming others for his adversity and discomfort. One must quit blaming parents, spouse, children, relatives, neighbors—and perhaps even God—for his problems. Forgiveness involves taking responsibility for one's own actions and leaving revenge to the Lord.

Regarding the idea that we shouldn't blame our troubles on anything in our environment, President Spencer W. Kimball said:

There are those today who say that man is the result of his environment and cannot rise above it. Those who justify mediocrity, failure, immorality of all kinds, and even weakness and criminality are certainly misguided. . . . [T]he fact remains that every normal soul has its free agency and the power to row against the current and to lift itself to new planes of activity and thought and development. . . . It is within [man's] power to lift himself by his very bootstraps from the plane on which he finds himself to the plane on which he should be. It may be a long, hard lift with many obstacles, but it is a real possibility. . . . In other words, environment need not be our limit. Circumstance may not need to be our ruler. ("The Abundant Life," pp. 6–7.)

President George Q. Cannon said it this way: "No man ought to say, 'Oh, I cannot help this; it is my nature.' He is not justified in it, for the reason that God has promised to give strength to correct these things and to give gifts that will eradicate them." (*Gospel Truth*, p. 155.)

7. *I found it helpful to listen to uplifting music.* This probably wasn't essential to my finding peace, but because of Heather, her story, her song, and her death, I can testify to the truth that there is great power in worthy music. Music has the potential to relieve pain and suffering and to bring feelings of comfort, joy, and happiness. It can be a great source of healing, and can even be a link with eternity.

8. *It helped to have a hobby or something I enjoyed doing.* Another helpful thing I found was to find something that took my mind off my problems, at least for two or three hours a week. For me, it was going to BYU football games or watching sports on television. For Bruce, it was building an addition on our home for Cindy, Heather, and Mark, and building a decorative retaining wall around our yard. For us together, it was going out on a Friday night "date" every week.

It is my testimony that doing the things listed above usually doesn't take away the problem that is causing the pain and suffering. Often the problem remains. Doing these things simply helps make us worthy to partake of the conditional part of Christ's atonement—for Christ to ease the pain by sending us peace and comfort. Our obedience doesn't restore the easy times we had before our adversity, and it doesn't shield us from additional adversity either. Knowing all these principles usually won't ease pain and suffering, as logic alone doesn't bring lasting peace. Lasting comfort comes only through personal faith in Jesus Christ and from His messenger, who is literally the Comforter.

How My Faith Developed

Because I grew up in a home where the gospel of Jesus Christ was taught and lived, I knew something of faith before I was married. I knew that faith is to trust in unseen things which are true (see Alma 32:21), and that to have faith in Jesus Christ is to trust in Him. I also vaguely understood that faith is a gift from God and is based on our righteousness.

Soon after I was married I discovered it is considerably easier to talk and learn about faith than it is to exercise it. I learned by experience that President Kimball was right when he said:

It takes faith—unseeing faith—for young people to proceed immediately with their family responsibilities in the face of financial uncertainties. It takes faith for the young woman to bear her family instead of accepting employment, especially when schooling for the young husband is to be finished. It takes faith to observe the Sabbath when "time and a half" can be had working, when profit can be made, when merchandise can be sold. It takes a great faith to pay tithes when funds are scarce and demands are great. It takes faith to fast and have family prayers and to observe the Word of Wisdom. It takes faith to do home teaching, stake missionary work, and other service, when sacrifice is required. (*Faith Precedes the Miracle,* p. 11.)

I learned more about faith after I had been married a year. Bruce and I were called to teach the family home evening class in Sunday School, which caused us to study the scriptures, listen to general conference talks, and read the writings of the Brethren. As we prepared lessons I learned from Elder Packer, who was then an Assistant to the Council of the Twelve, that there are two kinds of faith: "One of them functions ordinarily in the life of every soul. It is the kind of faith born by experience; it gives us certainty that a new day will dawn, that spring will come, that growth will take place." ("Faith," p. 62.) It is the kind of faith that motivates us to go to a doctor when we hope to get well, to plant a seed when we hope to reap a harvest, and to study and work when we hope for a college degree. In short, "it is the kind of faith that relates us with confidence to that which is scheduled to happen" (ibid., p. 62).

The second type of faith that Elder Packer described is the faith that causes things to happen. It is the first principle of the gospel and is specifically called "faith in the Lord Jesus Christ." Regarding that kind of faith, Elder Packer stated:

> Faith and humility go hand in hand. The person who can acknowledge his dependence upon God and accept a child-parent relationship with him has prepared a growing place for faith. . . .
>
> Faith, to be faith, must center around something that is not known. Faith, to be faith, must go beyond that for which there is confirming evidence. Faith, to be faith, must go into the unknown. Faith, to be faith, must walk to the edge of the light, and then a few steps into the darkness. If everything has to be known, if everything has to be explained, if everything has to be certified, then there is no need for faith. Indeed, there is no room for it. (Ibid., p. 62.)

Although Bruce and I were able to teach those concepts to people in our Sunday School class, much of what I now know in my heart about faith and my dependence upon God, as described by Elder Packer, has come from the experiences I have had in our home. For me, having children created an environment where I often found myself walking "to the edge of the light," "into the unknown," and even "a few steps into the darkness." Literally, in their individual ways Bruce and our children have become my "clinical material" (Maxwell, "If Thou Endure Well," p. 7) as the Lord has taught me what it means to walk by faith and to trust Him.

I now know that it is impossible to find lasting peace without having faith in Jesus Christ. I also know that in most cases faith grows gradually, "line upon line" and experience upon experience. It does not come merely by asking, but as a result of our individual faithfulness over a period of time—sometimes a long time. In other words, the gift of faith comes when we obey the law upon which the blessing of faith is predicated. As we show our faithfulness in doing God's will, He in turn blesses us with more faith. And great faith comes as we prove we can be trusted in all things.

From my own experiences I also know that patience is an important part of faith. Furthermore, I know that as people develop patience with their families, friends, neighbors, and others, they are learning the skills necessary to be patient with the Lord—and with His timing. That is necessary because, as Elder Maxwell states, faith in His timing is "one of the things most difficult for us to have faith in" (ibid., p. 2).

How true that statement is! It *was* difficult for me to have faith in the Lord's timing for Cindy, Heather, and Mark, because life was so hard every day. After Heather's death, however, I saw some of the blessings that were available when I was patient with the Lord and had faith in His timing, which makes it easier for me to be patient now.

For many years as I struggled to understand faith, I could never find the answers to several puzzling questions: Why is it that some people exercise faith and their loved one is healed, and other people, who seem just as faithful, exercise faith and their loved one is not healed? What makes the difference? Does one family have more faith than the other? Is one more righteous than the other? Thankfully, I found my answer in 1992 as I read a talk given by President J. Reuben Clark in the priesthood session of general conference: "I do not believe that the Lord, that God permits any man to have faith that would overrule His purposes. . . . I repeat, I think that the Lord never gives faith to any individual to enable him to overturn the purposes of His will. Always we are subject to what He wishes." And as President Clark said, even the Savior in Gethsemane "was not given the necessary faith at that time to enable Him to turn aside the purposes reached by Himself and the Father before and still remembered by the Father." (In Conference Report, April 1960, p. 21.)

And Elder Maxwell explained it this way:

Petitioning in prayer has taught me that the vault of heaven, with all its blessings, is to be opened only by a combination lock: one tumbler falls when there is faith, a second when there is personal righteousness, and the third and final tumbler falls only when what is sought is (in God's judgment, not ours) "right" for us. Sometimes we pound on the vault door for something we want very much, in faith, in reasonable righteousness, and wonder why the door does not open. We would be very spoiled children if that vault door opened any more easily than it does now. I can tell, looking back, that God truly loves me by the petitions that, in his perfect wisdom and love, he has refused to grant me. Our rejected petitions tell us not only much about ourselves, but also much about our flawless Father. ("Insights from My Life," p. 200.)

What a revelation! That meant that when Lara prayed for many months that Mark wouldn't become handicapped, it wasn't because she didn't have faith or wasn't righteous that her prayers were denied. The Lord didn't permit Lara to possess sufficient faith, because He knew our family needed other experiences. Similarly, when I prayed for Heather to be healed God knew I needed to learn to diligently seek Him, submit to His will, and pray continually. He also knew the effect Heather would have on many people later in her life. Consequently, He didn't permit us to possess sufficient faith for her to be healed.

It is my testimony that since God is all-knowing He is able to structure each of our individual "universes" (within the bounds of our agency) so that if we "search diligently, pray always, and be believing, . . . all things shall work together for [our] good" (D&C 90:24). In order for that to happen, however, we must always pray, "Thy will be done," and then continue to do everything we know we should do. That way we can be assured that whatever happens in that particular situation will be the Lord's will and what is best for us. For example, because Lara continued to pray, attend her meetings, keep the Sabbath day holy, pay her tithing, and obey the Word of Wisdom, even though her prayer wasn't answered the way she wanted it answered she could have the assurance that what happened was God's will and therefore for her best good.

As to the future, there are many things that will take faith for our children to do. It will take faith for them to be married in the temple; it may even take faith for them to stay married. It will take great faith for them to bear children, knowing that their parents have a genetic problem which resulted in their having three severely handicapped siblings, and knowing that they live in a time when many consider even healthy children to be a burden to parents. It will take great faith to "multiply and replenish the earth" when predictors of doom say the world is over-populated and running short of resources. It will take faith when they are mothers to remain at home to raise their children, as the prophets have admonished.

It is my testimony that it takes faith to keep the Sabbath day holy when so much of the world's "important" entertainment is on Sunday. It takes faith to pay tithing and to hold family home evenings. It takes faith to read, study, and ponder the scriptures. It takes faith to pray, saying, "Thy will be done," and to keep praying when prayers are not answered the way we want them answered. It takes great faith to follow the living prophets, especially when the prophet's words conflict with something we personally believe to be right and true. It takes faith to serve other people, especially when the world teaches that we as individuals are our own most important consideration. It takes faith to do the Lord's will in the season *He* desires. It takes faith to repent and cast our burdens on the Lord. It takes faith to turn our hearts to God. Those truths I know. But this I also know: If we have a repentant spirit and continually exercise faith in Jesus Christ, we eventually will find peace and joy in this world and eternal life in the world to come.

PART III

Bruce's Reflections and Perceptions

Bruce E. Erickson

CHAPTER 10

Why Me?

Although Joyce (Jo) and I experienced the same family adversity, we responded very differently. Elder Boyd K. Packer's words described our differences:

> The same testing . . . can have quite opposite effects on individuals. The Book of Mormon, which is another testament of Christ, [teaches] us that "They had had wars, and bloodsheds, and famine, and affliction. . . .
> But behold, because of the exceedingly great length of the war between the Nephites and the Lamanites many had become *hardened*, . . . and many were *softened* because of their afflictions, insomuch that they did humble themselves before God, even in the depth of humility." (Alma 62:39–41, italics added.)
> Surely you know some whose lives have been filled with adversity who have been mellowed and strengthened and refined by it, while others have come away from the same test bitter and blistered and unhappy. ("The Mystery of Life," p. 18.)

In our case Jo became "mellowed and strengthened and refined," and I initially was "bitter and blistered and unhappy." Although my experiences are probably very different from yours, I believe the principles I learned are universally applicable and that they can help you find happiness. Like Moroni, I share my imperfections and perspectives in the hope that you will "be more wise than [I] have been" (Mormon 9:31). That is the main reason I have tried to write the book I could never find. My prayer is that my honesty will be of value to you.

Early Years and Marriage

As one of eight children, I vividly remember enjoying fun activities with my family. We lived near Ogden, Utah, and once or twice a year we went to Yellowstone National Park. I remember packing the station wagon, setting up tents in driving rain, and shivering in a cold cabin as we built a fire in a cast-iron stove. Throughout the year we frequently went to the canyon for picnics or family home evenings. There we often had treasure hunts, played hide-and-go-seek, or sang songs around the campfire. I also recall the annual fathers and sons' hike to the top of Ben Lomond Peak, where we had a spectacular view in every direction. I loved those traditions, and I believed that when I married and had children we, too, would travel and go camping, hiking, and fishing, and those activities would help keep our family together.

I left home in 1964 to serve a mission in Germany, and upon my return became a student at Brigham Young University. There I met Jo, and we were married a year later in the Salt Lake Temple. Although she had one year of schooling left and I had four years of electrical engineering remaining, we made a commitment to follow the counsel of the Brethren and welcome children into our family when the Lord sent them. We also decided that Jo would not work outside the home once we had a child. That decision was confirmed a few months before we were married when I heard Elder A. Theodore Tuttle say in general priesthood meeting:

I would like to say a word about working mothers, brethren. I know I am not talking to working mothers. But I am talking to some fathers whose children have working mothers. You are the ones who cause, or at least permit, mothers to work. Brethren, before you count the profit of such an endeavor, count the *cost.* In our affluent society many of us cannot distinguish between luxuries and necessities. Too often mothers work to pay for luxuries that are not worth the cost. . . .

. . . I am not talking about widows or women who because of *necessity* must become a breadwinner, and I am not talking about women who have no children in the home at this particular time. Brethren, before you count the profit, count the cost of a working mother. Stable, secure, well-balanced individuals are not accidental. They are the result of prayerful, concentrated attention to parental responsibilities. ("On Being a Father," pp. 86–87, emphasis in original.)

While we struggled to graduate, we were blessed with two children, Michelle and Lara. As the family's sole provider, I worked an average of thirty hours a week and carried a heavy engineering class load. Consequently, camping, hiking, fishing, and similar activities were postponed until sometime after graduation, which finally occurred in May 1971. Jo and I both graduated, and I was commissioned an officer in the Air Force. Graduation day was exciting, but I worried about being sent to Vietnam.

Thankfully, my first assignment was to Keesler Air Force Base (AFB) in Biloxi, Mississippi, for seven months of communications-electronics training, after which we were transferred to March AFB, near Riverside, California. While relocating there, we were blessed with our third child. Cindy was a beautiful, healthy baby, and life was bright and exciting. College was finished, military training was complete, we had three wonderful children and finally a steady income. Now we could go camping, fishing, and hiking as a family. Truly my life was proceeding as I had expected and planned.

My World Turned Upside Down

Eight months later, on December 2, 1972, my entire world changed. Cindy lay down on the living room floor that evening and was never the same again. By New Year's Day she had spent four weeks in three hospitals. Michelle and Lara, who were four and two years old respectively, wondered why Cindy wasn't home for Christmas. I wondered too and was frustrated, since Christmas had always been my most joyful time of the year. I had never before experienced such intense heartache, grief, and disappointment.

When we finally brought Cindy home from the hospital, sleep became our number one need because she cried about twenty-three hours every day for many months. Doctors couldn't identify her illness nor explain why she was sick, but they said she had viral encephalitis—a catchall medical term—and that she exhibited symptoms of cerebral palsy. I wondered if she would ever be normal again and specifically if she would be able to start kindergarten in four years. Surely, with proper therapy, hard work, a positive attitude, and the Lord's help that could happen.

After many months of fasting and prayers, promises to the Lord, visits to the temple, priesthood blessings, and repeated hospital visits and tests, Cindy's condition deteriorated and her future was still uncertain. She lost all muscle control and was unable to hold up her head, voluntarily move her arms and legs, sit up, or control her tongue to eat. The cute little girl I loved and adored was now a crying, uncontrollable, totally dependent, handicapped child. Hiking, camping, and similar activities were no longer a choice for our family. I was frustrated and heartbroken, and wondered why she kept crying. Oh, how I hated to hear her cry.

I turned to the scriptures and the words of the Brethren for comfort, but I could not find answers to my questions: "Why me? What did I ever do to deserve this? Why doesn't God love me? Why is God punishing me?" I felt that my problems were far worse than other people's and that no one understood the burdens I was forced to bear.

My life surely wasn't proceeding as I had planned. I expected challenges, but I never thought I would have a handicapped child. Since my family seldom had medical problems while I was growing up, I believed that if family members kept the Lord's commandments they would be spared serious trials and medical problems. Now all my hopes and dreams were destroyed.

Besides those bitter disappointments, one of my greatest frustrations was that I felt that I had been wronged by the physician who refused to admit and treat Cindy the night she became ill. Surely the severity of her handicap was due to his faulty diagnosis and failure to act quickly. Friends even suggested that we had "just cause" to sue, so Jo and I discussed the possibility. However, because we felt that suing might canker our own souls, we concluded that litigation was not a righteous alternative for us. Later, the physician was discharged from the Air Force for several cases of malpractice.

No Answers

As I struggled with all my disappointments and frustrations, I continually prayed for Cindy to improve. When she didn't, I wondered why my prayers weren't answered. They had been answered when I was young. Once, I lost my pocketknife and prayed that I would find it, and I did. I prayed about the validity of the Book of Mormon and Joseph Smith's prophetic calling, and I received a sacred confirmation of their truthfulness. Why didn't the Lord answer my prayers now? Surely my petitions to heal Cindy were far more important than finding a pocketknife. Failing to receive answers to my prayers became a serious test of my faith.

Months passed as I struggled for answers. Perhaps it was my engineering background that prompted me to analyze problems, or maybe it was the result of my nature to question and wonder when a situation is unclear. Whatever the reason, I searched diligently for answers. As I did so, one sacrament meeting affected me in a profound way. I listened with great interest as the speaker, our stake patriarch, talked about his grandson becoming seriously ill and losing his hearing. After extensive evaluations the doctors determined that the boy would remain deaf unless he had surgery.

Several weeks before the operation, our patriarch gave his grandson a priesthood blessing and promised him that he would regain his hearing. The blessing was a great comfort to the boy and his parents, but when the boy's hearing didn't return, they proceeded with the surgery. Before operating, however, the surgeon rechecked the boy's hearing, and to his astonishment he could faintly hear. The surgery was postponed, and in a few days the boy's hearing was completely restored!

As I listened to our patriarch's talk, I thought, *It must be wonderful for a priesthood holder to have the gift of healing. Wouldn't it be great if he would bless Cindy.* Then I remembered—the patriarch *had* blessed Cindy! But he hadn't promised her a restoration of health. Why not? Why did God heal our patriarch's grandson and not Cindy? Weren't Jo and I deserving parents? Wasn't Cindy as important as the little boy?

Probably the most difficult aspect of coping with Cindy's illness was struggling to understand why she became handicapped when we were striving to keep God's commandments. As I pondered that seeming unfairness I became upset with God, and a bitterness developed within me. Why wouldn't He help us? Didn't He love us too? Initially I shared my feelings and frustrations with others, but I was repeatedly told, "You shouldn't feel that way." Well, I did feel that way, and ignoring those feelings didn't help. I concluded that it was useless to share my feelings, because no one seemed to understand me.

With time, I told only Jo about my bitterness, although those closest to me probably sensed it. It was embarrassing to share my feelings, because I had a testimony of the restored gospel and served in leadership positions in the Church, but I didn't have sufficient faith to overcome my adversity.

When Cindy remained severely physically handicapped in spite of all efforts, shamefully I longed for her to return to Heavenly Father. I thought that would be better for her and our family, because my family goals couldn't be achieved if we had to continually care for her. Besides, if our family couldn't enjoy fun activities together, how could we develop family traditions like I had experienced as a boy? Yes, I could take Michelle and Lara hiking or camping, but our whole family couldn't go together. In addition, Jo and I could never go on a vacation alone, since no one but Jo could feed Cindy. Family life certainly wasn't what I expected it to be.

In time I suppressed my bitterness in order to cope with the challenges of earning a living and raising a family. But I felt cheated. As I reflected on the unfairness I was experiencing, a thought came to mind: *What father, when asked for bread, would give his son a stone?* I had asked Heavenly Father for bread and He had given me a stone, and no matter how much I begged and pleaded, the stone remained.

Despite always wanting a large family, Jo and I had serious concerns about ever having more children, since caring for Cindy was so difficult and time-consuming. However, after considerable fasting and prayer and feeling that our family was incomplete, almost two years after Cindy became ill Heidi was born. To our great relief she developed normally and was a patient, loving, delightful child. Thankfully, the doctors were correct: Cindy's illness was a fluke, a rare act of nature.

Leaving the Air Force

In late 1975, after more than four years of active military duty, I was elated to learn that my next assignment would be Temple Hof AFB in West Berlin! I would be the commander of a 160-member communications squadron, our family would move to Germany, and I would return to the people whom I dearly loved. Finally the Lord was blessing me as I expected.

My excitement turned to extreme resentment several days later when I learned that there were no facilities for handicapped children of U.S. military personnel in West Berlin. I was devastated! I had the perfect assignment, but I couldn't accept it unless I deprived Cindy of medical care. Again, why had God given me a loaf and then replaced it with a stone? Once more I felt angry and betrayed.

I called my career counselor and told him I couldn't accept the assignment. His response was unexpected: "If it's not convenient for your family to go with you, we'll keep them at March AFB and give you a two-year remote assignment at a radar site in Turkey." What an alternative!

Jo and I spent the next several days praying, agonizing, and wondering what we should do. We had no intention of leaving the Air Force at that time, but we were forced to make a decision that was more permanent and far-reaching than we had planned.

If I stayed in the Air Force, Jo would have to care for the children alone, but Cindy could get proper care at minimal expense. If I left the military we would have to pay for all of Cindy's medical costs. We kept praying about our decision but received no answer. It seemed as if the Lord said, "You decide." Reluctantly we did—we would leave the Air Force.

I was apprehensive when I resigned my commission, because I loved serving my country and felt that the Air Force had been good to me. I had a bright future, promotions had come quickly, and I had received many significant recognitions. Our financial condition was steadily improving, we had paid off all but one student loan, had established a year's supply of food, and had a modest savings. However, we felt that keeping our family together was more important than financial security.

I was especially nervous about finding work, since I had never written a resume or interviewed professionally. I also wondered if we were doing what was best for our family and why Heavenly Father hadn't answered our prayers. He promised Oliver Cowdery that he could know the correctness of a decision if he followed certain steps (see D&C 9:8–9). We had followed those steps, but we received no confirmation. Why?

Our decision to leave the Air Force became irreversible in February 1976, when I was notified that my last day on active duty would be June 28. During those five months I interviewed with several firms and received an offer from a company in Logan, Utah. We prayed about the job, but again our prayers seemed to go unanswered. I wondered again why the heavens were sealed, and began to look for work locally. Finally, after several telephone discussions with the owner of the company that made Cindy's wheelchair, he offered me a job and invited me to visit him in Ventura. Jo and I prayed almost constantly for an answer regarding this new job offer, but again no answer came. *Why has God forsaken us?* I thought as I left for Ventura.

Confirmation Comes!

The traffic in Los Angeles was lighter than expected, and I arrived in Ventura an hour early. As I drove around the city, I traveled with the windows rolled down so I could enjoy the refreshing ocean breeze. The air was cool—not like the hot, smog-filled air of Riverside. While driving through the residential areas I saw flowers in bloom everywhere. I marveled at the beautiful homes, the meticulously manicured yards, and the tall, majestic palm trees that stretched against the cloudless blue sky. Ventura would be a heavenly place to live, I thought, but why hadn't the Lord confirmed our decision to move there?

As I drove I realized that I was humming a song. I thought nothing of it for several minutes, but when it persisted I listened as the words filled my mind:

> It may not be on the mountain height
> Or over the stormy sea,
> It may not be at the battle's front
> My Lord will have need of me.
> But if, by a still, small voice he calls
> To paths that I do not know,
> I'll answer, dear Lord, with my hand in thine:
> I'll go where you want me to go.
>
> (Mary Brown, "I'll Go Where You Want Me to Go," *Hymns*, no. 270.)

That was our answer! Our confirmation was in the words of the hymn I had been humming!

"It may not be on the mountain height"—we shouldn't return to the Rocky Mountains to live and work.
"Or over the stormy sea"—we shouldn't cross the Atlantic Ocean to live in Germany.
"It may not be at the battle's front"—we shouldn't remain in the Air Force.
"To paths that I do not know"—we should move to an unfamiliar city.

That morning, gratitude filled my heart. Heavenly Father *was* interested in us, and we would go where He wanted us to go!

Several months later Elder Boyd K. Packer said: "Once you really determine to follow that guide [the Holy Spirit], your testimony will grow and you will find provisions set out along the way in unexpected places, as evidence that someone knew that you would be traveling that way" ("Spiritual Crocodiles," p. 31). It was comforting to find a "provision" confirming our decisions.

Finding a Home

We became excited about buying our first home as soon as our decision to leave the Air Force became irreversible. We had already rented four homes during our nine years of marriage, and we were tired of moving. In addition, I resented getting no income tax deduction for rent. Although we could live in base housing until I separated from the military, we started looking for a home immediately because prices were rising rapidly.

Shortly after accepting the job in Ventura, I was shocked to learn that housing prices there were much higher than in the Riverside area. I checked neighboring cities and discovered that the only affordable housing with an acceptable family environment was in Santa Paula, a small city near Ventura. We consulted a real-estate agent, who quickly found several houses that met our needs. However, since only Jo could feed Cindy our house-hunting trips were frustrating and time-consuming. Every Saturday I drove for two and a half hours each way to look at homes. If I found a home I liked, Jo and I returned the following Saturday and evaluated it for about forty-five minutes before returning to feed Cindy. We could have taken her with us, but it would have meant being trapped with her, having to listen to her cry, and having no way to prepare her food.

After several weeks we made an offer on a house. Unfortunately, loan complications dashed our dreams. Thankfully, we soon found another house that was in a nicer neighborhood and better suited to our family. Our offer was accepted, but again the loan was denied. I was devastated! Why would the Lord treat us this way? We were trying to keep His commandments. We had waited patiently for almost nine years to buy a home. All of our friends owned their own homes. Why weren't we blessed like they were?

With the deadline to leave base housing less than two months away, I took vacation time each week and traveled to Santa Paula to find a house. Fortunately, we found one under construction that we liked even better than the others. Our offer was accepted, and again we waited anxiously for the loan approval.

Unbelievably, four weeks before my separation from the Air Force the Veterans Administration (VA) again denied our loan—once again because the house didn't meet some VA standard! How was this possible? Now there wasn't enough time to buy a house before we had to vacate government housing. What should we do?

Miraculously, the real-estate agent in Santa Paula found another house, which the owner agreed to rent for several months while our loan was processed. We had a home at last! Nevertheless, I was extremely frustrated and discouraged because even though the Lord had confirmed our decisions, nothing seemed to be coming together easily for us.

Then the unthinkable happened. Two days before we were to move Jo received a call from the owner of the home in Santa Paula, who said, "I'm terribly sorry to tell you this, but I just sold my home." How could she? Why hadn't she told us that she still was trying to sell her house? Again I felt betrayed and angry. Where could we go? Where would we send our belongings? The packers were coming the next day to pack our household goods and move us the following day. Why didn't Heavenly Father answer our prayers? All we were asking for was a place to live. We were caring for His special child. Didn't we deserve special blessings? I thought so, and my bitterness increased.

Paths That I Do Not Know

In desperation we called the bishop of the Santa Paula ward and asked him for help. He didn't know of any homes to rent but suggested we call several members in nearby Camarillo. After repeated tries we finally contacted the first counselor in the elders quorum presidency there. We explained our dilemma and were astonished when he said, "I'm the agent for a man who rents a house in our ward, and the renters are moving out." He then agreed to call the owner in Salt Lake City and tell him our plight.

Later that evening the owner called us and said he would rent us the house. He also agreed to significantly reduce the rent if we would renovate the yard and repaint the home inside and out. We were elated and agreed to his terms. Although we had only a brief description of the house and no knowledge of Camarillo, we finally had a place to live!

Two days later the movers loaded our household goods, and we said our good-byes to friends and neighbors in Riverside. Although we had experienced great discouragement and despair there, we hated leaving because of the friendships we had developed. Many people had rendered hundreds of hours of service in our behalf, and leaving them created anxiety in our hearts.

CHAPTER 11

Another Stone

W̲e were surprised when we saw our new home in Camarillo. It was attractive, spacious, located in a wonderful neighborhood, and had a large swimming pool! Although several
years would pass before I understood why the Lord called me
to "paths that I [did] not know," I was grateful we found a
beautiful home with rent less than half of what we were planning to spend for house payments. My bitterness was replaced
with thanksgiving—for a time.

New Employment

Developing electronic products for severely handicapped
people was an exciting job. Even though it required a cut in
salary, from $20,000 to $12,000 per year, we believed we could
survive until I received royalties from products I designed.
Unfortunately, that was a bad assumption. First, the plans for
the product I was developing changed, so after almost a year of
effort the project was suspended, and I began developing a new
product. Second, because I had never produced a product before I greatly underestimated the time required to design, pro-
totype, debug, test, document, and manufacture a complex,
portable, state-of-the-art electronic product. Third, company

medical insurance benefits were not adequate for our family, so it wasn't long before Cindy's medical expenses created a serious financial burden. In retrospect, we should have carefully reviewed our medical insurance benefits before I signed my employment contract, but we were so excited about working for a company that helped handicapped people that we didn't consider insurance limitations.

To compound our financial problems, less than two months after I left the Air Force Jo had a miscarriage and required surgery. Our entire family was unhappy about losing a baby, and I was devastated when I learned that the surgery was not covered by medical insurance. Perhaps $746 isn't much today, but it was a small fortune then as I struggled to support a family of six in Southern California. Our savings were nearly gone, and the only way I could get Jo out of the hospital was to pay with a credit card.

After deciding against seeking different employment, to minimize expenses we utilized food that we had stored for emergencies. Except for breakfast, most of our meals were made with beans, rice, or wheat, complemented with fresh potatoes and other vegetables. We enjoyed hamburger or chicken only once or twice a month, and we never had other cuts of meat.

The result of our financial problems was that I became very discouraged, and my suppressed bitterness returned. My life certainly wasn't progressing as I had expected after obtaining a college degree and serving five years in the Air Force. I was now thirty-six years old, I didn't own my own home, and I felt we had been cursed with a handicapped child. Life seemed so unfair. I was honest, hardworking, and tried to keep the commandments. But why weren't we blessed? Why weren't we prospering as prophets had promised (see Mosiah 1:7)? Why did the Lord continue to place obstacles in our path? I continued to struggle, with little hope in sight.

Heather

In May 1977 Jo and I were blessed with our fifth child, Heather. Although she was born five weeks prematurely, she was strong and healthy for her size, and by November she was rolling over and sitting up. Then it happened. Shortly before Christmas Jo thought she saw Heather posture her hands like Cindy! It couldn't be—but it was. The day we learned that Heather was "developmentally delayed," I was heartsick. Why had God punished us again when we were trying to live as we should and after we had followed inspiration to have another child? We had trusted Him, and yet He had abused that trust. We had fasted and prayed and promised Him renewed dedication after Cindy became ill. Didn't that mean anything? I drove home from work with a heavy heart, wondering how our family could survive financially and emotionally. The more I tried to plan my life, the worse things got. Why didn't Heavenly Father love me and care about our family?

Several days later I had a quarterly interview with a stake high councilor. I didn't want to go, but I felt he might be able to comfort my troubled heart. As he greeted me he said, "How are you, Brother Erickson?" "Rotten," I replied, hoping to share my grief. "You can't be rotten," he said. "The gospel's true, and that's all that matters." As he proceeded with the interview I wondered, *Isn't he interested in me? Can't he tell my heart is ready to break and that I need his help? Isn't my welfare more important than a church program?*

Ward members were extremely understanding and helped ease our pain, but my heartache was almost more than I could bear. Why us? Wasn't one severely handicapped child enough? Why were we cursed with two? How could we care for Cindy and Heather and give Michelle, Lara, and Heidi the love and attention they needed? The healthy girls were already taunted by their peers for having one "retarded" sibling. How would they be treated now?

Since caring for Cindy and Heather was more than a full-time job, doing things together as a family became nearly impossible. How unfair! My goals and desires couldn't be achieved, my life's plans were ruined, and I felt cheated out of a normal family life. Furthermore, we had to listen to Cindy cry almost constantly, we weren't buying our own home, and we were deeply in debt. And worst of all, my relationship with Jo was not satisfying. I was envious of other couples because Jo and I had so little time for each other and no time for fun activities together. Several months earlier I had learned that 85 percent of married couples who have a handicapped child get divorced. How could our marriage survive with two handicapped children? Life seemed so unfair. Once again Heavenly Father had given me a stone.

A Priesthood Blessing

Not long after we learned of Heather's illness, Jo told me she felt Heather could be healed by a priesthood blessing. I was hesitant and troubled, because years earlier I had blessed Cindy, and our bishop, stake patriarch, and a visiting General Authority had blessed her, but her condition never improved. I was troubled, too, because I had tried earlier to understand priesthood blessings but found little material to study. I had read President Spencer W. Kimball's talk "Tragedy or Destiny," but it didn't calm my troubled heart. I had also read Elder Matthew Cowley's talk "Miracles," but it left me discouraged and bitter. He shared many experiences of children who were healed, but he never told of a child who wasn't healed—every story was of a priesthood "success." Why wasn't Cindy healed like the children he described in his talk? Didn't the Savior love Cindy too?

As I pondered on priesthood blessings again, I wondered why I hadn't received a feeling like Jo did that Heather could be healed. Was Heather really supposed to be healed? I hoped Jo was correct, but I wondered if I had the necessary faith, especially since Cindy hadn't been healed. I wanted time to think, pray, and fast, so we set a date to bless Heather in six weeks. Actually, I delayed the blessing as long as Jo would let me.

During the next six weeks I studied, prayed, pondered, and fasted like never before. I reviewed my life and promised Father that I would correct things that were displeasing to Him. All I asked in return was that He heal Heather. As I pondered I tried to understand the principle of faith and wondered why Heather should suffer if I lacked faith or wasn't worthy enough. I also wondered if I had sufficient faith to change something that medical experts didn't understand. Finally, after diligently searching for answers, I decided that even if I didn't have sufficient faith, Jo did, and the brethren who would assist me certainly did. Still, I wondered if the Lord wanted Heather healed.

I reflected often on priesthood blessings I had participated in earlier. I remembered a tiny infant in an incubator who was healed, a lady with a broken back whose health was completely restored, and a blind boy who was freed of severe eye pain. I knew that the priesthood could heal and that I had that authority. It had been restored to the Prophet Joseph Smith by a visitation of the ancient Apostles Peter, James, and John, and it had been properly conveyed to me. But did Heavenly Father want Heather healed? Jo felt so. Why didn't I? And why was there so little written about priesthood blessings?

As I struggled for understanding I wondered if I should find a priesthood bearer with the gift of healing. I actually wanted our bishop to perform the blessing, but I concluded from my studies that God would honor a healing petition from any worthy Melchizedek Priesthood holder. I didn't have to search out a General Authority or a person with the gift of healing, as I did when Cindy became ill. Such requests of General Authorities or brethren in leadership positions were unnecessary and placed additional burdens on their limited time. I also learned that the outcome of a priesthood blessing would be whatever the Lord wanted as long as worthy Melchizedek Priesthood holders performed the blessing and sufficient faith was exercised. Therefore, I decided I would do as the Brethren had counseled—I would bless Heather. Surely, with Heather's name on temple prayer rolls and our extended families fasting and praying for her, there would be sufficient faith to heal her.

As the weeks passed I worried constantly about how Jo and the children would feel if Heather weren't healed, and I questioned why the Lord would heal Heather when He didn't heal Cindy. I wondered what I should say as I blessed Heather. Would I say what Jo and I wanted or what the Lord wanted? I had never appreciated the pressure stake patriarchs must feel when they speak for the Lord as they pronounce patriarchal blessings.

Finally the time arrived to bless Heather. I was very nervous that Sunday morning in early spring 1978 as several priesthood holders met in our home. Surely the Lord would recognize their faith and righteousness. As Jo held Heather, our bishop anointed her and I sealed the anointing. I listened carefully as I blessed her. Where were the healing words that confirmed Jo's feeling that Heather could be healed? I continued the blessing, but I didn't say what we wanted to hear. Instead I said that Heather would be a joy and a blessing in our home and would bless the lives of others.

After the blessing I felt like a total failure. Why did Jo get the distinct feeling that Heather could be healed? Why wasn't she healed after all we had done? We had followed the Savior's counsel to His apostles when they tried to heal a handicapped boy: "This kind goeth not out but by prayer and fasting" (Matthew 17:21). Should we now find another priesthood holder to bless her, since Jo and I both felt I had failed? Why should our family suffer because I apparently lacked sufficient faith to heal Heather as Jo felt I could?

I wanted with all my heart to pronounce a healing blessing, but I couldn't. Was I not in tune with the Spirit? Was I afraid to pronounce a healing blessing for fear that it wouldn't be fulfilled? I didn't know, and therefore I became confused and frustrated with priesthood blessings. How was I to know what was right when giving blessings? I thought I had followed the Spirit when I blessed Heather, but Jo said Heather could be healed. Again my bitterness increased and I wondered why the Lord had forsaken me.

Not long after Heather's blessing, a close friend told us that his mother was cured of cancer by a tribal faith healer in the Philippines. For a moment, because I was desperate and wanted Cindy and Heather healed so badly I wondered if we should take them to the Philippines. I decided, however, that I would only put my trust in the restored priesthood—not in a faith healer.

Increased Bitterness

After many months I quit trying to understand my adversity, and my despair increased dramatically. I lost all hope that my life would ever be enjoyable. In my mind it was just another case of asking Heavenly Father for bread and getting a stone instead. Other families were able to go places and do things together. Why couldn't we? Yes, we could go places as a family, but pushing two wheelchairs made me feel awkward and embarrassed. I felt self-conscious not only because the wheelchairs were strange, mechanical "straightjackets" on wheels, but also because Cindy and Heather looked so different. Their arms and legs were abnormally skinny, and even though they occasionally smiled, their heads drooped down and they drooled and slobbered all over themselves. Michelle, Lara, and Heidi felt the embarrassment too and referred to those who turned and stared as "lookie-looks."

Besides feeling embarrassed, many other things bothered me as well. I resented the time it took to care for Cindy and Heather. I felt cheated when people testified in church meetings of miraculous healings. I struggled when fathers blessed new infants with health and strength. I resented the blessings that others received, and I was bitter because with two severely handicapped children we surely could never afford to buy a home. In addition, I was bitter because married life wasn't what I expected. I felt cheated because other couples were able to get away for a few days to have fun or to sort out problems in their relationships. Not Jo and I. We were lucky to get away for two hours. Would I have married if I had known how unfulfilling and unromantic my marriage would be? I didn't know.

My heart ached, and I wondered why the Lord treated me so unfairly. My experiences certainly weren't anything like those of my family when I was growing up. My parents had purchased a home after only two years of marriage, and later they purchased a farm. Dad and my brothers and I worked outside, and Mom and my sisters took care of the shopping and domestic responsibilities inside the home. Mom was a super cook, and it seemed that each meal was a carefully prepared feast. She was proficient at getting everything on the table at the same time, and it was always hot. We enjoyed baked bread, rolls, biscuits, fresh muffins, or scones almost every meal, and our desserts included scrumptious fruit pies, cakes, cookies, brownies, or other treats. Also, since Mom was always the first one up every morning, she always fixed a hot breakfast—even if we went to school or work at 5:00 A.M. She did all that while raising eight children. Certainly all mothers could do the same for their families, I thought, especially those with fewer than eight children.

With two handicapped children, our family circumstances were drastically different. We were still renting after nine years of marriage—with little hope of ever owning a home. Since Jo spent a major portion of every twenty-four hours feeding and caring for Cindy and Heather, her meals were hastily thrown together with little variety, and nothing tasted as good as my mom's cooking. Rarely was there dessert. Also, since Jo usually spent much of the previous night awake with one of the children, she was always too tired to get up and fix breakfast. Seldom was she even awake when our junior- and senior-high-school-age children left for school or when I left for work at 7:00 A.M. I never enjoyed a warm breakfast and a good-bye kiss like my dad did. In addition, limited sleep left Jo physically and mentally exhausted, and it seemed that she always had bad headaches. She never had time to shop for groceries or run errands, so year after year I did all of the family grocery shopping. I knew that she couldn't do things differently, but I still resented doing "her" work.

There were other expectations that were not met either. Jo never kept our home orderly like I expected, she seldom folded laundry like I wanted, and she rarely mended clothes. We simply struggled for survival each and every day. The emotional stress we suffered was nearly more than I could bear, and it increased whenever Cindy or Heather were ill. If Cindy was hospitalized, Jo would live in the hospital and care for her and I would stay home and tend the rest of the family. Grudgingly I used vacation time to watch sick children rather than for relaxation. In short, I was extremely frustrated because I had believed that if I was prayerful, served the Lord, and kept His commandments, He would bless me with happiness.

Ever-Increasing Debt

In addition to our physical and emotional struggles, Jo and I also faced the burden of ever-increasing debt. Jo's miscarriage was a financial crisis, but Heather's birth was the backbreaker. There were bills for the hospital, obstetrician, pediatricians, consulting doctors, and anesthesiologists—nine medical bills each month for almost three years. With no other choice we used credit cards to pay bills, but the monthly card payments became more than half my salary. Consequently we were deeply in debt only one year after leaving the Air Force.

We desperately needed additional income, so I found work as a night custodian. Although the job was not difficult, it was humiliating for me, a trained electrical engineer, to mop floors and clean toilets. Furthermore, it meant spending a minimum of ninety hours each week working two jobs, which left me thoroughly exhausted. I resented Jo's not being able to bring home a paycheck like so many mothers, but I tolerated the situation because I thought we would soon receive additional income from product royalties. Unfortunately, more than a year would pass before that would happen.

Despite the additional income from my second job, our debts continued to mount. Although our extended family provided significant financial support, because of continual medical expenses and the high inflation rate we concluded that the only way to survive financially was to get a loan and consolidate our medical bills and credit card charges into one monthly payment. That would buy us time until I began receiving royalties.

I left work early one hot July afternoon in 1978 to visit our bank. While waiting for the loan officer, I completed an application and reflected on our finances. I wondered why we struggled financially. I was honest, hardworking, and dedicated to helping handicapped people. We had always kept our financial commitments to our fellowmen and to the Lord. Why didn't He keep His commitments to us? Why weren't we receiving financial blessings as I believed the prophet Malachi had promised? (See Malachi 3:8-11.) Why weren't we prospering as Book of Mormon prophets had repeatedly promised? (See Mosiah 1:7.) We had not pushed Cindy's or Heather's care to the State as some thought we should, but were committed to caring for them at home as long as we were physically and emotionally able. Why were people who didn't keep the commandments blessed much more than we were? Why didn't God treat all of His children fairly?

The loan officer interrupted my thoughts and invited me into his office. We chatted briefly and then he reviewed my application. During his review I imagined how wonderful it would be to have our medical bills and credit card charges paid so we could finally get some peace of mind. I was shocked when he said, "I can't approve your loan. You're on the verge of bankruptcy. You can try other banks, but I'm sure you'll get the same answer."

Years earlier we had easily borrowed money for college and a new van, so I protested his decision. Surely he could tell that I was an honest, hardworking person, that I would repay the loan. I told him of people who weren't as dependable as we were who had loans. Besides, we weren't asking for that much. I refuted his statements, but to no avail.

As I drove home, my puzzlement turned into anger. The pent-up emotions and frustrations of once more being abandoned by my Maker caused bitter tears to run down my face. Why wouldn't God help us? My patriarchal blessing said we would be blessed financially. Why weren't we?

When I arrived home thirty minutes later, my anger had changed to fear. How could we survive financially? Should we file for bankruptcy? Should we move and find a new job? Who would hire me? How could we take care of our family? What about the handicapped people who needed the products I could develop? Where would we live? We couldn't rent a home for much less than we were paying.

Indeed, we had exhausted all of our resources and possibilities. Our extended family had helped us as much as I believed they should. We wondered about government assistance but remembered Elder Boyd K. Packer's counsel: "If a member is unable to sustain himself, then he is to call upon his own family, and then upon the Church, in that order, and not upon the government at all" ("Self-Reliance," p. 85). Our bishop had offered assistance earlier, but my pride got in the way. *We don't need church welfare. That's for long-term welfare cases*, I thought. So, not wanting to impose on my extended family any more than we already had and not willing to ask for church assistance, we sold possessions to pay bills. I became so desperate that I even checked the local blood bank to see how much they would pay for Jo's rare blood! I learned, however, that the price for all blood was the same—only sixteen dollars a pint. At that price, we both would have to sell our blood for a decade to pay our debts. Indeed, our financial future was bleak.

An Inspired Home Teacher

At church a few days later I was approached by my home teacher, a wonderful man, who asked if he could visit us that afternoon. When he arrived he greeted us and asked if he and I could talk privately. Although that was unusual I didn't give it a second thought, and we subsequently chatted about a variety of subjects for several minutes. Then he asked about my work and our family's financial status. Under most circumstances I wouldn't have been as forthright with my answers, but since I desperately needed to talk with someone, and since he was genuinely interested, I told him about our problems. Perhaps it was because he worked with many people in his profession, maybe it was because he also had a large family, possibly it was because the Spirit of the Lord was there; whatever it was, his questions were kind and unthreatening. He listened intently, never interrupting.

Within an hour he clearly understood our financial dilemma. I didn't feel embarrassed telling him about our problems, since he didn't criticize me or my decisions. Instead, he lauded Jo and me for our thriftiness, resourcefulness, and food storage, for receiving financial assistance from our extended family, and for my willingness to work two jobs. He then complimented us for our resolve to not have Jo work outside the home, our determination to shun government assistance, and our efforts to care for Cindy and Heather at home.

As he concluded his comments he took a checkbook from his pocket, wrote a check, and handed it to me. I protested, but he refused to take the check back and said he wanted to help us until we started receiving royalties. He was so sincere that I felt I would hurt his feelings if I protested further. I stared at the check in amazement. My home teacher had given me one thousand dollars! I told him I couldn't accept the money, because I didn't know when or how I could repay him. He said we would worry about that later.

Many prayers of thankfulness were offered in our home that evening. We were grateful for a home teacher who had listened to the Spirit and sacrificed his personal resources to help us, and that Heavenly Father had answered our prayers through him. Although I told Jo and the girls about our home teacher's gift, I was grateful he had given it to me privately.

Several weeks later, in a kind, gentle, and courteous manner our home teacher determined that we needed more money because royalties still were not forthcoming. Again he gave me a check. Again I protested, but accepted it. As before, I told him I didn't know how I could repay him, and again he said we would worry about that another time.

Final Farewell

Six months later, the Liberator 912 was completed. It was a small, portable, battery-operated device with an electronic printer, and it enabled severely handicapped people to write using only movements of the head, arm, hand, leg, or tongue. The local newspaper carried a lengthy article describing the device and included a picture of a severely handicapped young man writing his first words. Finally my product was helping someone! Unfortunately, the royalties were not sufficient to significantly improve our financial position, so when my father was diagnosed with leukemia we decided to move to Utah to be closer to him. A close friend found work for me there, in a different career field but with a significant pay increase.

Before leaving Camarillo we visited our home teacher and thanked him again for rescuing us from financial ruin. I told him that I would repay his loan with interest as soon as possible, but I was astonished at his reply: "I don't want the interest, nor do I want the money. Sometime, and it might be twenty to thirty years in the future, when you are financially able, give the money to someone who needs it. I don't want it back."

While I tried unsuccessfully to change his mind, I thought, *We truly have been blessed with an outstanding home teacher.* Later, as I pondered his generosity and goodness, I realized that our home teacher served as Elder Packer stated: "[Home teachers] are guardians of the individual and of the family" ("The Saints Securely Dwell," p. 88).

As we prepared to move, we did so with heavy hearts. The love and assistance we had received from Church members in Camarillo was probably more than any family deserved. I especially felt a deep love and gratitude for them because they had helped us bear heavy burdens, and because the young men I had worked with were like my sons. The only thing that eased the pain of leaving was a spiritual feeling that our work there was finished.

CHAPTER 12

Yet Another Stone

The moving van had left, the house was cleaned, and our car and van were packed. But as we prepared to leave, we couldn't start the van. Unfortunately, it had to be towed to a repair shop, where we waited most of the day while the ring gear was replaced. Even the van didn't want to leave Camarillo! Although we had lived there only three years, leaving was hard because we had developed so many wonderful friendships. That was why Jo cried most of the way to Salt Lake City.

Prior to moving we had searched in vain for a house in Salt Lake City that met our special needs. We needed a house with low rent that was near a pediatric clinic, a hospital, and a school for the handicapped. It had to be wheelchair accessible and have at least four bedrooms. Although it seemed that no such house existed, the Lord knew where one was, and He let us know through another person. Ironically, we found the house because the young daughter of our close friend—the one who found the job for me in Utah—burned her hand. While the pediatrician dressed the girl's wound, her mother asked him if he knew of a house for rent. He did—and the renters were moving out! Again, after all our efforts had failed, the Lord helped us find a home.

A Stumbling Block

We had lived there a little more than a year when I encountered another obstacle in my life, and, strangely, it was due to a talk given at general conference. After my mission I always looked forward to hearing inspired counsel from the Lord's prophets in those meetings, but during the October 1980 session Elder Boyd K. Packer, one of my favorite speakers, said that unhappiness and trouble "are part of the lessons of life, part of the test. Some are tested by poor health, some by a body that is deformed or homely. Others are tested by handsome and healthy bodies; some by the passion of youth; others by the erosions of age. Some suffer disappointment in marriage, family problems; others live in poverty and obscurity. Some (perhaps this is the hardest test) find ease and luxury." ("The Choice," p. 21.)

I concurred with his comments, but then he continued, "All [of life's challenges] are part of the test, and there is more equality in this testing than sometimes we suspect" (ibid., p. 21). The phrase "equality in this testing" caused me to pause in disbelief. Surely he had made a mistake. His statement upset me because I had two severely handicapped children who required enormous amounts of care, attention, and financial support, and Jo and I had sacrificed nearly all of our resources caring for them. Surely our trials were much greater than those my neighbors were experiencing. Only two years earlier a neighbor had told Jo that during her fifty years of life she never had a significant trial. How could there be equality in testing when her life had been free of trials and our trials were more than a full-time job? Certainly the emotional and financial stresses we were experiencing were far worse than those she experienced in her $500,000 home.

I was distressed by Elder Packer's comments because I loved his carefully prepared conference addresses. They were always clear, concise, and inspirational, and they always "felt" correct to me. But how could there be equality in testing? I wrestled with his comment for almost four weeks before I received the *Ensign* with the conference proceedings. Over the years I had noted slight differences between the spoken and the written word, and

I was sure Elder Packer's comment would be corrected in the written conference record. I quickly scanned his talk, and to my great disappointment the troublesome phrase was still there!

Because the Brethren speak for the Lord (see D&C 1:38), and because what they say "when moved upon by the Holy Ghost shall be scripture" (D&C 68:4), Elder Packer's comments became a major stumbling block for me. I tried to dismiss his words, but they haunted me whenever I had difficulties. Unfortunately it would be almost a decade before I would know that, indeed, Elder Packer was correct—there is more equality in our testing than we suspect.

My Fishing Companion

In 1981, after living in Utah for two years, doctors still didn't know why Cindy and Heather had become handicapped, nor could they give us a prognosis. Nor could they explain why Michelle, Lara, and Heidi were not affected, or why Cindy's condition was more severe than Heather's. In addition, geneticists couldn't find any abnormalities with Jo, me, or the children, although they thought that two severely handicapped children in the same family was more than a coincidence. Admittedly, Jo and I were very concerned about having more children after Heather became handicapped, but I felt strongly that there was another member of our family waiting to come to earth. Consequently, when we learned Jo was expecting I was overjoyed. I felt strongly it would be a boy—and I had wanted a boy for almost fourteen years.

Several weeks before the delivery, Lara, who was eleven years old, said, "Dad, I have been praying and asking Heavenly Father to bless us with a boy and that he won't become handicapped." Surely God would answer her prayers, I thought. Surely He would answer all of our prayers.

On July 25 we were blessed with a beautiful boy, whom we named Mark. I was elated because he was strong and healthy, and I now had my fishing and hiking companion. He had a pleasant and loving personality, and unlike Cindy, he seldom cried. In addition, since I wasn't working the long hours I had worked when the other children were young, I had more time to play with him. And, since our financial situation was much improved, after fourteen years of renting we were finally building a home of our own!

In December Mark was active, strong, and inquisitive, and we worried that he might pull the Christmas tree over. Then, shortly before Christmas, Jo was horrified when she saw him posture his hands like Cindy and Heather. No, it couldn't be! Perhaps she was wrong. But she wasn't. The little boy who jumped, crawled, and made others laugh would become handicapped! I was devastated. Why? Why was God so cruel? And again at Christmas! Three times during the previous nine years the spirit of the Christmas season was ruined by the realization that our youngest child would be severely handicapped. My grief was almost unbearable. There would be no hiking, fishing, or camping with my son—only another wheelchair to push. It just wasn't fair. Where was justice? Where was mercy? What was the value of living the gospel if it didn't make me happy? What value was there in planning or setting goals? Oh, why did Heavenly Father give me yet another stone?

Overwhelming Bitterness

As I looked to 1982, my bitterness reached new heights. If this latest challenge was to help our family, what could we learn from three severely handicapped children that we couldn't learn from two, or even one? How would Michelle, Lara, and Heidi respond? Their perspective of family life was already centered around severely handicapped children. Was that fair to them? I struggled to understand, but understanding didn't come. Prayers, blessings, fasting, and promises to the Lord went unanswered—Mark remained handicapped.

Why did Jo and I even have handicapped children? We had never smoked, drunk alcoholic beverages, used illicit drugs, or drunk tea or coffee. We had always tried to eat wholesome foods and be physically fit, yet strict adherence to the Word of Wisdom hadn't helped. Three of our children were not healthy. What was the value of living the gospel? Those who didn't live it seemed to be happier and blessed more than many who did. I didn't know of any couples who lived the gospel who had more than one handicapped child, much less three. But I knew many, many couples who weren't living the gospel who had normal, healthy children. How was that fair? Furthermore, we had welcomed another child into our family, and yet we were still punished. We had sacrificed so much to keep Cindy and Heather at home instead of putting them in an institution. How could we now find the time, energy, emotional strength, and financial resources to adequately care for Michelle, Lara, and Heidi, plus three severely handicapped children? Why wouldn't God help us? What was the point of our suffering?

Besides those questions, I was plagued by the thought, *Father, I asked for bread and Thou gavest me a stone,* and by Lara's remark, "I prayed the whole time Mom was pregnant that the baby wouldn't be handicapped. Why didn't Heavenly Father answer my prayers?" Wasn't the faith of an innocent child sufficient? How would Lara ever develop faith in prayer? Why did the Lord continue to kick us when we were down? I had so many unanswered questions. And oh, how embarrassing—three handicapped children!

To make matters worse, no one understood how much Jo and I were chained to Cindy, Heather, and Mark, or the stress they placed on our relationship. We had spent so little time alone together since Cindy became ill nine years earlier. How could our rocky relationship survive now? In addition to raising Michelle, Lara, and Heidi, we were forced to spend ten to fifteen hours each day caring for Cindy, Heather, and Mark and countless sleepless nights worrying about them—*every day* for the rest of their lives. Setting goals was useless. When we planned an activity it was usually postponed by a medical crisis. Furthermore, unlike other couples we couldn't plan to serve a mission when our children left home. Cindy, Heather, and Mark had to die before we could serve a mission together! How was that "equality in testing"? Those thoughts kept going through my mind over and over and over.

Before Mark became handicapped I tried to be patient as I encountered new trials. For example, I didn't complain when our entire basement flooded with raw sewage from our neighbors' homes, when the car that the young men in Camarillo had restored was stolen and never recovered, or when the car we replaced it with caught fire. Still, our trials seemed endless.

As previously mentioned, I was bitter when Cindy became handicapped, but I accepted her condition because I considered her illness to be a strange circumstance of nature. Then, when Heather became handicapped the earlier bitterness returned, except stronger. As time passed my bitterness subsided to some degree because of the wonderful ward members in Camarillo, especially the kindness of the members of the priests quorum and our home teacher. But now that Mark was handicapped, my new adversity fueled my bitterness again.

One of the feelings that returned was a resentment for people with more money than I had. I worked at least as hard as many of the wealthy people I knew, yet I didn't seem to be blessed like they were. Some had purchased homes with money from their parents, while others had inherited large sums of money. It didn't seem fair that many people who weren't working as hard as I was were more prosperous—neither did it seem fair that many families where the mother worked outside the home in order to provide luxuries were blessed. Why not us? We had tried to keep all of the commandments and follow the counsel of the Brethren, but what did we have to show for it?

I also resented the fact that the Lord seemed to punish us financially. When we began construction of our home the interest rate was 13 percent, but when the loan closed three months later it was at 16.5 percent for thirty years. Consequently, more than half of our monthly salary went to house payments! In contrast, our friends had financed their homes many years earlier when interest rates were 8 or 9 percent for fifteen years. Their monthly payments were low, and their homes were nearly paid off. Additionally, the value of their homes appreciated two or three times during the real-estate boom of the seventies. I felt punished even more when many young couples built homes in our subdivision. Why didn't each of them have to wait many years to buy a home? Why did the Lord bless them? In my bitterness, living the gospel seemed to be of little value.

Whenever I heard someone talk about enjoying camping, backpacking, or a similar family activity, I felt cheated. If our family attended parties we spent most of our time feeding Cindy, Heather, and Mark and shooing flies away from them while Michelle, Lara, and Heidi waited for us to finish. Consequently, ward campouts became impossible. Then there were the "lookie-looks" whenever we went anywhere in public. I always believed people thought, *Look at the stupid parents with three handicapped kids. Why do they keep having retarded children?* Some comments were unintentionally hurtful. For instance, one of the many doctors we worked with said, "If you had quit with two children like you should have done, you wouldn't have the problems you have now." That mocking comment hurt me deeply, because I felt strongly that the Lord wanted us to have all of our children.

Probably the thing that hurt most, however, was listening to Church members tell how someone they knew had been healed by a priesthood blessing. Their successes left me feeling that our children weren't healed because we didn't have sufficient faith, we weren't worthy, or we weren't as good as they were. It seemed that they bragged about their healings. Couldn't they keep them to themselves? I dreaded hearing healing successes or talks on adversity in church meetings. And I became really irritated when I heard the phrase, "If God hands you a lemon, make lemonade." I wasn't making lemonade! I was trying to cope with problems others couldn't possibly understand.

At times I felt trapped and wanted to quit everything and run away from my family and responsibilities. My problems were overwhelming, and my depression was intense. Nobody had problems as bad as mine, and nobody understood the heartache I was suffering. And at times the relationship Jo and I had was almost unbearable. Why continue? Often I told her, "Don't bother me with family problems. I have enough of my own to worry about."

The gospel wasn't bringing me happiness, and I couldn't find enjoyment in anything—not with Jo, my children, the Church, or my employment. What was the point of life? Why should I continue to struggle? Reluctantly, and sometimes in anger, I prayed for understanding—probably out of a sense of duty—but the answers I wanted didn't come. Heavenly Father had abandoned me.

As time passed, caring for Cindy, Heather, and Mark became all-consuming. Although Cindy didn't cry as much as before, she became more difficult to feed, and each meal was a frustrating multi-hour ordeal. Jo had to hold her at the proper angle so her pureed food would slide down her throat and into her stomach, not into her lungs. Occasionally we considered having a feeding tube surgically implanted into her stomach so Jo could feed her quickly. But after talking to parents who used that procedure, we decided the problems outweighed the advantages.

Not only were Cindy, Heather, and Mark difficult to feed, but they also slept poorly. In fact, one year I counted only six times that they all slept through the same night! Because they frequently woke up screaming with a cramp in an arm or leg, Jo was always tired and didn't feel well. Consequently, she never seemed to have time for me. From my perspective romance was something others enjoyed—but not us. Oh, for a romantic weekend away from the children!

People occasionally asked us why we didn't put Cindy, Heather, and Mark in an institution "so you can lead a normal life." We discussed that idea with Michelle, Lara, and Heidi, but they always rejected it. Together we felt that as long as we were physically, emotionally, and financially able we would care for Cindy, Heather, and Mark in our home, where we could enjoy each other's love.

As the years passed I continued to attend my church meetings, read the scriptures, study the gospel, attend the temple, and pray. I tried to live the commandments, but answers to my questions still didn't come. Consequently, my bitterness increased or decreased depending on our circumstances. If things went well financially and the children weren't sick, I thanked the Lord. If not, I became upset because He was unfair. At times my frustration placed an unbearable strain on our family, and I questioned the meaning of life. Was there really a God? Did I have a personal Savior? If so, where was He? Why had He abandoned me? Shouldn't He help me if I kept His commandments? Wasn't He supposed to open the windows of heaven and help me prosper? Where were His promised blessings? Why couldn't I plan my life? I continued to ask these questions, but I received no answers or comfort.

Unfulfilled Goals

Shortly after graduating from BYU I had read President Heber J. Grant's words:

> As a boy of seventeen, I dreamed in my mind about my future life—what I was going to do until I became thirty-five years of age. . . . I had planned everything I was going to do and where I was going to get, and from the time I was seventeen until I was twenty-four years old I accomplished every one of the things that I had planned to do and dreamed about in my mind and worked for. I never would have done so without planning—we do not accomplish things without having the idea. ("Dream, O Youth! Dream Nobly and Manfully," p. 524.)

President Grant's message excited me—I could plan my life and accomplish whatever I wanted. As an engineer I considered the process of setting goals as merely fulfilling an equation. After all, the Lord said that all blessings were based upon law, "and when we obtain any blessing from God, it is by obedience to that law upon which it is predicated" (D&C 130:21). How simple—fulfill the law and get the promised blessing. I therefore set goals for myself, Jo and me, and our family, as well as church- and employment-related goals. It worked! The first year after graduation, my goals were fulfilled as I had planned.

Then, shortly after relocating to March AFB in 1972, a co-worker introduced me to the book *Think and Grow Rich* by Napoleon Hill, which essentially conveyed the same message that President Grant's words did. The concept was simple and logical, and I was confident in the validity of the book. I memorized a portion of a well-known poem that expressed this idea:

> If you think you are beaten, you are;
> If you think you dare not, you don't.
> If you like to win, but think you can't,
> It's almost a cinch you won't.
> If you think you'll lose, you're lost,
> For out in the world we find

> Success begins with a fellow's will;
> It's all in the state of mind.
> . . . .
> Life's battles don't always go
> To the stronger or faster man;
> But soon or late the man who wins
> Is the man who thinks he can.

(Walter D. Wintle, as quoted in Monson, *Favorite Quotations from the Collection of Thomas S. Monson,* p. 131.)

Further study reaffirmed my belief that I could achieve anything I desired if I kept the commandments, had faith, and worked accordingly. For example, the prophet Alma said that the Lord blesses us according to our desires (see Alma 29:1–6), and Christ said, "If ye will have faith in me ye shall have power to do whatsoever thing is expedient in me" (Moroni 7:33). In addition, whenever I attended time management and goal setting seminars I always left feeling that all things were possible if I had a positive mental attitude, believed in myself, and worked diligently. I also heard Church leaders talk about the importance of setting and achieving goals.

My life went according to plan until Cindy became ill, but from that moment forward I seemed to have little control. Yes, I could set and achieve simple goals such as reading the Book of Mormon, but I couldn't achieve major goals. For instance, in spite of my positive mental attitude, goals, prayers, desires, fasting, promises to the Lord, and extensive therapy, Cindy never learned to walk, talk, or voluntarily do anything. Similarly, when I set financial goals such as reducing our debt, they were disrupted by having to pay for a piece of medical equipment, a two-thousand dollar wheelchair, or unexpected hospital bills. Or when Jo and I planned to get away for a few hours, often one of the children became ill.

As I struggled to understand why the words of President Grant, Alma, and the Savior weren't fulfilled for me, I wondered what I was missing. My friends were able to set and achieve important goals. Why couldn't I? After many years I finally concluded that setting goals was a waste of time.

The Heavens Are Sealed

Whenever my prayers weren't answered I became confused, irritated, and angry because I felt that Heavenly Father didn't care about me. During those times I hated hearing: "God always answers prayers. Sometimes he just says no by withholding an answer." But how was no answer an answer? If a child asked, "Mother, do you love me?" and the mother never replied, would that be an answer of love? I didn't think so.

Over the years I also hated hearing talks on prayer, especially if the speakers quoted the words of the Savior: "Whatsoever thing ye shall ask the Father in my name, which is good, in faith believing that ye shall receive, behold, it shall be done unto you" (Moroni 7:26). I had fulfilled the Savior's requirements, but my children weren't healed. Elder Spencer W. Kimball described my condition perfectly: "Some become bitter when oft-repeated prayers seem unanswered. Some lose faith and turn sour when solemn administrations by holy men seem to be ignored and no restoration seems to come from repeated prayer circles." ("Tragedy or Destiny," p. 210.)

Enos's experience bothered me too. He said: "And my soul hungered; and I kneeled down before my Maker, and I cried unto him in mighty prayer and supplication for mine own soul; and all the day long did I cry unto him; yea, and when the night came I did still raise my voice high that it reached the heavens. And there came a voice unto me, saying: Enos, thy sins are forgiven thee, and thou shalt be blessed." (Enos 1:4–5.) He made the process seem so simple, so straightforward. He asked and received the answer he wanted. Why couldn't I? I asked hundreds of times, but I never received the answer I wanted. I decided Enos probably had his prayers answered because he was a prophet—but couldn't I expect to have mine answered as other people did?

I also hated hearing about other's spiritual experiences. I had never had a spiritual dream, seen an angel, had a vision, or heard the voice of the Lord. Why? Even wicked men had spiritual manifestations. Alma the Younger saw an angel, even though he was "a very wicked and an idolatrous man. And . . . he led many of the people to do after the manner of his iniquities. And he became a great hinderment to the prosperity of the church of God; stealing away the hearts of the people; causing much dissension among the people; giving a chance for the enemy of God to exercise his power over them." (Mosiah 27:8–9.) Saul also saw an angel, even though he "made havock of the church, entering into every house, and haling men and women committed them to prison" (Acts 8:3). Surely I was living far better than Alma or Saul were when they saw an angel. Why were those wicked men blessed with spiritual manifestations? Such seeming inconsistencies fueled my bitterness.

Too Much to Do

Another frustration was that it seemed impossible to live the whole gospel. For instance, Heavenly Father expected me to attend my church meetings, but as Cindy's and Heather's health deteriorated I often had to miss church to stay with them. Essentially, because we cared for God's "special children" there were many things that I didn't have time to do, and I often felt guilty and became depressed because I was falling short in every aspect of my life.

How could I do everything God expected? I was to be a good father, husband, and provider; fulfill a church calling and be a good home teacher; improve myself; help in the community; go to the temple; do missionary and genealogy work; visit the sick; comfort those who mourned; pray for my enemies; keep the Sabbath day holy; teach my children to pray; spend time with my wife; pray unceasingly; overcome pride, selfishness, and greed; avoid the appearance of evil; fast often; pay tithes and generous fast offerings; study the scriptures; get out of debt; store a year's supply of food; honor my parents; support the Boy Scouts; control my temper; help the poor; seek good, wise, and honest people for public office; organize my time well; grow a garden; have a beautiful yard; hold family home evening; let virtue garnish my thoughts unceasingly; work at the welfare project; help quorum members; plant berry bushes and fruit trees; attend priesthood and sacrament meetings; partake of the sacrament with the proper spirit and attitude; eat wholesome foods; select proper reading materials for my family; ensure that my children seek wholesome entertainment; learn a foreign language for a mission later in life; become physically fit; and much more.

As I pondered my duties, the list grew. It seemed endless. How could I do all that God required when I had so little time? The Lord said He couldn't look on sin "with the least degree of allowance" (D&C 1:31), so how could I ever return to Him? Additionally, I thought I needed to serve in a Church leadership position in order to improve myself—but since I couldn't do that and care for Cindy, Heather, and Mark, it seemed I was denied the opportunity to become perfect. The Savior said, "My yoke is easy, and my burden is light" (Matthew 11:30). Why, then, was the gospel so complicated and difficult for me to live? Wasn't it supposed to bring peace into my life? Where was that peace?

CHAPTER 13

A Changing Heart

Just when it seemed that I could endure no more, God gave me an additional stone that challenged my faith but eventually led to a change of heart.

My Pearl Harbor Day

My bitterness and frustration reached new heights on September 7, 1986—my Pearl Harbor Day. That day my employer announced that the Salt Lake City operation would close and all employees would be terminated unless they relocated to Troy, Michigan. I was devastated! How could the Lord let this happen to me after everything I had been through? How would I support my family and care for His "special children"? A feeling of inferiority overcame me, and I felt God had handed me yet another stone.

I struggled to be positive as I looked for new employment, but I was angry and bitter. Several weeks earlier my employer told all employees that the Salt Lake City operation was most important. Then, without notice, he changed his mind. I had always believed that only bad employees were laid off, that if I was honest, hard-working, and dependable I would always have work. Was I an inferior, incompetent employee? I didn't believe so, but I would soon be unemployed. As I looked for work my attitude shifted frequently from optimism to depression. When I wasn't looking for work, I reviewed my life. I couldn't believe how different reality was from my plan and expectations. Being laid off certainly hurt my self-esteem—I felt like a total failure!

As I searched for peace and comfort, I read and reread scriptures on adversity, many conference talks, and portions of Church books. Nothing I read changed my attitude, and praying didn't help either. So, with the workplace closure only weeks away, I went to a bookstore and searched for a book about overcoming adversity and bitterness. I couldn't find one that I hadn't already read, so I looked at books by non-LDS authors. I finally found one that caught my interest: *When Bad Things Happen to Good People* by Harold S. Kushner. I read it but still found no peace or comfort.

Weeks passed as I looked for work locally, but nothing seemed promising, so I interviewed out of state. We didn't want to move, but we didn't see any other alternative. I worried about caring for our family if I didn't find work soon, and about having another medical emergency with no insurance.

Finding Employment

Fortunately I found job opportunities in Chicago and Dallas. Interviews in Chicago went well, and I had a job offer before returning home. Interviews in Dallas were successful too, and I was invited back for more discussions.

When I returned to Dallas, I interviewed with a vice president who asked me to convince him that I could overcome difficult challenges. I paused, wondering what to say, when I felt impressed to tell him about our family. *No,* I thought, *he wants an example from my employment. It would be too embarrassing to tell him about our family.* However, since he was waiting for an answer and nothing else came to mind, I followed the prompting. I told him we had six children, three of whom were severely handicapped and required total care. I explained how we cared for them at home, and that in spite of it all my wife and I had kept the family together, were actively involved in our church, and had faithfully supported my employer, and that I was an elected city councilman. I told him that 85 percent of all marriages with a handicapped child end in divorce, and that despite our problems Jo and I were still married. I explained how adversity had made me a better person and that because of my trials I was better able to understand people and cope with the stresses and challenges of management.

As I explained our challenges, I was surprised by my remarks. I told him things that I had never thought about before! He was surprised too and said, "You certainly have convinced me. Anyone who has overcome the challenges you have can certainly handle the challenges of this job."

On the flight home I reflected on my comments. I wondered why I had said what I did, and concluded that most of my comments were prompted by the Spirit. As I pondered that thought, the words of President Marion G. Romney came to mind: "I always know when I am speaking under the inspiration of the Holy Ghost because I always learn something from what I've said" (as quoted in Packer, *Teach Ye Diligently*, p. 304). I truly had learned from my comments.

Several days later I received a lucrative job offer from the firm in Dallas—$109,000 for the first year! Although I wanted to accept it, we really didn't want to move. So I continued to pursue job opportunities in the local area while we considered the offers in Chicago and Dallas. Soon I had an offer from a local firm. We prayerfully considered all offers and decided to accept the local opportunity, even though it paid less than half the offered compensation of the Dallas job and 25 percent less than I had previously earned. It required a career change, but we felt it was more important for us to keep the family close to friends and relatives, and the children in the same schools, than it was to earn a lot more money. We strongly agreed with the Brethren's counsel that our family should feel a sense of tradition and stability and "not [be] relocated on a whim" (*Father, Consider Your Ways*, pp. 1–5). Later, Lara commented, "Money isn't everything."

My new job began October 31, the same day my previous employment ended. Besides being in an unfamiliar industry and requiring considerable time and effort to learn, my first assignment was a very difficult one with an extremely challenging customer. It was humbling trying to simultaneously learn a new technology, manage the program, and become familiar with new people and a new company. I called upon Heavenly Father frequently for guidance, always thanking Him for helping me find a superb company with genuinely helpful people. Not only was my new company more financially sound than my three previous jobs, but it was also the most enjoyable.

As I began my new employment I reflected on the positive things that were a direct result of my previous job being terminated. I pondered on my comments to the vice president in Dallas and his job offer. I thought about how blessed we were that we would have two incomes for six months, and that we were able to acquire life insurance for Cindy, Heather, and Mark—something we had never been able to do.

A Change of Attitude

Soon after my final job interview in Dallas, something wonderful happened to me. My entire attitude began to change, and I experienced more peace and contentment than ever before. As I reflected on the reasons for that change, I realized that it wasn't a single incident, but many factors that finally contributed to a remarkable change of heart.

The Saints' Generosity

I believe very strongly that the kindness and generosity of the youth, our home teacher, and Church members in Camarillo actually initiated the remarkable change in my life. Although I was bitter about having handicapped children and about how different my life was from what I expected it to be, the selfless sacrifices of the ward members there touched my heart again and again. My parents and grandparents had always set an outstanding example of generosity, but it wasn't until people outside my family helped us bear our burdens that my attitude finally began to change.

Unconditional Love

During my periods of intense bitterness, a major source of strength was Jo's love. In spite of the problems in our family and her desire to have me improve, she never complained about my bitterness, my shortcomings, or the standard of living I provided, or nagged me to change. If she had done so, I probably would have left!

The girls also cheered me up, and Mark helped immeasurably. I enjoyed being with him and doing things for him because of his wonderful spirit. Unlike Cindy or Heather, he could speak a few distinguishable words, and we became best friends early in 1987, when Jo had to spend more time caring for Heather. Whenever I was home I cared for Mark. That included changing his diapers—even the dirty ones. Previously I had rarely changed diapers because that was something "only a mother could love."

As I cared for Mark I felt closer to him, and my love for him grew. Not only was he appreciative of my help, but he loved me unconditionally. He often said, "Da, I luv oo" ("Dad, I love you") at very unexpected times, and he never forgot to say "tank oo" ("thank you"). Despite his disability he never complained about his inability to play like other children, or that life was unfair. Even at a very young age he chose to be happy and seemed to understand the principle taught by Sister Donna Packer: "I know that we do not find happiness. We choose happiness by making righteous decisions. We don't *have* to be happy. We *get* to be happy. We have our free agency, and we get to choose." (In Packer, *That All May Be Edified*, p. 324, emphasis in original.)

Mark determined his attitude, regardless of his circumstances. That was something I couldn't do. My attitude depended on whether I felt the Lord was blessing me. Heather also was an outstanding example. She attempted to be positive even when she was in intense pain. Often I watched her muster a partial smile and suffer in silence as tears flowed down her cheeks. Experiencing Mark's happiness and unconditional love and Heather's determination to be happy slowly changed my outlook on life.

Another example of how Mark chose to be happy took place when Heather suffered with severe back pain. Every night Jo rubbed Heather's back or held her until she fell asleep— often not before 1:00 A.M.—while I took Mark to bed with me and massaged his tight muscles. As I rubbed, he sighed loudly with approval and said, "O Da, I luv oo," or, "Tanks, Da." After I finished rubbing his back, we raced to see who could go to sleep first. I believe I always won, although he claims he did.

"Koz"

Since our family wasn't able to go camping together, beginning in 1983 all of us except Cindy and Heather attended BYU home football games. Mark quickly developed an understanding and love for the game, and in 1985, when he was four years old, an event occurred that touched my heart deeply. It involved Glen Kozlowski ("Koz"), a BYU wide receiver who was one of Mark's idols. Doug Robinson of the *Deseret News* reported:

> After his first injury, . . . Kozlowski was devastated. For two weeks he moped around the house. Thinking the worst, he broke down watching Monday night football. "I came so close (to playing pro) and then to have it taken away on one play," he told his wife, Julie.
>
> During those two weeks he didn't even try to come back. One BYU trainer noted at the time, "I don't think he's coming back. He's not even working out. He hasn't been around here."
>
> In the meantime, Kozlowski was receiving dozens of phone calls and letters wishing him well, and that alone seemed to reach something in him. . . . He also got a letter from a Centerville family enclosed with two pictures of a boy in a wheelchair. The boy, the letter explained, could say only a few words but one of them was "Ka," for Koz, and he knew his number and could recognize his picture. He had cried when he saw Koz was hurt.
>
> "You've brought him a lot of happiness," the boy's parents said. "Our family hopes you will play in a Cougar uniform again."

"We just sat there and cried," says Julie. "That got Glen going. He was in deep depression. It was like he didn't even care."

"Here I was feeling sorry for myself," says Koz, "but I am so blessed physically. At least I knew I would be able to walk and run again. It really made me determined."

. . . For the next three weeks, Koz worked out twice a day. . . . He lifted weights and, when he was ready, ran. Each evening he would progressively crutch/walk/jog/run through pass patterns, catching passes thrown by Julie, a former intramural wide receiver. . . .

Eventually Kozlowski got the go-ahead from doctors to play against Wyoming, and he arranged for the boy from Centerville to attend the game. It had all the makings of a movie-like comeback—except that in the third quarter Koz injured the same knee and this time it required surgery to repair. . . .

Immediately after the game, however, Koz was thinking nothing about the knee or his future. Hopping around on one leg, he showed his young friend in the wheelchair around the locker room, introducing him to teammates and getting their autographs.

"He's learned a lot during all this," said one coach.

Koz readily agrees. "I've learned that all things happen for a purpose," he says. ". . . A lot of good things have come out of this. I've gotten a lot closer to my family and God. I've spent more time with my little boys. It's been a plus for me in so many ways . . . I feel humbled by this whole thing." ("Kozlowski's Injury Isn't Holding Him Back," pp. D1, D6.)*

---

* Originally appeared in the *Deseret News*, November 12, 1985, by Doug Robinson. Reprinted by permission.

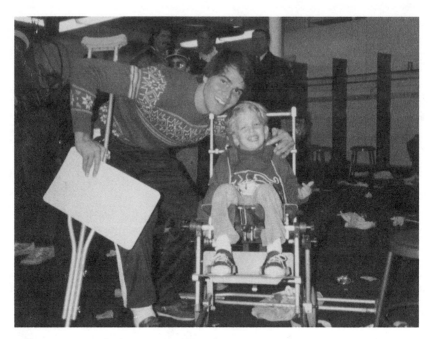

Mark and "Koz"

Later, Glen sent an autographed picture with the following inscription:

Dear Mark and Erickson Family,

Thanks for the letter. It has cheered me up. I will be back and Mark had a great deal to do with inspiring me. God bless you always.

Your friend, Glen Kozlowski #7

P.S. Give Mark a hug for me.

A Shining Example

While addressing survivors of the Teton Dam disaster, Elder Boyd K. Packer said, "I know there are times when you would want to give up, or to weep, or to yield, but you have got to stand steady as an example to others" (Mitchell, "Thousands of Saints," p. 70). While I suffered in bitterness, President Spencer W. Kimball was my "adversity role model." Although Christ and

Joseph Smith each suffered persecution and eventually sacrificed their lives for their teachings, I related better to President Kimball. Consequently, shortly after his death in November 1985 I reread the book *Spencer W. Kimball* and marveled how his life was filled with serious physical problems and personal frustrations, even though he was righteous and served the Lord. His struggles touched my heart deeply, and I was comforted and uplifted by his faith. I truly appreciated his sharing his personal experiences, because they gave me courage to struggle on.

Reading Heather's Story

In August 1986, just prior to my "Pearl Harbor Day," Jean Ernstrom asked Jo to review the story "Jesus, Listening, Can Hear." That story moved me to tears every time I read it, and I believe it was the catalyst for many of the thoughts that I shared with the company vice president in Dallas several weeks later.

Embarrassment No More

While we were living in California, occasionally people asked, "Did you adopt your handicapped children?" When I answered, "No, we're their natural parents," I usually got a strange look—a look which I felt meant, "Why didn't you stop having children when you had the first handicapped child? Are you also retarded?" Consequently, when we moved to Salt Lake City I didn't voluntarily tell my business associates that Cindy and Heather were handicapped, nor did I keep a picture of my family at work. Similarly, I didn't tell them when Mark became handicapped, because it was too embarrassing.

However, after I told the vice president in Dallas about our family, I wasn't embarrassed anymore! For the first time I felt that the adversity I was experiencing was of value. As a result, my attitude about my handicapped children changed, and when I later spoke with interviewers of the company that eventually hired me, I told them about Cindy, Heather, and Mark. The first day on my new job, I put a picture of my family on my desk—the first I had displayed at work since Cindy became ill fourteen years earlier.

A Speaking Challenge

Another event that contributed to my change of heart occurred when I was assigned to speak about adversity in our
ward sacrament meeting. That talk was a challenge, because although my heart had started to change, I still didn't have answers to my questions. I struggled with the assigned subject and
finally decided to tell two stories. The first was about the
Martin handcart company, as told by Elder James E. Faust,
which Jo quoted in chapter 3, and the second was about a currant bush, as told by Elder Hugh B. Brown. Although I had
previously read both stories several times, telling them touched
me deeply and helped me better understand my adversity. Elder
Brown said:

> I was living up in Canada. I had purchased a farm. It
> was run-down. I went out one morning and saw a currant
> bush. It had grown up over six feet high. It was going all to
> wood. There were no blossoms and no currants. I was raised
> on a fruit farm in Salt Lake before we went to Canada, and
> I knew what ought to happen to that currant bush. So I got
> some pruning shears and went after it, and I cut it down,
> and pruned it, and clipped it back until there was nothing
> left but a little clump of stumps. It was just coming daylight,
> and I thought I saw on top of each of these little stumps
> what appeared to be a tear, and I thought the currant bush
> was crying. . . . I looked at it, and smiled, and said, "What
> are you crying about?" You know, I thought I heard that cur-
> rant bush talk. And I thought I heard it say this: "How
> could you do this to me? I was making such wonderful
> growth. I was almost as big as the shade tree and the fruit
> tree that are inside the fence, and now you have cut me
> down. Every plant in the garden will look down on me, be-
> cause I didn't make what I should have made. How *could*
> you do this to me? I thought you were the gardener here."
> That's what I thought I heard the currant bush say, and I
> thought it so much that I answered. I said, "Look, little cur-
> rant bush, I *am* the gardener here, and I know what I want
> you to be. I didn't intend you to be a fruit tree or a shade

tree. I want you to be a currant bush, and some day, little currant bush, when you are laden with fruit, you are going to say. 'Thank you, Mr. Gardener, for loving me enough to cut me down, for caring enough about me to hurt me. Thank you, Mr. Gardener.' "

Time passed. Years passed, and I found myself in England. I was in command of a cavalry unit in the Canadian Army. I had made rather rapid progress as far as promotions are concerned, and I held the rank of field officer in the British Canadian Army. And I was proud of my position. And there was an opportunity for me to become a general. I had taken all the examinations. I had the seniority. There was just one man between me and that which for ten years I had hoped to get, the office of general in the British Army. I swelled up with pride. And this one man became a casualty, and I received a telegram from London. It said: "Be in my office tomorrow morning at 10:00," signed by General Turner in charge of all Canadian forces. I called in my valet, my personal servant. I told him to polish my buttons, to brush my hat and my boots, and to make me look like a general because that is what I was going to be. He did the best he could with what he had to work on, and I went up to London. I walked smartly into the office of the General, and I saluted him smartly. . . . He said, "Sit down, Brown." Then he said, "I'm sorry I cannot make the appointment. You are entitled to it. You have passed all the examinations. You have the seniority. You've been a good officer, but I can't make the appointment. You are to return to Canada and become a training officer. . . ." That for which I had been hoping and praying for ten years suddenly slipped out of my fingers.

Then he went into the other room to answer the telephone, and I took a soldier's privilege of looking on his desk. I saw my personal history sheet. Right across the bottom of it in bold, block-type letters was written, "THIS MAN IS A MORMON." . . . When I saw that, I knew why I had not been appointed. I already held the highest rank of any Mormon in the British Army. He came back and said, "That's all, Brown." I saluted him again, but not quite as smartly. . . . I got on the train and started back to my town, 120 miles away, with a broken heart, with bitterness in my soul. And every click of the wheels on the rails seemed to say, "You are a failure. You will be called a coward when you get home. You raised all those Mormon boys to join the army, then you sneak off home." I knew what I was going to get, and when I got to my tent . . . I clinched my fists and I shook them at heaven. I said, "How could you do this to me, God? I have done everything I could do to measure up. There is nothing that I could have done—that I should have done—that I haven't done. How could you do this to me?" I was as bitter as gall.

And then I heard a voice. . . . It was my own voice, and the voice said, "I am the gardener here. I know what I want you to do." The bitterness went out of my soul, and I fell on my knees by the cot to ask forgiveness for my ungratefulness and my bitterness. . . .

I arose from my knees a humble man. And now, almost fifty years later, I look up to him and say, "Thank you, Mr. Gardener, for cutting me down, for loving me enough to hurt me." ("The Currant Bush," pp. 14–15, emphasis in original.)

The statements "[That is] the price we paid to become acquainted with God," from Elder Faust's talk (see "The Refiner's Fire," p. 53) and "I am the gardener here. I know what I want you to do," from Elder Brown's talk kept running through my mind for many months after I spoke. Even today those phrases come to my mind during difficult times.

Later, as I mentally reviewed my talk, I realized how valuable it had been for me to prepare and give it. That in turn reminded me that I had heard Elder LeGrand Richards say many years earlier that when he served as bishop, he found that one of the best ways to reactivate or help ward members was to ask them to speak in sacrament meeting on a subject they were struggling with. He also gave them several weeks to prepare so they might feel comfortable with the subject. I was thankful that I was asked to speak on adversity and that I had adequate time to ponder and prepare.

An Unexpected Testimony

Probably the most important event that helped soften my heart occurred in 1987 during spring vacation as our family visited many natural wonders in Utah, Nevada, and Arizona. We rented a large motor home so we could prepare meals and feed the handicapped children while we traveled, thus avoiding the hassle of continually packing and unpacking their food, clothes, and special equipment. For five days and nights we traveled and visited Bryce Canyon, Zion National Park, the Grand Canyon, and many places in-between. During that time we played, ate, sang, talked, and slept together in the motor home. While driving I reviewed nearly twenty years of marriage and the changes in my attitude that had occurred since my Pearl Harbor Day.

On the evening of the fourth day we camped, ate dinner, and had family home evening before retiring. As part of our activity we had a testimony meeting, and I bore my testimony. I explained how bitter I had become because Cindy, Heather, and Mark were severely handicapped and weren't healed, and how my resentment was fueled by our financial problems. I told them how Heavenly Father recently had softened my heart and blessed me with sufficient faith to overcome my bitterness and trust Him with my life. I testified that I no longer became angry with God when bad things happened to me, that I recognized adversity as being a part of life and that it could have real value. I had finally realized, as Elder Spencer W. Kimball said, that "suffering can make saints of people as they learn patience, long-suffering, and self-mastery," and that, as Elder James E. Talmage said, "no pang that is suffered by man or woman upon the earth will be without its compensating effect . . . if it be met with patience" (as quoted in *Faith Precedes the Miracle,* p. 98).

I testified that I finally understood that when I keep the commandments and bad things happen to me, they probably aren't punishments but can teach me patience and help me grow. I also said that I finally recognized that I really had been blessed—I had a loyal and dedicated wife and a wonderful family; we enjoyed the blessings of the gospel; our children had embraced its teachings; we had a thoughtful and supportive extended family and many remarkable friends. From an eternal perspective, what more could I want? I finally recognized that the things I had been bitter about didn't really matter, and that adversity was part of my development and training.

I also apologized to my family—especially to Jo—for the way I had treated them during the long years of my bitterness. I explained that several weeks earlier, while reading my patriarchal blessing, I discovered that I had been told I would be *blessed* with handicapped children! Although my blessing was given almost thirty years earlier, and I had read it dozens of times, I had never caught the significance of a particular phrase: "Your children, which the Lord shall give you in numbers, will be yours to *keep* and to *hold* and to *nourish* through life and will be your blessing" (emphasis added). That phrase literally had been fulfilled. All of our children were a blessing to us, and, in the case of Cindy, Heather, and Mark, we were required to keep them, hold them, and nourish them through life. As I reread that statement I knew the interpretation was correct. Again I remembered Elder Boyd K. Packer's statement about finding "provisions set out along the way" ("Spiritual Crocodiles," p. 31), and marveled that there was another "provision" along my path. What a comfort to know that!

That night as I finished my testimony, my bitterness was gone. My heart—the part of me dealing with my inner feelings—was softened, and I finally felt at peace. Apparently my bitterness couldn't be completely removed until I had apologized to my family for my lack of faith and the way I had treated them. I finally agreed with the message of a poem quoted by President Spencer W. Kimball—adversity is our friend:

> Pain stayed so long I said to him today,
> "I will not have you with me any more."
> I stamped my foot and said, "Be on your way,"
> And paused there, startled at the look he wore.
> "I, who have been your friend," he said to me,
> "I, who have been your teacher—all you know
> Of understanding love, of sympathy,
> And patience, I have taught you. Shall I go?"
> He spoke the truth, this strange unwelcome guest;
> I watched him leave, and knew that he was wise.

He left a heart grown tender in my breast,
He left a far, clear vision in my eyes.
I dried my tears, and lifted up a song—
Even for one who'd tortured me so long.

(Author unknown, as quoted in *Faith Precedes the Miracle*, p. 99.)

That night as I tried to sleep I pondered Elder Packer's troublesome statement regarding equality in testing. I finally knew that he was correct. I realized that since the Lord gives us weaknesses to make us strong (see Ether 12:27), and since each of us is at a different stage in our eternal development, we experience trials that we each need for our personal progress. From His perspective, there is equality in testing—not that all trials are equal, but that many of our trials test us in areas that require strengthening, and they test us to our limit. God will judge each of us according to our individual circumstances. I believe it is these factors, as well as the pain, anxiety, and heartache we suffer, that provide equality in testing.

As we traveled home I reflected on my testimony of the previous night. Not only had I learned from what I said, but after my testimony was borne I finally understood why my bitterness was gone and why I then had the faith to trust Heavenly Father with my life. Later, as I read Elder Boyd K. Packer's explanation, I understood why that knowledge came when it did:

Oh, if I could teach you this one principle. A testimony is to be *found* in the *bearing* of it! Somewhere in your quest for spiritual knowledge, there is that "leap of faith," as the philosophers call it. It is the moment when you have gone to the edge of the light and stepped into the darkness to discover that the way is lighted ahead for just a footstep or two. . . .

It is one thing to receive a witness from what you have read or what another has said; and that is a necessary beginning. It is quite another to have the Spirit confirm to you in your bosom that what *you* have testified is true. Can you not see that it will be supplied as you share it? As you give that which you have, there is a replacement, with increase! ("The Candle of the Lord," pp. 54–55, emphasis in original.)

Balm Of Gilead

Another story that significantly impacted my changing heart was one Elder Packer shared in October 1987 general conference. I had previously realized that good people suffer from adversity, but not until I heard this talk did I realize that *even good people can become bitter.* This talk was a second witness to me that what happened the night I bore my testimony in the motor home truly was the key to my overcoming adversity and finding peace.

> My message . . . [is] an appeal to those who are not at peace, those whose lives are touched with bitterness, with hostility, or with resentment. It is a plea to those who anxiously struggle with worry, or with grief or disappointment, with guilt, or with shame. . . .
>
> If the burden is guilt, then repentance is the Balm of Gilead. . . .
>
> If you suffer from worry, from grief or shame or jealousy or disappointment or envy, from self-recrimination or self-justification, consider this lesson taught to me many years ago by a patriarch. He was as saintly a man as I have ever known. He was steady and serene, with a deep spiritual strength that many drew upon.
>
> He knew just how to minister to others who were suffering. On a number of occasions I was present when he gave blessings to those who were sick or who were otherwise afflicted. His was a life of service. . . .
>
> On one occasion, when the Spirit was right, he gave me a lesson for my life from an experience in his own. Although I thought I had known him, he told me things about his life I would not have supposed.
>
> He grew up in a little community with a desire to make something of himself. He struggled to get an education.
>
> He married his sweetheart, and presently everything was just right. He was well employed, with a bright future. They were deeply in love, and she was expecting their first child.
>
> The night the baby was to be born, there were complica-

tions. The only doctor was somewhere in the countryside tending to the sick.

After many hours of labor, the condition of the mother-to-be became desperate.

Finally the doctor was located. In the emergency, he acted quickly and soon had things in order. The baby was born and the crisis, it appeared, was over.

Some days later, the young mother died from the very infection that the doctor had been treating at another home that night.

John's world was shattered. Everything was not right now; everything was all wrong. He had lost his wife. He had no way to tend both the baby and his work.

As the weeks wore on, his grief festered. "That doctor should not be allowed to practice," he would say. "He brought that infection to my wife. If he had been careful, she would be alive today."

He thought of little else, and in his bitterness, he became threatening. Today, no doubt, he would have been pressed by many others to file a malpractice suit. And there are lawyers who would see in his pitiable condition only one ingredient—money!

But that was another day, and one night a knock came at his door. A little girl said simply, "Daddy wants you to come over. He wants to talk to you."

"Daddy" was the stake president. A grieving, heartbroken young man went to see his spiritual leader.

This spiritual shepherd had been watching his flock and had something to say to him.

The counsel from that wise servant was simply, "John, leave it alone. Nothing you do about it will bring her back. Anything you do will make it worse. John, leave it alone."

My friend told me then that this had been his trial—his Gethsemane. How could he leave it alone? Right was right! A terrible wrong had been committed and somebody must pay for it. It was a clear case.

But he struggled in agony to get hold of himself. And finally, he determined that whatever else the issues were, he should be obedient.

Obedience is powerful spiritual medicine. It comes close to being a cure-all.

He determined to follow the counsel of that wise spiritual leader. He would leave it alone.

Then he told me, "I was an old man before I understood! It was not until I was an old man that I could finally see a poor country doctor—overworked, underpaid, run ragged from patient to patient, with little medicine, no hospital, few instruments, struggling to save lives, and succeeding for the most part.

"He had come in a moment of crisis, when two lives hung in the balance, and acted without delay.

"I was an old man," he repeated, "before I finally understood! I would have ruined my life," he said, "and the lives of others."

Many times he had thanked the Lord on his knees for a wise spiritual leader who counseled simply, "John, leave it alone."

And that is the counsel I bring again to you. If you have a festering grudge, if you are involved in an acrimonious dispute, "Behold what the scripture says [and it says it fifty times and more]—man shall not smite, neither shall he judge; for judgment is mine, saith the Lord, and vengeance is mine also, and I will repay."(Mormon 8:20.)

I say therefore, "John, leave it alone. Mary, leave it alone." . . .

Some frustrations we must endure without really solving the problem. Some things that ought to be put in order are not put in order because we cannot control them. Things we cannot solve, we must survive.

If you resent someone for something he has done—or failed to do—forget it. . . .

If you brood constantly over a loss or a past mistake, look ahead—settle it.

We call that forgiveness. Forgiveness is powerful spiritual medicine. To extend forgiveness, that soothing balm, to those who have offended you is to heal. And, more difficult yet, when the need is there, forgive yourself!

I repeat, "John, leave it alone. Mary, leave it alone."

Purge and cleanse and soothe your soul and your heart
and your mind and that of others.
A cloud will then be lifted, a beam cast from your eye.
There will come that peace which surpasseth understanding. ("Balm of Gilead," pp. 16–18.)

A New Person

Since our family testimony meeting in the motor home, I am
a different person. I still face daily frustrations and struggle with
the weaknesses of the flesh, but my attitude and outlook is vastly
different. Now I am not bitter when the car won't start or the
washer breaks. I'm not upset with God when the children are
sick or I have financial problems. I'm no longer envious when
others have greater wealth or opportunities than I have. I'm not
covetous when I see those with superior intellect, talents, or
physical capabilities. As one of God's children, I now realize that
I am unique and must not compare myself with others. I also
understand that Heavenly Father customizes a curriculum for
each of us, with many of our challenges tailored to help us
progress (see Maxwell, "Insights from My Life," p. 192).
Additionally, Elder Neal A. Maxwell's words comforted me: "We
soon discover in the quietude of our ponderings and our think-
ings upon the Lord that he is a tutorial and activist God. He is
not a passive being somewhere in space. He is active in the tutoring of each of us." Earlier in the same talk he said, "Let us not
misread God's tutoring love. He would not be a loving Father if
He ignored our imperfections. We must not forget that. He
would not be a true Father if he were content with you and me
just as we now are." ("If Thou Endure Well," pp. 9, 6.)

I have shared my feelings of bitterness because it is important to note that they distorted my perspective, so much so that
I truly believed my trials were much worse than other people's
trials, that God wasn't interested in me, that God treated me
unfairly, and that there was no value in adversity. Now, with a
softened heart and a new perspective on life, I believe many
people experience similar feelings when they encounter challenges and trials.

To demonstrate how my attitude changed, I share four experiences that would have greatly fueled my bitterness had my heart not been softened. The first experience occurred in April 1989.

Emergency!

My secretary interrupted me. "Come quickly. Your daughter is very ill," she said as we hurried to the telephone.

I wondered what was wrong with Cindy. Twice in the last three years she had been rushed to the hospital with her heart beating more than 250 beats per minute. Since then her physical condition had deteriorated and she was confined to bed. As I picked up the telephone I was sure her life was in jeopardy. However, as I spoke with Jo I was surprised to learn that it was Heather, not Cindy, who was ill. Heather, who was younger and healthier than Cindy, had stopped breathing!

I immediately left work and considered exceeding the speed limit, but felt I shouldn't. Consequently, the thirty-minute drive home seemed to take an eternity. Although I kept asking myself, *Why Heather? Why did she stop breathing?* a calm feeling came over me, and I felt that everything would be all right. It didn't relieve my anxiety, but I felt that what was happening was Heavenly Father's will. The faith He had blessed me with to overcome my bitterness enabled me now to trust Him and say aloud, "Father, thy will be done."

As I neared home an ambulance left our driveway and sped away with its lights flashing and siren blaring. Thinking that Heather was probably still alive, I stopped and asked the neighbors gathered there how she was. Unfortunately, they didn't know.

When I arrived at the hospital the paramedics were reloading their equipment, and the scene was one of peace and tranquillity. I ran into the emergency area, where I met Jo and our pediatrician. He quietly said, "Heather is gone." Jo and I embraced, and my tears came freely as we stood alone with Heather in a private emergency room. With her spirit gone, her small, severely deformed body wasn't the Heather we knew, but Jo and I had a heartfelt prayer with her before leaving the hospital.

That night as I tried to sleep I thought about Heather. She really was gone. Death seemed so permanent, so final. We hadn't had a chance to tell her good-bye. Why her? Why now? Just weeks before her twelfth birthday. What a loss! As I reviewed her life I was grateful for everything we had done together—especially her baptism—and for all she had done for our family. She was such a joy, a help, a friend, a peacemaker, an angel. I concluded, as Jo did, that I was thankful that she was not healed when she was an infant. I wanted her healed, but I didn't need her healed.

Some people might feel that Jo and I would have been relieved to be free of the burden of caring for a severely handicapped child. Sometimes when we struggled to care for Heather I thought I would feel that way too. But I missed her as I believe I would miss any of my children if they passed away, and I felt her loss just as intensely as I felt the loss of my father several months later, when he died after many years of illness. In fact, I discovered that I miss and mourn for loved ones regardless of how easy it might be when they are gone. I also learned that it doesn't help for someone to say, "I'm sure you'll miss her, but now life will be much easier for you." Although Heather's passing was extremely difficult, I was thankful that the Lord had softened my heart before calling her home. I'm not sure how I would have reacted if I still had been bitter.

Emergency Again

As Jo mentioned earlier, the day after Heather died Cindy developed severe breathing problems and we had to take her to the hospital at 2:00 A.M. As I stood in the same small emergency room where Heather's body lay just thirty-six hours before, I was tired and frightened that we might have a double funeral—but I was not bitter or angry with God. If this emergency had happened before my heart was softened, I know I would have been bitter.

Festival of Trees

The third experience occurred during the Christmas season in 1989, when Jo and I attended the Festival of Trees, a fund-raising event for a local hospital. The spirit of the occasion was warm and peaceful as we viewed the beautiful tree that my employer had donated and Jean Ernstrom and friends had decorated to commemorate Heather's life. I was deeply touched as I realized volunteers had spent hundreds of hours preparing it. Unfortunately, our joy was short-lived. When we arrived at our baby-sitter's home, we learned that Cindy had been rushed to Salt Lake City in an ambulance. We were told she could barely breathe and was turning blue.

During the twenty-five-minute drive to the hospital, we wondered if Cindy was still alive. Was this her last struggle for life? We soon discovered that she was in critical condition. Her heart was beating more than 250 beats per minute, and she was struggling to breathe. We assisted doctors for many hours, and by morning she was stabilized and out of danger.

Despite this crisis at Christmastime, the feelings of bitterness that I had experienced so many times before were gone. I didn't question the Lord. Instead, though anxious about Cindy's welfare I was calm and had the courage to say again, "Father, thy will be done."

A Stroke

The fourth experience occurred a year later, on Christmas morning. We awoke early, and upon entering Cindy's bedroom Jo found her highly distressed. Sometime during the night she apparently had suffered a stroke. The left side of her face was paralyzed, she was lethargic, her eyes "danced," and her breathing was labored. It was many hours before she was stabilized and we were able to open presents. During the entire ordeal my attitude was one of sorrow and concern for her and our other children—not one of anger because our holiday was spoiled. If this experience had occurred before my heart was softened, it would have fueled my bitterness, and I would have become upset with God for disrupting the beautiful Christmas season again.

PART IV

Blessings of a Changing Heart

Bruce E. Erickson

CHAPTER 14

Understanding Myself

As my heart softened and my outlook on life changed, fresh new insights and many blessings came in unexpected ways and at unexpected times. In the process I began to understand myself better. Also, my relationship with God, Jo, and my children changed, and I began to feel at peace.

Surprising Insight

One of the most surprising insights came after Heather died as I reflected on my personal relationships and previous bitterness. I wondered what caused that bitterness, what helped me overcome it, and what brought peace to my troubled soul. Why did it take so much adversity to soften my heart, and why was I tested the way I was? Jo suggested that it was because I had low self-esteem. "Impossible," I said. "I've always had high self-esteem. I had perfect grades in high school and many, many achievements since then." I couldn't understand how I could possibly have low self-esteem, or how that might cause my bitterness.

Initially I thought it would be easy to determine if I had high or low self-esteem. However, the more I pondered and studied, the more conflicting information I found, and the more confused I became. I was especially surprised to read the words of President Ezra Taft Benson and several of the Brethren, whose comments were not based on clinical theories but were related to obedience to the laws of God. What did keeping the commandments have to do with self-esteem? Wasn't self-esteem increased by accomplishments and achievements? Didn't playing the piano well, getting good grades, or learning a sport build one's self-esteem? I was sure those assumptions were correct, because I had heard many parents say they shuttled their children to baseball, soccer, and basketball games; swimming lessons; music lessons; dance lessons; and a host of other activities to build better self-esteem.

Jo compounded my confusion by insisting that Heather had high self-esteem (as related in chapter 8). How could she? She couldn't read, work, sing, play the piano, participate in sports, or voluntarily move. Her face and body were severely distorted by her disease, she had buck teeth, and some people thought she was ugly. Lacking achievement, talent, and beauty, how could she have high self-esteem?

Although Jo developed an understanding of self-esteem long before I did, I was sure she was wrong. Hence, I struggled for many months to understand self-esteem, but because of contradictory information I finally decided to follow President Ezra Taft Benson's wise counsel: "No matter how the world uses the term, we must understand how God uses the term so we can understand the language of holy writ and profit thereby" ("Beware of Pride," p. 4). Although he was speaking of pride when he made that statement, it seemed applicable to my study. Therefore, I abandoned my interest in secular writings on self-esteem and restricted my study to the words of the Brethren and the scriptures.

With that new approach, a major clue came as I read Elder Boyd K. Packer's statement about a seemingly unrelated subject: "There is a practice, now quite prevalent, for unmarried couples to live together, a counterfeit of marriage. . . . However much they hope to find in a relationship of that kind, they will lose more. Living together without marriage destroys something inside all who participate. Virtue, *self-esteem,* and refinement of character wither away." ("Marriage," p. 13, emphasis added.) From that I concluded that failure to keep God's commandments causes a loss of self-esteem. As I wondered what produced self-esteem, President Ezra Taft Benson provided the answer: ["The proud] depend upon the world to tell them whether they have value or not. Their *self-esteem* is determined by where they are judged to be on the ladders of worldly success. They feel worthwhile as individuals if the numbers beneath them in achievement, talent, beauty, or intellect are large enough. . . . If we love God, do His will, and fear His judgment more than men's, we will have self-esteem." ("Beware of Pride," p. 6, emphasis added.)

As I read and reread President Benson's statement, it seemed that he described two types of self-esteem. Curious, I checked the World Book dictionary and found two meanings for the term *self-esteem.* One read, "the thinking too well of oneself; conceit"; and the other, "the thinking well of oneself; self-respect." With that insight, I labeled the two types of self-esteem the "world's self-esteem" and "God's self-esteem," and then categorized the elements of each by evaluating the words of President Benson and other Brethren:

World's Self-Esteem

- Our value or worth is based on:
    —Where we are on the ladder of worldly success (wealth, social position, fame, honor, achievement, talent, beauty, intellect).
    —Competition: "If you succeed, I am a failure."
    —Comparing ourselves with others.
- We feel ashamed or embarrassed if we don't measure up to society's standards.
- We are unwilling to admit our mistakes or apologize for them.
- We depend on others to tell us if we are good enough.
- We disregard, forget, or give "lip service" to God. "They draw near to me with their lips, but their hearts are far from me" (Joseph Smith–History: 1:19).
- Our hearts are set upon the vain things of the world.
- We ask, "What do I want out of life?"
- We receive no lasting peace or happiness from our achievements.

God's Self-Esteem

- Our value or worth is based on:
  — Our relationship with God and our fellowmen. Do
  we truly love both?
  — How we keep God's commandments.
  — Whether we fear God's judgment more than men's
  judgments. We worry more about what God thinks
  than what men think.
  — The truth that everyone can succeed.
- We live independent of the praise of the world.
- We admit our mistakes and apologize for them.
- We repent daily and retain a remission of our sins.
- We forgive others of their trespasses against us, even if
  we are the victims.
- We turn our hearts to God.
- We give our time and talents to build God's kingdom.
- We ask, "What would God have me do with my life?"
- We keep our covenants, and the Spirit confirms that we
  are fulfilling our life's mission and blesses us with lasting
  peace and happiness.

As I reviewed the elements of the world's self-esteem and
God's self-esteem, they "felt" correct to me, and there came to
mind the dreams that father Lehi and Nephi had of the tree of
life. I visualized the tree, the path leading to it, the rod of iron
near the path, and the great and spacious building nearby. I
imagined people pressing forward to the tree, and remembered
that the people in the building mocked them. I recalled that
some on the path became embarrassed, forsook the fruit, and
wandered away. It seemed that the people in the great and spacious building were pursuing the world's self-esteem, while those
who held fast to the iron rod were pursuing God's self-esteem.

That was it! Combining the ideas about self-esteem with
Nephi's dream helped me understand my past behavior. In
essence, I had struggled to hold on to the iron rod, but I listened
to the people in the great and spacious building as I slowly
moved toward the tree of life. My self-esteem was based on
what people thought of me; getting outstanding grades in

school; how much money I made; the type of house, car, and furniture I had; the brand of the clothes I wore; the church calling I had; my accomplishments at work; my children's appearance, achievements, grades, and awards; and even how many children I had. I believed that excelling in my work and achieving success according to society's standards increased my self-esteem.

I finally understood why my efforts to obtain success left me confused, unhappy, and without peace. I wanted both the world's self-esteem *and* God's self-esteem! That was why I always compared myself with others and criticized and judged their actions, why I felt cheated, why I was embarrassed about my family, and why I felt life was so unfair. That was why I didn't receive lasting peace and happiness from my accomplishments, why they were never enough, and why there was always more that I could or should do. I didn't know of President Brigham Young's warning, "The man or woman who tries to live according to the Gospel of the Son of God, and at the same time clings to the spirit of the world, has trials and sorrows acute and keen, and that, too, continually" (*Journal of Discourses,* 16:123).

That was also why my life was one of competition as I struggled to be better than my peers. I had forgotten Elder Boyd K. Packer's words: "In this life we are constantly confronted with a spirit of competition. Teams contest one against another in an adversary relationship in order that one will be chosen a winner. We come to believe that wherever there is a winner there must also be a loser. To believe that is to be misled." ("An Appeal to Prospective Elders," p. 105.) That also explained why I was not content with my lot in life. I didn't realize, as Alma did, that "I ought to be content with the things which the Lord hath allotted unto me" (Alma 29:3), because He tailored my circumstances to my specific needs. If I want a different allotment, I put my wisdom above the Lord's.

Weeks later I reread President Ezra Taft Benson's talk on pride ("Beware of Pride," pp. 4–7) and was surprised to learn the true meaning of my definitions for self-esteem. He called the world's self-esteem *pride* and God's self-esteem *humility.* How could that be? Surely something was wrong, because I was a humble person. A person with my trials couldn't be proud!

After considerable soul-searching I concluded that my definitions were correct: I was a proud person! My life was focused mainly on the world's self-esteem, not on God's self-esteem. I finally understood why the building in Lehi's dream represented the "pride of the world," and why the proud people in it mocked those who followed Christ as they pressed forward to the tree of life. Although I initially didn't think pride was so serious, I later remembered that Alma regulated the Church in Zarahemla by excommunicating those who remained proud! (See Alma 6:1-5.) Yes, my pride was a serious sin.

With a clearer perspective of pride and humility, I began to understand myself even better. I understood why I thought I needed a leadership position in the Church to feel good about myself and why I expected the Lord to prosper me with worldly wealth. Because I was blinded by pride, I didn't recognize that God was blessing me and my family with spiritual gifts such as increased testimony, faith, humility, charity, and patience. As President Benson testified:

> The greatest blessings of the Lord are, after all, spiritual in nature. Perhaps that is the deeper meaning to the expression, "I will open you the windows of heaven and pour you out a blessing, that there shall not be room enough to receive it" (Malachi 3:10). The late Elder Melvin J. Ballard, an Apostle, said that "the Lord has promised that the man and woman who pay their honest tithing shall be provided for, [but] He doesn't promise to make them rich, not in material things. The greatest blessings of the Lord are spiritual, and not material." (*The Teachings of Ezra Taft Benson*, pp. 472–73.)

Truly, while I was seeking worldly success the Lord blessed me with eternal riches. I perceived He had given me stones, when in reality He had given me bread. I then realized that serving others and turning my heart to Him, not holding positions of leadership in His Church, are the keys to His kingdom.

Finally, the words of Elder George Albert Smith gave me the peace I needed: "It is not necessary for a man to be a president of a stake, or a member of the Quorum of the Twelve, in order to attain a high place in the celestial kingdom. The humblest member of the Church, if he keeps the commandments of God, will obtain an exaltation just as much as any other man in the celestial kingdom. The beauty of the Gospel of Jesus Christ is that it makes us all equal in as far as we keep the commandments of the Lord." (As quoted in *A Royal Priesthood*, p. 48.)

Knowing that pride was the source of many of my problems helped me understand why it had been painful for me to change my life and why it took large doses of adversity to humble me. President Ezra Taft Benson said: "God will have a humble people. Either we can choose to be humble or we can be compelled to be humble. . . . We can choose to humble ourselves by conquering enmity toward our brothers and sisters, esteeming them as ourselves, and lifting them as high or higher than we are." ("Beware of Pride," pp. 6–7.) However, as I pondered that thought I became confused. Didn't God violate my moral agency by forcing me to be humble? Didn't He take away my right to choose? Further study helped me see that I still had my agency even though He had compelled me to be humble. Alma said, "Because ye are compelled to be humble blessed are ye; for a man *sometimes,* if he is compelled to be humble, seeketh repentance" (Alma 32:13, emphasis added). Although I was compelled to be humble when Cindy, Heather, and Mark became handicapped, I chose not to repent. I remained proud. It wasn't until I was compelled to be humble when I lost my job that I sought to repent and change my life. God didn't force me to repent; I finally chose to repent.

Understanding the differences between the world's self-esteem and God's self-esteem helped me realize that Jo was correct. Heather had high self-esteem—not the self-esteem of the proud, worldly person, but the self-esteem of the humble, Christlike person—and I had low self-esteem. I was a perfect example of Elder Neal A. Maxwell's words: "Usually a crisis of faith involves a crisis of self-esteem" (*Wherefore Ye Must Press Forward*, p. 101). I had lacked the faith to trust God completely, because my self-esteem was based on the world's standards—and, to complete the circle, my pride kept me from developing sufficient faith (see Stephen L Richards, in Conference Report, April 1935, pp. 30–31).

A New Focus

My new understanding of self-esteem caused me to further review my life and to wonder why I had pursued the world's self-esteem when I was raised by loving parents who lived and taught the gospel in word and deed. As I tried to answer that question, Jo suggested I reread *The Divine Center* by Stephen R. Covey. I had read it in 1983 at her insistence, but found it of little value because I believed my life already was focused on God.

With a softened heart and a more teachable mind, however, I reread *The Divine Center.* Surprisingly, without the proud, know-it-all attitude I had when I first read the book, I discovered many new insights. The author noted that people focus their lives on one or more centers, including God, church, family, friends, leaders, enemies, work, recreation, self, or possessions. As I read I realized that my life had been centered on a combination of church, family, work, and self—all important centers, but not the "sure foundation" the prophet Helaman described:

> And now, my sons, remember, remember that it is upon the rock of our Redeemer, who is Christ, the Son of God, that ye must build your foundation; that when the devil shall send forth his mighty winds, yea, his shafts in the whirlwind, yea, when all his hail and his mighty storm shall beat upon you, it shall have no power over you to drag you down to the gulf of misery and endless wo, because of the rock upon which ye are built, which is a sure foundation, a foundation whereon if men build they cannot fall. (Helaman 5:12.)

I was also surprised to learn that my actual behavior in many situations was highly predictable based on the focus of my life. As I read, Elder Bruce R. McConkie's words described a weakness of mine:

> Our tendency—it is an almost universal practice among most Church leaders—is to get so involved with the operation of the institutional Church that we never gain faith like the ancients, simply because we do not involve ourselves in the basic gospel matters that were the center of their lives.

We are so wound up in programs and statistics and trends, in properties, lands, and mammon, and in achieving goals that will highlight the excellence of our work, that we "have omitted the weightier matters of the law." And as Jesus would have said: "These [weightier things] ought ye to have done, and not to leave the other undone." (Matthew 23:23.) . . .

We are not saved by Church programs as such, by Church organizations alone, or even by the Church itself. It is the gospel that saves. . . .

Salvation comes because "Jesus Christ," as Paul said, "hath abolished death, and hath brought life and immortality to light through the gospel." (2 Timothy 1:10.) It is the gospel that raises men "in immortality" and "unto eternal life." (D&C 29:43.) The gospel is the plan of salvation by which we can change the souls we possess into the kind of souls who can go where God and Christ are. (As quoted in *The Divine Center,* pp. 60–61.)

After reading Elder McConkie's comments I understood once again that the focus of my life had been on worldly things, not on God and Christ. It was focused on the number of awards, trophies, and scholarships I received, the number of times my name appeared in the newspaper, the promotions and bonuses I received, and many other prideful goals. I realized that I gave lip service to God, but my heart was centered on my accomplishments and in "programs and statistics and trends, in properties, lands, and mammon, and in achieving goals that [would] highlight the excellence of [my] work." Because I was proud, my virtues became vices, my strengths became weaknesses (see Oaks, "Our Strengths Can Become Our Downfall"), and my sins kept me from understanding God's will for me.

As I pondered further I realized that I resented rich people because I was envious and coveted their wealth. Because I was poor, I thought I was poor in heart (see Alma 32:3, 8). I now know, however, that poor people are those who lack sufficient sustenance, and the poor in heart are those who, regardless of their financial status, have centered their lives on the Savior and are striving to follow Him. Later, I was surprised that President Benson described my condition:

Most of us consider pride to be a sin of those on the top, such as the rich and the learned, looking down at the rest of us. There is, however, a far more common ailment among us—and that is pride from the bottom looking up. It is manifest in so many ways, such as fault-finding, gossiping, back-biting, murmuring, living beyond our means, envying, coveting, withholding gratitude and praise that might lift another, and being unforgiving and jealous. ("Beware of Pride," p. 5.)

I truly had been envious and jealous of others' success. I coveted their blessings and opportunities, and I hadn't forgiven those who had wronged me.

As I reflected further I remembered President Spencer W. Kimball's temple dedicatory prayer: "Bless all people, our Father, that they may prosper, but not more than their faith can stand. . . . We pray that they may not be surfeited with flocks and herds and acres and barns and wealth which would bring them to worship these false gods." (*The Teachings of Spencer W. Kimball,* p. 354.) I realized I was one of the Saints for whom President Kimball was praying, because I was proud, covetous, and selfish. I hadn't recognized that earlier, and Elder Boyd K. Packer ably described why I hadn't: "Selfishness can attach itself to an individual without his being aware that he is afflicted with it. It can become imbedded so deeply and disguised so artfully as to be almost indistinguishable." (*That All May Be Edified,* p. 192.)

As I tried to center my life on God and Christ, I finally understood the Savior's words: "He that loveth father or mother more than me is not worthy of me: and he that loveth son or daughter more than me is not worthy of me" (Matthew 10:37–38). Regarding that, Elder Joseph Fielding Smith said:

Anyone who *loves* his father, mother, wife, and all that is dear to him, even his own life, *more* than he loves Christ, is not worthy of him and cannot be his disciple. The thought is very clear in this instruction that all who seek eternal life are required to come to Christ willing to give up all that they possess, if necessary. Should they be unwilling to do so, even to the laying down of life in his cause, then they are not worthy of his kingdom. This is reasonable; no unjust demand is made by our Savior, for he came and laid down his life for us that we might have life everlasting. He suffered for us; should we not love him more than we love our own lives? (*The Way to Perfection*, pp. 272–73, emphasis in original.)

Unrighteous Dominion

As my heart softened I also began to understand why Jo and I hadn't enjoyed a happy, fulfilling, and romantic relationship. In part it was because I had entered marriage with false expectations and ideas. I believed that if a couple married in the temple and kept the commandments, they would be wonderfully blessed in their relationship—that problems would be minor and that their relationship would be romantic and fulfilling. I had reached that conclusion because my parents, grandparents, aunts, and uncles were all married in the temple, all seemed happy, and none were divorced.

Once married, however, I discovered that there was much more to a happy marriage than being married in the temple. Yes, I knew that a couple must work on their relationship, but I didn't understand what that meant, and I certainly didn't understand how each partner's past experiences as well as the differences between men and women would make marriage so challenging.

Jo and I had problems early in our marriage, but I attributed them to the pressures I felt while supporting a family and being a full-time student. Later, I thought our problems were due to Cindy's illness. Still later, I believed our marriage would be happy if Cindy, Heather, and Mark were healed.

Not until after my heart was sufficiently softened did I recognize the real cause of my unhappy marriage: I was proud and selfish, and had a distorted view of my role as a husband and father. I knew what was best for our family, and my way was the only correct way to do things, whether it had to do with food preparation, how our home was cleaned, how our children were disciplined, or a hundred other things. I decided what brand of products we bought and how we spent our money, and if I really wanted something I usually bought it. As the lord and ruler of our home, my wants and needs came first—everyone had to do as I directed. I didn't have to help with the children or assist Jo with her responsibilities when I was tired, since I deserved to relax after a hard day's work. After all, I was the breadwinner and the priesthood bearer. I was supposed to lead the family and make the major decisions, because my responsibilities were far more important and challenging than Jo's. Although she was able to voice her opinions, I recently learned that she simply "rubber-stamped" my decisions to keep peace in the family.

Truly, because of my pride, selfishness, and misconceptions about being a husband and father, I exercised "unrighteous dominion" (see D&C 121:39). Although I thought that only ruthless, inconsiderate, abusive men exercised unrighteous dominion, I realized that I did too. I was unwilling to apologize, I was judgmental and critical of everyone in our home, and I blamed Jo for all the problems in our marriage. I criticized everything from the way she cooked to the way members of her family spoke and acted. Furthermore, I felt my extended family was far better than hers because, among other things, all members of my family were active members of the Church, all had been married in the temple, and none were divorced. Since that was not the case with her extended family, I believed they didn't have the strength and religious convictions that my family did. Therefore, she needed to do things my way, the way my family did things. To me, my perceptions literally were reality.

Cindy's illness brought Jo and me closer together for a time, but when Cindy wasn't healed I resented God's unfair treatment, and my domineering attitude again applied tremendous strain on our marriage. Then with each additional handicapped child I felt so trapped that I often thought divorce was the only escape. Fortunately, however—perhaps out of a sense of duty—I resisted the desire to solve my problems with divorce because of the collective counsel of the Brethren. President Kimball's admonition was clear:

> Every divorce is the result of selfishness on the part of one or the other or both parties to a marriage contract.

Someone is thinking of self-comforts, conveniences, freedoms, luxuries, or ease.

Divorce is not a cure for difficulty, but is merely an escape, and a weak one. . . . The divorce itself does not constitute the entire evil, but the very acceptance of divorce as a cure is also a serious sin of this generation. Because a program or a pattern is universally accepted is not evidence that it is right. Marriage never was easy. It may never be. It brings with it sacrifice, sharing and a demand for great selflessness. (*The Teachings of Spencer W. Kimball*, pp. 313, 314.)

Now, with a softened heart, I recognize the heartache and grief that I caused Jo and the children, and that I was one of the men Elder H. Burke Peterson admonished: "Unfortunately, too many men may be denied the blessings of heaven because they have failed to understand and heed the Lord's counsel concerning unrighteous dominion" ("Unrighteous Dominion," p. 11). With a clearer view I finally realized how Jo felt when I exercised unrighteous dominion in our home. Recently she shared her feelings:

Before Bruce's heart began to change, every day I wondered what he would criticize me or the girls for next. I never knew what I should or shouldn't say to him, and it seemed like I had to justify and explain everything I did. If I questioned the way he did something or the way he handled one of the children, he felt I was judging him or questioning his authority or his knowledge. Truly, those were the days when I felt like I walked on eggshells as I tried to make sure nothing upset him, and when I honestly didn't think we would ever see eye to eye on much of anything.

After pondering the scriptures, Jo's feelings, and Elder Peterson's article on unrighteous dominion, I know he was correct when he said:

A man needs to understand that his power to influence his wife or children for good can only come through love, praise, and patience. It can never be brought about by force or coercion.

Many women carry heavy burdens raising children and attending to household responsibilities. They often accomplish near-miracles in balancing all the demands made upon them. A husband who is critical of his wife and communicates censure for what hasn't been done rather than thanks for what has been done fosters discouragement. . . . Criticism has a negative influence on the feelings of love for and interest in one's spouse. Women need love, affection, and emotional support from their husbands. (Ibid., p. 9.)

I now recognize that my judgmental and critical attitude had a very negative influence on Jo's feelings of love for me. The romance I wanted was inhibited by my pride and criticism, not by a lack of her love. Earlier I had felt that our marriage would be more romantic if we could get away to Hawaii, the Caribbean, or some other exotic place, like other couples did. The paradox was that *romance came because of my repentance and change of heart, not by getting away on an exotic vacation* or spending more time together.

In contrast to how Jo felt about our relationship before, she recently said:

The difference between Bruce now and Bruce before his change of heart is like the difference between day and night. It's not that he was mean or terrible before, but that he was probably like many men whose nature and disposition is to exercise unrighteous dominion (D&C 121:39) as soon as they become responsible for a wife and children.

Now, with a changed heart, Bruce sincerely tries to influence me and our children by persuasion, long-suffering, gentleness, meekness, and kindness (see D&C 121:41-42). He no longer makes decrees about what our family will do, but he works with me to make joint decisions, and he even accepts my viewpoint. He sincerely recognizes the difficulty of my tasks, and he appreciates and compliments me for what I have done rather than criticizes me for what I haven't done. He gives me genuine love, affection and emotional support, and he even helps me with my domestic tasks. He is patient when I am slow to understand something that is obvious to him, and he is quick to say, "I'm sorry; I was wrong"—even when the problem was mostly my fault. He also makes it a point to be happy and positive when he comes home from work, and he is now friendly and loving with his in-laws. Truly, doing those things is what validates my value to him, as well as my value as a wife and mother.

Because he has changed, I no longer "walk on eggshells," but look forward to him coming home from work each day. I can say what I really think without fear of censure, and we now actually see eye to eye on most subjects. In short, although we still have our struggles and disagreements—which probably is not unusual for two very strong-willed individuals—our relationship is now a happy, loving, and rewarding one, and it certainly is much more romantic. Truly, it's so much easier to give of myself when I feel emotionally supported.

Incidentally, although I previously thought saying "I'm sorry" was of little value, I now see that an unwillingness to admit mistakes and apologize is a sure sign of pride and a major stumbling block in personal relationships. I also realize that saying "I'm sorry," and really meaning it, is a sign of humility and a necessary step to repentance.

A Fresh View

One day as Jo and I discussed my change of heart, she noted that the process was actually initiated by repentance. As I pondered her comment I discovered the following definition for repentance in the LDS Bible Dictionary: "The Greek word of which this is the translation denotes a change of mind, i.e., a fresh view about God, about oneself, and about the world. . . . Repentance comes to mean a turning of the heart and will to God, and a renunciation of sin to which we are naturally inclined. Without this there can be no progress in the things of the soul's salvation."

What an incredible discovery! That process is exactly what I experienced. After I had repented of my pride, selfishness, and unrighteous dominion, and apologized to Jo and the children for the way I had treated them, my heart began to change, and I began to understand myself, others, and God in a way I had never done before. *Repentance* was the key to my changed perceptions, my softened heart, and the change in my behavior. It also was the key to my receiving peace in the face of continuing adversity.

As I pondered that conclusion, I wondered if repentance could do the same for everyone. I discovered the answer when I read the words of two prophets. Samuel the Lamanite said that many "are led to believe the holy scriptures . . . which leadeth them to faith on the Lord, and unto repentance, which faith and repentance bringeth a change of heart unto them" (Helaman 15:7). And President Benson noted:

> Repentance means more than simply a reformation of behavior. Many men and women in the world demonstrate great willpower and self-discipline in overcoming bad habits and the weaknesses of the flesh. Yet at the same time they give no thought to the Master, sometimes even openly rejecting Him. Such changes of behavior, even if in a positive direction, do not constitute true repentance. . . .
>
> . . . Repentance involves not just a change of actions, but a change of heart. ("A Mighty Change of Heart," p. 2.)

As I contemplated his counsel, the thought occurred to me that although I had never been addicted to habit-forming drugs, I had been addicted to pride, selfishness, and unrighteous dominion. But unlike many people who are able to exercise "great willpower and self-discipline in overcoming bad habits and the weaknesses of the flesh," I did not have sufficient self-control to overcome my addictions. It was only through repentance that I was able to obtain the spiritual help I needed to change my life.

I Missed the Mark

As my perspective broadened I saw the fourth article of faith in a new light. I had always believed that after I had faith in Jesus Christ, repented of my sins, accepted baptism, and received the gift of the Holy Ghost I had completed the basic requirements of the gospel. I felt that I then needed to gain more knowledge by studying "advanced" gospel subjects such as unanswered questions about the fall of Adam, the history of the earth, the location of Nephite cities, and inconsistencies in Church history. After all, Joseph Smith said: "Whatever principle of intelligence we attain unto in this life, it will rise with us in the resurrection. And if a person gains more knowledge and intelligence in this life through his diligence and obedience than another, he will have so much the advantage in the world to come." (D&C 130:18.) The Lord even commanded us to learn "all things that pertain unto the kingdom of God . . . of things both in heaven and in the earth, and under the earth; things which have been, things which are, things which must shortly come to pass; things which are at home, things which are abroad; the wars and the perplexities of the nations, and the judgments which are on the land; and a knowledge also of countries and of kingdoms" (D&C 88:78–79). Didn't I therefore need to learn as much about the world and mysteries of the gospel as possible?

With a softened heart I discovered that due to my pride, I often had been spiritually blinded and searched for gospel knowledge according to man's reasoning, not God's reasoning. I was guilty of "looking beyond the mark" when seeking gospel knowledge. The prophet Jacob explained: "The Jews were a stiffnecked people . . . and sought for things that they could not understand. Wherefore, because of their blindness [footnote: 'spiritual blindness'], which blindness came by looking beyond the mark, they must needs fall." (Jacob 4:14.) I hadn't understood that the Spirit distills knowledge line upon line as a person needs it and is worthy to receive it.

I now know that faith in Jesus Christ isn't required just for baptism, it is the key to eternal progression. The way to godliness, knowledge, and intelligence is a spiral of faith, repentance, and obedience—not "wresting" the scriptures (see Alma 13:20; 41:1; D&C 10:63). As I exercise more faith in the Lord, repent, and keep the commandments, my testimony of His plan increases and I see it more clearly. For instance, as my heart softened I didn't find answers to my questions about gospel mysteries and the earth, as I thought I needed, but I began to see and feel a fuller meaning and appreciation for the purpose of mortality, the role of the Savior, and the understanding that this life is a continuation of the war in heaven (see *The Teachings of Ezra Taft Benson*, pp. 24, 658). And I received new insights about "God's master plan" (see 2 Nephi 9:13), "Satan's master plan" (see 2 Nephi 9:28), the need to fortify myself against Satan's evil ways, and my responsibility to help my spirit brothers and sisters who are "wounded" or "missing in action."

Now I no longer seek answers to the mysteries but instead feel as Elder Dean L. Larsen stated so eloquently:

> I am much more concerned about understanding the admonitions of Samuel the Lamanite as he stood on the walls of the city of Zarahemla and called the rebellious Nephites to repentance than I am about identifying the location of that city in today's geography.
>
> I am more vitally interested in what the Father and the Son commissioned Joseph Smith to do, and the fruits of his prophetic labors, than I am in whether he made mention of one divine personage or two in his initial recounting of the First Vision.
>
> I am going to make a greater effort to be worthy of holding an ordained office in the priesthood of God, and be less concerned about confirming the exact date and place of the appearance of Peter, James, and John to restore this divine authority and power. ("Looking Beyond the Mark," p. 12.)

Surely I should learn of the earth, history, and other things so I can serve others and help build God's kingdom, but I must remember President Benson's caution that "not all knowledge has the same worth—nor are all truths equally valuable. The truths upon which our eternal salvation rests are the most crucial truths that we must learn." (*The Teachings of Ezra Taft Benson*,

p. 295.) I must also remember the counsel of Elder Neal A. Maxwell: "The vision of those in the celestial kingdom (seen by the Prophet Joseph Smith) was of those 'who overcome by faith'—*not* because while in mortality they had it all figured out, being perpetually able to give a logical, precise explanation for everything. (D&C 76:53.)" (*All These Things Shall Give Thee Experience*, pp. 34–35; emphasis in original.) Thankfully, I am no longer troubled by unanswered questions or seeming inconsistencies in the written word.

CHAPTER 15

New Perspectives

President Spencer W. Kimball said, "The more we follow the teachings of the Master, the more enlarged our perspective becomes. . . . One of the advantages of the gospel of Jesus Christ is that it gives us perspective about the people on this planet, including ourselves, so that we can see the things that truly matter." ("The Abundant Life," p. 4.) That is exactly what I experienced. As my heart softened I found answers to puzzling questions and obtained a new perspective on gospel subjects that had perplexed me for many years.

My New Glasses

One new insight came as I tried to understand why Jo and I saw things so differently for the first twenty years of our marriage. As I pondered that, I remembered the statements of two ancient prophets. The Apostle Paul noted, "For now we see through a glass, darkly" (2 Corinthians 13:12), and Nephi said that the Lamanites' and Jews' "scales of darkness [footnote: 'spiritual blindness'] shall begin to fall from their eyes" (2 Nephi 30:6). As I reflected on those scriptures I reasoned that Jo and I had vastly different perspectives because my vision had been clouded. I saw "darkly" through the eyes of a natural man until the time when my spiritual blindness was removed.

As I reflected on that thought, I remembered that Stephen R. Covey compared a person's perceptions to a pair of glasses. He said, "Normally each person sees himself and the world through the lens of his past experiences. Those glasses, his frame of reference, become the center through which he sees and interprets and explains everything else." (*The Divine Center,* p. 19.)

Using Stephen Covey's analogy, I concluded that for me my perceptions were reality, and that often our perceptions are influenced by many things, including:

- Our eternal spirit—the being that possesses our body when we come to mortality—and the characteristics of that spirit.
- Our gender and our mortal genetic imperfections.
- Our environment, including family, friends, and where we live.
- The traditions of our fathers (D&C 93:39), both inherited and learned.
- Our faith and commitment to covenants we have made.
- The degree to which our spirit is able to control our mortal body.

I realized that Jo and I experienced many of the same events and had the same religious goals, but with different "lenses" it was often impossible to "see" what the other person saw or felt. After I truly repented and "focused" my life on God and Christ, however, I began to see myself, God, and the world from a new perspective, through a new set of lenses. Truly Christ's light "enlighteneth [my] eyes" and "quickeneth [my] understandings" (D&C 88:11).

I believe that only through the help of the Lord can we see the world as it really is. In a very real sense, only if our "eye be single to [His] glory" (D&C 88:67) can we establish lasting relationships, avoid the deceptions of this world, and become one with Him.

Perspective on Adversity

As I mentioned earlier, one of the most significant new insights that came from my adversity and subsequent softened heart was an understanding that much of my inability to find peace and comfort during my trials was the result of pride and lack of faith. My pride kept me from receiving the Lord's help and letting go of things I thought were important to success and happiness in this life. Consequently, I lacked the faith to ask Him to help me overcome my adversities and recognize that they were for my own good—that often He chastened me to help me.

Unfortunately, much of my life I was tormented by the false belief that all adversity is a consequence of sin. That distorted view caused me considerable anguish because I felt the Lord was punishing me far worse than my sins deserved. In one respect I was like Laman and Lemuel, who "did murmur because they knew not the dealings of that God who had created them" (1 Nephi 2:12). I didn't understand the concept taught by President Marion G. Romney: "If we can bear our afflictions with the understanding, faith and courage, . . . we shall be spared the torment which accompanies the mistaken idea that all suffering comes as chastisement for transgression" (as quoted in *To Make Thee a Minister and a Witness,* p. 80).

I now realize that much of my peace came when I finally knew that adversity had value beyond punishment for sin. Brigham Young said:

> Every vicissitude we pass through is necessary for experience and example, and for preparation to enjoy that reward which is for the faithful. . . .
>
> Joseph [Smith] could not have been perfected, though he had lived a thousand years, if he had received no persecution. If he had lived a thousand years, and led this people, and preached the Gospel without persecution, he would not have been perfected as well as he was at the age of thirty-nine years. (*Discourses of Brigham Young,* pp. 345, 351.)

With that understanding, it was helpful for me to divide adversity into two major categories: "Self-Inflicted" and "No-Fault."

Self-Inflicted Adversity

Personal Sins. When I break God's commandments I become unhappy, discouraged, and even depressed. Of this, President Spencer W. Kimball said, "Moroni tells us that despair comes because of iniquity (see Moroni 10:22). This means that individuals can be caught in a terrible trap—the greater the iniquity, the greater the sense of despair and hopelessness. A deteriorating society, therefore, will see a lessening of real hope and an increase in despair. . . . Sin brings . . . a sense of despair." (As quoted in *Lay Hold Upon the Word of God,* p. 104.)

Although a certain amount of discouragement is a natural part of mortality, if it is caused by willfully sinning then the associated depression will be difficult to overcome. Repentance is the only therapy that brings lasting comfort when adversity is the consequence of willfully sinning. One may soothe the conscience temporarily through counseling and therapy, but the only way to remove that despair and discouragement is to repent.

The Lord explained why the early Saints suffered horrible persecution: "Verily I say unto you, concerning your brethren who have been afflicted, and persecuted, and cast out from the land of their inheritance—I, the Lord, have suffered the affliction to come upon them, wherewith they have been afflicted, in consequence of their transgressions. . . . Behold, I say unto you, there were jarrings, and contentions, and envyings, and strifes, and lustful and covetous desires among them." (D&C 101:1–2, 6.)

It is important for me to remember that God would never desire that I purposely choose sin so that I may learn from its resulting adversity. In fact, Elder Spencer W. Kimball stated, "That man who resists temptation and lives without sin is far better off than the man who has fallen, no matter how repentant the latter may be" (*Miracle of Forgiveness,* p. 357).

Personal Mistakes. Often adversity comes when we make mistakes that are due to poor judgment. For instance, I was extremely frustrated when I didn't look carefully and backed into a passing car, when I was late for an important event because I made a wrong turn, and when I purchased the wrong part to fix the washing machine. Adversity may be the result of diving

head first into shallow water, making a poor business invest-
ment, or damaging a car engine when forgetting to check the
oil.

"No-Fault" Adversity

Living in Mortality. We are tested as a consequence of living
in a mortal world where we might experience drought, excessive
heat and cold, dust, earthquakes, tornadoes, cyclones, hurri-
canes, lightning, fires, too much moisture, animals, weeds, in-
sects, rodents, vermin, bacteria, and viruses. Similarly, we are
tested when cars malfunction, clothes tear, metals rust, our
bodies grow old, and countless other things.

I have learned that even "no-fault" adversity can have value.
The Lord told Moses, "And unto Adam, I, the Lord God, said:
Because thou hast . . . eaten of the fruit of the tree of which I
commanded thee, saying—Thou shalt not eat of it, cursed shall
be the ground *for thy sake*" (Moses 4:23, emphasis added). God
didn't curse the earth to punish Adam and Eve for their transgression—he cursed it for their good, and for *our* good.

Elder Boyd K. Packer, while visiting the failed Teton Dam,
heard someone ask, "What did we do wrong to deserve such a
disaster?" "The answer is," he said, "probably nothing. If you attach tragedy or suffering or disaster to sin only, how do you explain the suffering of Christ? Fine people, living worthily, can
be subject to disasters such as you have faced here. The difference will be in how you face it." (In Mitchell, "Thousands of
Saints," p. 70.) On another occasion Elder Packer said: "It was
never intended that we float in an effortless environment at 72
degrees and bathe constantly in the sensation of physical, sen-
sational, and spiritual pleasures. We are here to grow." (*Let Not
Your Heart Be Troubled,* p. 252.)

Being a Victim. We are tested when others make mistakes or
purposely choose sin. Examples of the former might be people
who suffer because of faulty products or doctors' mistakes.
Examples of the latter might be those who suffer because another person chooses to lie, steal, gossip, exercise unrighteous
dominion, commit adultery, use pornography, inflict abuse, or
act in any other selfish way. Each of those choices causes adver-

sity and pain to come into the lives of everyone involved, just as my pride and unrighteous dominion caused suffering in our home. Elder Richard G. Scott commented that even this type of adversity can have value for the victim: "Adversity, even when caused willfully by others' unrestrained appetite, can be a source of growth when viewed from the perspective of eternal principle. (See D&C 122:7.)" ("Healing the Tragic Scars of Abuse," p. 32.) Particularly to victims of abuse, Elder Scott also counseled, "Don't view all that you experience in life through lenses darkened by the scars of abuse" (ibid., p. 33).

God's Polishing Process. Adversity can come as a consequence of God's polishing process, which He gives to help us grow, develop, and become like Him. This is the adversity Joseph Smith talked about when he compared himself to a rough stone rolling down a mountain and having rough edges ground off by coming in contact with difficulties (see *Teachings of the Prophet Joseph Smith,* p. 304).

For me, the adversity associated with personal sin, personal mistakes, and living in mortality didn't test my faith like the adversity associated with the polishing process. That was because I could logically understand the first three causes, but the "polishing" adversity seemed irrational and unfair, since I thought life should be fair. I didn't realize that even when I tried to live righteously God would allow me to experience unfair situations, and that trials, by their very nature, are unfair (see Maxwell, *All These Things Shall Give Thee Experience,* p. 31). And as Elder Neal A. Maxwell noted, "The customized challenges are often the toughest and the most ironical" ("Endure It Well," p. 34).

Elder George Q. Cannon clarified God's polishing process when he explained Abraham's trial to sacrifice Isaac:

Now, why did the Lord ask such things of Abraham? Because, knowing what his future would be and that he would be the father of an innumerable posterity, he was determined to test him. God did not do this for His own sake; for He knew by His foreknowledge what Abraham would do [Abr. 1:22–23]; but the purpose was to impress upon Abraham a lesson, and to enable him to attain unto knowledge that he could not obtain in any other way. That is why God tries all of us. It is not for His own knowledge for He knows all things beforehand. He knows all your lives and everything you will do. But He tries us for our own good, that we may know ourselves, for it is most important that a man should know himself. He required Abraham to submit to this trial because he intended to give him glory, exaltation and honor; He intended to make him a king and a priest, to share with Himself the glory, power and dominion which He exercised. (As quoted in Doxey, *Latter-day Prophets and the Doctrine and Covenants,* vol. 3, p. 369.)

I now know that Heavenly Father is the "Master Gardener" and that He has a very different plan for my life than I had originally planned or expected. Since He knows what is best for me, He is attempting to prune my sins and imperfections so I can return to Him. Much of my adversity comes because His plan and my plan are very different.

I also now realize that the struggles we have with our spouse, children, extended family, friends, ward members, associates, and others are often the means for our growth. In the words of Elder Maxwell, we are often each other's "clinical material," just as Jo stated in chapter 9 (see "If Thou Endure Well," p. 7). Now, when Jo and I have a disagreement, we often give each other a smile or a hug and say, "I'm sorry that I was your clinical material again."

The Role Of Moral Agency

After my heart was softened I finally understood the correlation between adversity and moral or free agency. As President Spencer W. Kimball said:

If all the sick for whom we pray were healed, if all the righteous were protected and the wicked destroyed, the whole program of the Father would be annulled and the basic principle of the gospel, free agency, would be ended.

If pain and sorrow and total punishment immediately followed the doing of evil, no soul would repeat a misdeed.

If joy and peace and rewards were instantaneously given the doer of good, there could be no evil—all would do good and not because of the rightness of doing good. There would be no test of strength, no development of character, no growth of powers, no free agency. ("Tragedy or Destiny," p. 210.)

I further understood the relationship between moral agency and adversity when I read the words of Elder Maxwell: "You will see some men and women without faith who will rail at God because they do not understand that much of human misery is caused by misused human agency. If God were to take away that agency, those who rail would then rail at Him for taking away their agency! These individuals want a smooth flow of blessings in life but no consequences from misused agency." ("If Thou Endure Well," p. 14.)

Indeed, one reason God permits human suffering and man's inhumanity to man is to protect moral agency. Unfortunately, I couldn't see that until I began to observe life through my new lenses.

Appreciation for Mothers

With my new perspective I saw a mother's role differently. Although I earlier had complained about doing domestic tasks such as changing diapers and doing the family shopping, I now know that managing a household, providing care and training for children, and meeting family members' needs are much more challenging, demanding, and important than I had ever imagined. A mother's work is difficult to do day after day, especially if she or the children are sick or if she is unsupported, criticized, or unappreciated.

Recognizing that a mother's role is highly demanding helped me develop a greater appreciation for the service Jo and the girls render in our home. Now, to show my appreciation and to help them rest from their labors, every Sunday I prepare the meals, clean the kitchen, and wash the dishes. Initially, doing those tasks was a chore, but now, doing them helps me appreciate and understand why the Lord has put so much emphasis on the role of mothers. I now know the validity of President Joseph Fielding Smith's remark: "The most noble, exalting calling of all is that which has been given to women as the mothers of men" (as quoted in *A Royal Priesthood*, p. 93).

Men and Women

Another new perspective was a clearer understanding of two differences between men and women—which are best explained with a joke and two experiences. First, the joke: "What is one of the reasons why a female astronaut was on the recent space shuttle flight?" Answer: "So if they became lost in space there would be one astronaut who would ask for directions."

Next, a personal experience: Jo and I had the first quarrel of our marriage while driving to Portland, Oregon, for our wedding reception. I took a detour from the main highway, and we became lost. As I searched in vain for the interstate, Jo suggested that we backtrack to find it. I became irritated at her recommendation and insisted that doing so would be a waste of both time and gasoline. When I was still lost fifteen minutes later, she then proposed that I stop at a store and ask for directions. With that suggestion I became angry—I didn't need anyone to help me find my way back.

It is now my perception that the joke and the experience typify one of the many differences between men and women. Since most women seem to be able to admit that they need help, and men generally do not, I suspect many men would have acted as I did. Call my attitude self-sufficiency, pride, or arrogance; whatever it was, that attitude caused problems in our marriage. For some reason, receiving counsel from Jo was most difficult for me until my heart began to change.

The second experience occurred when an associate remarked, "I finally understand a major difference between my wife and me. I tend to be task-oriented and she tends to be process-oriented." Puzzled, I asked him what he meant, and he replied:

> I came home from work yesterday and my wife said that Bobby had an accident and she had to take him to the hos-

pital. I asked if he was okay, and she proceeded to explain how he got injured. Her explanation began with Bobby getting up that morning and included all the chronological details about *her* activities and *her* schedule. I listened patiently, because I knew from previous experiences that if I interrupted her lengthy explanation and asked for the "bottom line"—was Bobby okay—that she would be upset and I probably wouldn't get dinner. So, I listened for almost twenty minutes before I finally got the answers I wanted: "Yes," Bobby was okay, and "no," he wasn't in the hospital.

As Jo and I discussed my friend's experience, we concluded that his assessment also applied to us. I generally want a "summary statement" or bottom-line answer, while she usually wants an answer to be an informative process with full explanations and feelings. Although I believe Jo and I should not try to change our innate differences, just being aware of them has helped immensely. Now I can say, "Jo, I know that you want to start at 600 B.C. to explain the problem, but I only have a couple of minutes before I must leave. Can you please give me the bottom line?" We both smile, and she quickly summarizes her comments. Other times, when I'm not rushed, my new understanding makes it easier for me to be patient as she starts at 600 B.C. and moves forward to the present day to explain an issue. I must admit, however, that sometimes it is hard not to interrupt her.

This new perspective is significant because if someone had identified those differences before my heart was softened, I wouldn't have appreciated the importance of both points of view. Instead I probably would have laughed and thought that my way was right and Jo's way was wrong.

Reverence for Life

The first time I felt a special reverence for life was when I began my missionary work near Nuernberg, Germany. Although World War II had ended nineteen years earlier, I was surprised to see many disabled people. I frequently saw men who were missing an arm or a leg or had other notable injuries, and I occasionally saw people with large, ugly scars on their faces and hands. As I spoke with some of these people I learned that they had indeed been injured during the war, that they were productive and, for the most part, happy citizens. I concluded that although they were "imperfect," they still contributed to society.

The next time I felt that special sensitivity for life was when I visited Dachau, one of the Nazi death camps. Anguish filled my heart as I walked through the camp where hundreds of thousands of men, women, and children were humiliated, tortured, and murdered. My senses were shocked as I saw gas chambers where people were gassed, and cremation ovens where their lifeless bodies were reduced to ashes. I was so appalled that I reflected on that experience again and again. How could human life be treated with such contempt? How could Hitler believe people had no value, or that some were needed and others were not? What insensitivity for life!

Years later I asked similar questions when abortion was legalized in the United States. How could human life be "legally" sacrificed? How did legalized abortion differ from the destruction of individuals in Dachau? Obviously the ages of the victims were different, and one group of victims wasn't developed to the same degree as the other, but each person certainly had worth and deserved to live.

Today many neonatal problems can be detected long before birth, and couples face decisions never confronted in an earlier day. When told their baby might be "abnormal," they might ask, "Should we abort it?" Unfortunately, many "experts" tell patients that abortion is a solution for "imperfection."

Abortions are so prevalent today that Elder Russell M. Nelson noted:

> In the first two hundred years as a nation, the lives of over one million Americans were lost due to war.
>
> Regrettable as is the loss of loved ones from war, these figures are dwarfed by the toll of a new war that *annually* claims more casualties than the total number of fatalities from all the wars of this nation.

It is a war on the defenseless—and the voiceless. It is a war on the unborn.

This war, labeled "abortion," is of epidemic proportion and is waged globally. Over fifty-five million abortions were reported worldwide in the year 1974 alone. . . . In the United States of America, over 1.5 million abortions are performed annually. ("Reverence for Life," p. 11, emphasis in original.)

As a parent of three severely handicapped children—children who are considered imperfect by society—it hurts me deeply to know that "imperfect" or unwanted babies are aborted. Who is to judge what perfection is? Certainly Cindy, Heather, and Mark are imperfect by society's standards and might be "unwanted" because they require full-time care and significant financial sacrifice. Are they productive? By society's standards, no. Have they required others to sacrifice and render service? Absolutely. Have they been detrimental to society? Unequivocally not! In fact, I believe that the positive impact they have had on thousands of lives in their few short years has been more profound than that of most "perfect" people who live and produce for a lifetime.

Because of a greater perspective of God's eternal plan and my experiences with Cindy, Heather, and Mark, I know that the worth of *every* soul is great in the sight of God, and that it is a problem of disastrous proportions when society "legally" removes imperfect, unwanted, or unproductive citizens. As Elder Russell M. Nelson said, "Life comes from life. It is a gift from our Heavenly Father. It is eternal, as he is eternal. Innocent life is not sent by him to be destroyed! This doctrine is not of me, but is that of the living God and of his divine Son." (Ibid., p. 14.)

I now feel so strongly about the value of human life that I am often overcome by Elder Boyd K. Packer's remarks:

Just a short time ago, I had a young couple come to see me in company with their bishop who had made the appointment. She, a student, wife of a student, had measles afflict their two-year-old daughter; and it was a very severe case of measles. She contracted it and underwent the usual adult experience of having it hit her harder than it had the youngster. It was only when she was recovering that she found she was pregnant. Her doctor immediately recommended an abortion. She was concerned about it and sought other counsel. Two other doctors confirmed the recommendation. Two of the three doctors were members of the Church.

And there came a Gethsemane to that young husband and wife—what to do? The best medical advice they could get agreed in counsel, but she said, "What does the Church teach?" The doctor alleged to her that the Church approved it. Finally, after their Gethsemane, this young couple determined that they would take the course of living with whatever problems presented themselves; but that they would keep their child. And they had come for a special blessing.

I told this young mother that not too long ago I had seen someone who fifteen years ago had been in the same situation, but who had taken the other course. With the best knowledge and information that the world could provide and considering some supposedly very important ethical principles involved, they had decided that it would be better for all concerned not to bring into the world a possibly handicapped child. And I said to this young mother, "You can imagine what happened to that mother when they moved to another city and became close to another family. One day as they were talking about moments of crisis, the other mother, pointing to a laughing, beautiful, healthy child, said, "We were really afraid about our little girl. We weren't sure she would be normal because I had the measles just after I got pregnant, and the doctors. . . ." You know the rest. (*That All May Be Edified*, p. 268–69.)

The Lord said not one of us is perfect, that all "come short of the glory of God" (Romans 3:23), and that He gives us weaknesses, or imperfections, to make us humble (see Ether 12:27). The words of Elder Nelson and Elder Packer are true—the worth of souls is great, regardless of a person's imperfections and the sacrifice required to care for them. Truthfully, I would not change my challenges of raising three severely handicapped children, for that is the price I am paying to know God.

Not from the Slime

One day, while our family was undergoing genetic testing at a university medical center, the attending physician briefly explained the genetic blueprint of the human body and then remarked unexpectedly, "I don't know where man came from, but his creation wasn't an accident." Today as I ponder her comments I am amazed by man. I marvel at the functionality of the human body, that it is an orchestrated symphony of systems and subsystems. I'm impressed that it contains a highly intelligent processing center and systems for heating, cooling, energy conversion, communication, rejuvenation, reproduction, defense, mobility, sensing, repair, and much more. I'm awed that it is so highly adaptable, that it can climb the face of an ice-covered cliff, swing on parallel bars, perform microscopic brain surgery, create a work of art, fly an airplane, and do innumerable other things.

Because of Cindy's, Heather's, and Mark's inability to consciously control their muscles, I am amazed when I see fully functioning infants and young children. I marvel as they run, play, hold an object in their hands, and speak, and I'm awed that they can learn a language at a very early age. In fact, one of the things that surprised me earlier when I arrived in Germany was that little children could speak German so well! They pronounced difficult words correctly and even conjugated verbs without knowing the rules.

I also marvel at the order, balance, beauty, and perfection of the animal and plant kingdoms. Alma truly was inspired when he refuted the comments of the atheist Korihor: "And now what evidence have ye that there is no God, or that Christ cometh not? I say unto you that ye have none, save it be your word only. But, behold, I have all things as a testimony that these things are true; and ye also have all things as a testimony unto you that they are true." (Alma 30: 40–41.) That testimony became my testimony one day while I observed two magpies building a nest. As I watched I was filled with the feeling that all things do speak of God and that truly I am living amid the work of a glorious masterpiece, with man as the ultimate creation.

As I pondered our doctor's comments on the origin of man, I remembered Elder Packer's experience:

Some years ago I returned home to find our little children waiting in the driveway. They had discovered some newly hatched chicks under the manger in the barn. When they reached for them, a protective hen rebuffed them. So they came for reinforcements.

I soon gathered a handful of little chicks for them to see and touch.

As our little girl held one of them, I said in a teasing way, "That will make a nice watchdog when it grows up, won't it?" She looked at me quizzically, as if I didn't know much.

So I changed my approach: "It won't be a watchdog, will it?" She shook her head, "No, Daddy." Then I added, "It will be a nice riding horse."

She wrinkled up her nose and gave me that "Oh, Dad!" look. For even a four-year-old knows that a chick will not be a dog, nor a horse, nor even a turkey. It will be a chicken. It will follow the pattern of its parentage. She knew that without having had a course in genetics, without a lesson or a lecture.

No lesson is more manifest in nature than that all living things do as the Lord commanded in the Creation. They reproduce "after their own kind." (See Moses 2:12, 24). They follow the pattern of their parentage. Everyone knows that; every four-year-old knows that! A bird will not become an animal nor a fish; a mammal will not beget reptiles; nor "do men gather . . . figs of thistles" (Matthew 7:16).

In the countless billions of opportunities in the reproduction of living things, one kind does not beget another. If a species ever does cross, the offspring generally cannot reproduce. The pattern for all life is the pattern of the parentage.

This is demonstrated in so many obvious ways, even an ordinary mind should understand it. Surely no one with reverence for God could believe that His children evolved from slime or from reptiles. . . . The theory of evolution, and it is a theory, will have an entirely different dimension when the workings of God in creation are fully revealed. ("The Pattern of Our Parentage," p. 67.)

My testimony of man's divine parentage was further strengthened when I read the words of President Joseph F. Smith and his counselors: "It is held by some that Adam was not the first man upon this earth, and that the original human being was a development from lower orders of the animal creation. These, however, are the theories of men. The word of the Lord declares that Adam was "the first man of all men" (Moses 1:34). . . . There is nothing . . . to indicate that the original man, the first of our race, began life as anything less than a man, or less than the human germ or embryo that becomes a man." (As quoted in Doxey, *Latter-day Prophets and the Doctrine and Covenants*, vol. 3, p. 71.)

Although I never really questioned man's origin, I am grateful that a softened heart brought me a much stronger sense of my divine parentage. How can I possibly have faith, keep the commandments, and have true self-esteem if I don't know I am truly His child? How can I effectively communicate with Him if I don't believe He is listening? What a blessing to know that I am His son and that the human race didn't have its origin in the slime of the earth. Knowing that has brought me much closer to Him.

Receiving and Giving

Recently Jo and I discussed the kindness and generosity of our home teacher in Camarillo. We concluded that if people are to be blessed for giving, there must be those who are willing to receive. The Lord said, "For what doth it profit a man if a gift is bestowed upon him, and he receive not the gift? Behold, he rejoices not in that which is given unto him, neither rejoices in him who is the giver of the gift." (D&C 88:33.) If I had allowed my pride to interfere and had rejected assistance from my home teacher, as I previously had done with my bishop, I might have hurt his feelings or denied him blessings, and, most certainly, my family would have continued to suffer. In addition, my children probably would have been denied a valuable lesson, for as Elder Neal A. Maxwell stated, "One of the many reasons some of today's children have not learned to give is that some parents do not know how to receive" (*All These Things Shall Give Thee Experience,* p. 62).

Jo and I also realized that gifts need not always be given anonymously. If our home teacher had done so, we would have missed the blessing of a close, lasting friendship with him and his family. Later, as I pondered that thought, I realized that the Savior didn't always give anonymous service. I concluded that I must follow the Spirit when deciding what, to whom, and how to give.

In retrospect, the lessons Jo and I learned from church members, our generous home teacher, and our extended families changed our lives forever. We were so overwhelmed with their charity and generosity that after my heart was softened we decided that if it were ever possible we would "invest" in people, as the Camarillo Saints and our families had done with us, rather than in gold, silver, stocks, or bonds. Consequently, we have gained an unshakable testimony of the truthfulness of President Marion G. Romney's counsel: "*May I remind you that you cannot give yourself poor in this work; you can only give yourself rich.* I have satisfied myself regarding the truthfulness of the statement made to me by Elder Melvin J. Ballard as he set me apart for my mission in 1920: 'A person cannot give a crust to the Lord without receiving a loaf in return.' " ("Welfare Services: The Savior's Program," p. 93, emphasis in original.) Likewise, the words of President Spencer W. Kimball are true: "If we give a generous fast offering, we shall increase our own prosperity both spiritually and temporally" ("Welfare Services: The Gospel in Action," p. 79).

Use of Wealth

Many years ago while stationed at March AFB, I assisted with the Combined Federal Campaign and solicited money from approximately one thousand officers and enlisted personnel. As I counted the money and pledges I observed that, with few exceptions, the more a person earned, the less he or she contributed. At the time I wondered why. Now, with my new "lenses," I see that one reason is that the natural man is never satisfied. In the words of Elder George Q. Cannon: "There is no person living, however rich he or she may be, who is entirely satisfied. There is something that he or she does not have that he or she would like to have. It is not given to men and women on the earth to be entirely satisfied, if they seek for satisfaction and happiness in worldly things." (*Gospel Truth*, vol. 2, p. 317.)

I believe that is one of the reasons ease and luxury is perhaps the hardest test in this life (see Packer, "The Choice," p. 21). Even when we gain wealth honorably through hard work, we risk becoming proud and selfish. Alma explained: "The people of the church began to wax proud, because of their exceeding riches, and their fine silks, and their fine-twined linen, and because of their many flocks and herds, and their gold and their silver, and all manner of precious things, which they had obtained by their industry; and in all these things were they lifted up in the pride of their eyes, for they began to wear very costly apparel" (Alma 4:6).

As I pondered the proper use of wealth, I remembered the parable of the talents (see Matthew 25:14–30) and recalled that as a youth I learned that a talent was a measure of gold. I then concluded that if I was blessed with any degree of wealth, I should invest it to produce greater wealth, and the Lord would reward me as I multiplied my resources. However, I have a new perspective because of the generosity of many people who rendered assistance to our family. I now realize that whatever "talent" the Lord blesses me with, be it faith, testimony, wealth, a skill, or intelligence, He expects me to multiply it, paradoxically, by sharing it. As President Spencer W. Kimball explained: "The more we serve our fellowmen in appropriate ways, the more substance there is to our souls. We become more significant individuals as we serve others indeed, it is easier to 'find' ourselves because there is so much more of us to find!" ("The Abundant Life," p. 3.)

I now realize that even if I prosper it isn't just the work I do to obtain wealth, but the physical abilities, intelligence, wisdom, health, and opportunities the Lord blesses me with that enable me to produce it (see Mosiah 2:21). Consequently, I believe He expects me to use a portion of it to help others.

When Jesus told the rich young ruler who had kept all the commandments from his youth to sell all that he had, give it to the poor, and follow Him, "he went away sorrowful: for he had great possessions. Then said Jesus unto his disciples, Verily I say unto you, That a rich man shall hardly [*Greek,* with difficulty] enter into the kingdom of heaven" (Matthew 19:22–23). Truly, if I am selfish, fail to share what I have with others, and remain unrepentant, I will lose my eternal reward.

King Benjamin taught the importance of serving others: "And now, . . . for the sake of retaining a remission of your sins from day to day, that ye may walk guiltless before God—I would that ye should impart of your substance to the poor, every man according to that which he hath, such as feeding the hungry, clothing the naked, visiting the sick and administering to their relief, both spiritually and temporally, according to their wants" (Mosiah 4:26). And President Kimball said:

> Many people spend most of their time working in the service of a self-image that includes sufficient money, stocks, bonds, investment portfolios, property, credit cards, furnishings, automobiles, and the like to *guarantee* carnal security throughout, it is hoped, a long and happy life. Forgotten is the fact that our assignment is to use these many resources in our families and quorums to build up the kingdom of God—to further the missionary effort and the genealogical and temple work; to raise our children up as fruitful servants unto the Lord; to bless others in every way, that they may also be fruitful. Instead, we expend these blessings on our own desires. ("The False Gods We Worship," p. 4, emphasis in original.)

Elder Ezra Taft Benson suggested the role possessions should play in our lives: "Our affections are often too highly placed upon the paltry perishable objects. Material treasures of earth are merely to provide us, as it were, room and board while we are here at school. It is for us to place gold, silver, houses, stocks, lands, cattle, and other earthly possessions in their proper place. Yes, this is but a place of temporary duration. We are here to learn the first lesson toward exaltation—obedience to the Lord's gospel plan." (*The Teachings of Ezra Taft Benson,* p. 26.)

One of the greatest challenges Jo and I face is determining how to use the resources we have been blessed with. My prayer is that my sentiments will always be those of the hymn "Because I Have Been Given Much."

Because I have been given much, I too must give;
Because of thy great bounty, Lord, each day I live
I shall divide my gifts from Thee
With ev'ry brother that I see
Who has the need of help from me.

Because I have been sheltered, fed by thy good care,
I cannot see another's lack and I not share
My glowing fire, my loaf of bread,
My roof's safe shelter over head,
That he too may be comforted.

Because I have been blessed by thy great love, dear Lord,
I'll share thy love again, according to thy word.
I shall give love to those in need;
I'll show that love by word and deed:
Thus shall my thanks be thanks indeed.*

By the Sweat of My Brow

One of my most important new perspectives was an understanding of the value of work. Because I grew up on a small farm I had morning and evening chores in the garden, in the orchard, and with the animals. The work was never ending, and I hated it because I wanted to do other things. I loved to play with friends and to hunt frogs in the marsh near our home, build and launch rockets, and climb the nearby foothills. I thought life would be much more enjoyable if I didn't have to work. Then as I became older and saw people retire, I looked forward to the day when I could retire too.

---

* "Because I Have Been Given Much" from *Light of the Years* by Grace Noll Crowell. Copyright 1936 by Harper and Row, Publishers, Inc. Copyright © renewed 1964 by Grace Noll Crowell. Reprinted by permission of Harper-Collins Publishers, Inc.

My attitude about work began to change following my Pearl Harbor Day. My employer kept the building open so employees could use company resources to help find employment. I didn't have to work for seven weeks, and yet I would receive full pay. In addition, I had fourteen weeks of severance pay and six weeks of accumulated vacation. In total, I would receive a full salary for twenty-seven weeks without working! Initially it was great to sleep in and do whatever I wanted. However, after a few days of going to work only when I needed to use the phone or make copies of my resume, I realized that I needed work to help motivate me. I needed rules, regulations, and routines in order to be productive.

Later I remembered that God commanded Adam to earn bread by the sweat of his brow *all* the days of his life (see Genesis 3:19). And Elder Bruce R. McConkie taught: "We are here on earth to work—to work long, hard, arduous hours, to work until our backs ache and our tired muscles knot, to work all our days. This mortal probation is one in which we are to eat our bread in the sweat of our faces until we return to the dust from whence we came. Work is the law of life; it is the ruling principle in the lives of the Saints." ("Stand Independent above All Other Creatures," p. 93.)

President David O. McKay provided additional insight: "Learn to like your work. Learn to say, 'This is my work, my glory, not my doom.' God has blessed us with the privilege of working. When he said, 'Earn thy bread by the sweat of thy brow,' he gave us a blessing. . . . Too much leisure is dangerous. Work is a divine gift." (*A Royal Priesthood*, p. 65.) And Elder Spencer W. Kimball said, " 'Six days shalt thou labor, . . .' (Exodus 20:9). Yet ever-increasing hours of leisure provide ever-increasing opportunities for Sabbath breaking and commandment ignoring, and strikes and lobbying go on to increase damaging leisure and decrease work hours further." ("Listen to the Prophet's Voice," p. 939.)

As I reflected on "damaging leisure," I remembered Elder Neal A. Maxwell's words: "For many reasons, work is a spiritual necessity. . . . Idleness is not in itself a vice, but a rust that attacks all virtues. In Ezekiel, we read that one of the sins of

Sodom was an 'abundance of idleness' made possible, apparently, by some affluence or 'fulness of bread.' (Ezekiel 16:49.)" (*Wherefore Ye Must Press Forward,* p. 7.) I also remembered that Elder L. Tom Perry counseled:

> Teaching children the joy of honest labor is one of the greatest of all gifts you can bestow upon them. I am convinced that one of the reasons for the breakup of so many couples today is the failure of parents to teach and train sons in their responsibility to provide and care for their families and to enjoy the challenge this responsibility brings. Many of us also have fallen short in instilling within our daughters the desire of bringing beauty and order into their homes through homemaking.
>
> Oh, how essential it is that children be taught early in life the joy that comes from starting and fashioning a job that is the workmanship of their own hands. Teach children the joy of honest labor. Provide a foundation for life that builds confidence and fulfillment in each life. ("The Joy of Honest Labor," p. 62.)

Since work is so important, choosing to avoid it surely has eternal consequences. For that reason I'm saddened when people win large sums of money and no longer have to work. It seems to me that such income violates the law of the harvest, that "whatsoever ye sow, that shall ye also reap" (D&C 6:33). President Kimball noted: "The dignity and self-esteem that honest work produces are essential to happiness" ("Listen to the Prophets," p. 78). Additionally, it seems to me that the focus of my work must be correct, for surely work, like any virtue, can become a vice if I don't find the proper balance. Finding that balance, I believe, is one of the great challenges of life.

Incidentally, I also believe that Heather and Mark understood the importance of work. Heather always wanted to help Jo with housework, and Mark always wants to help me with my chores. Even if my work requires physical exertion, such as lifting a large rock or digging a hole, Mark always "helps" by grunting and groaning as I strain with the task.

CHAPTER 16

Guidelines for Living

Another blessing that came as the Lord softened my heart was a clearer understanding of some principles to help guide me through life.

Never Give Up

One of the most important guidelines I learned was that when I struggle under the weight of trials and my life is filled with stress and despair, I must not let go of the iron rod as I press forward to the tree of life. I must keep doing the basic things I know are right and remain steadfast, even when life is difficult. (See 2 Nephi 31:20; Alma 1:25.) For instance, I might be tested by a lack of understanding of why something isn't as I believe it should be or why someone acted as they did. I might be troubled by a Church doctrine or policy, a Church leader who sinned or received a calling I don't believe was deserved, or a friend, neighbor, or relative who offended me. It might be that promises made in my patriarchal blessing can't be fulfilled during mortality. Whatever the trial, I need to remain steadfast in my testimony of Jesus and to not lose faith in Him or His Church. As Elder Mark E. Petersen said: "You know we are on the 'Old Ship Zion.' We are in the midst of the ocean. A storm comes on, and, as sailors say, she labors very hard. 'I am not going to stay here,' says one; 'I don't believe this is the "Ship Zion."' 'But we are in the midst of the ocean.' 'I don't care, I am not going to stay here.' Off goes the coat, and he jumps overboard. Will he not be drowned? Yes. So with those who leave this Church. It is the 'Old Ship Zion.' Let us stay in it." ("Salvation Comes Through the Church," p. 110.)

Essentially, I must keep doing what I know I should while I patiently wait for further guidance and understanding, because as Elder Boyd K. Packer stated:

> You cannot force spiritual things. Such words as compel, coerce, constrain, pressure, demand, do not describe our privileges with the Spirit. You can no more force the Spirit to respond than you can force a bean to sprout, or an egg to hatch before its time. You can create a climate to foster growth, nourish, and protect; but you cannot force or compel: you must await the growth.
>
> Do not be impatient to gain great spiritual knowledge. Let it grow, help it grow, but do not force it or you will open the way to be misled. ("The Candle of the Lord," p. 53.)

Some might find answers to their questions very quickly, while others might not receive them until after this mortal probation. Whatever time is required to understand our adversity, we must not give in to Satan. We must keep struggling and press forward, always holding on to the iron rod. Otherwise, the unhappiness that follows is sure; it's just a matter of when it will come. Thankfully, during the years I suffered in bitterness I was blessed with sufficient faith to study the words of the prophets, pray, attend church and the temple, and fulfill my church and family responsibilities. Although I questioned my adversity and continually wondered why the Lord didn't heal my children, my faith kept me from totally rebelling against the truth. That was a key to my overcoming adversity.

Now that I better understand the way to perfection, my challenge is to do what I know is right. Of that challenge Elder Melvin J. Ballard said, "The greatest conflict that any man or woman will ever have . . . will be the battle that is had with self" (*Melvin J. Ballard . . . Crusader for Righteousness*, p. 179).

Forgive Others

A guideline that I had known but only gave lip service to was the principle of forgiveness. The Savior taught, "For if ye forgive men their trespasses, your heavenly Father will also forgive you: But if ye forgive not men their trespasses, neither will your Father forgive your trespasses" (Matthew 6:14–15). The Savior, the only sinless person to ever live on this earth, set the pattern for us by forgiving those who crucified Him (see Luke 23:34). To receive peace and comfort I must forgive others as He did, even if I am the innocent victim.

With a new understanding of forgiveness, I have changed my approach to dealing with people. For example, each day as I travel to and from work I drive several miles on a two-lane highway where passing is prohibited and the posted speed limit is forty miles per hour. Almost daily someone pulls out in front of me and proceeds at twenty miles per hour, thus forcing me to slow down. Previously I became very irritated in those situations and cursed the driver for being inconsiderate. Now, instead of getting angry I often say, "I forgive you, for you don't know how you've offended me," and I have much more patience to let people in front of me. It is amazing how forgiving others helps me feel better about myself and the people around me.

Set Proper Goals

As I explained earlier, I believed I could have anything I wanted if I planned, worked diligently, and kept the commandments. Now, after more than two decades of failing to achieve most major goals, I realize I needed to seek the Lord's inspiration as I set goals, because only He knows my true needs. For instance, after Cindy became sick I should have sought the Lord's help to determine if it was needful for her to attend kindergarten four years later. Since I didn't do that, I set goals for her that were my wants rather than my needs. I could have spared myself considerable frustration if I had sought to know God's will before I set goals regarding Cindy's future.

I also set improper goals when I tried to become prosperous.

I wanted that, but I didn't need that as long as I was proud and selfish. From an eternal perspective, I needed to repent of my pride and selfishness so I could achieve my eternal desire to eventually live in the celestial kingdom. I should have followed Jacob's counsel: "But before ye seek for riches, seek ye for the kingdom of God" (Jacob 2:18).

Now, when setting personal goals, I do the following:

- Determine my most important eternal desire, always remembering that the Lord will honor that desire (see Alma 29:4) and, within the limits of my moral agency, help me attain it. Then I set intermediate goals that will help me achieve that eternal desire.
- Determine intermediate goals by pondering, praying, seeking the will of the Lord, and separating wants from eternal needs. These goals must reflect my righteous desires. It is important that they are "needful" and that I "ask not amiss" (see 2 Nephi 4:35). Often I consult my patriarchal blessing for guidance, because I believe it reflects the personality and desires I had while I lived in my premortal home.

Judge Not

While striving to understand self-esteem, I realized that prior to my softened heart I was highly critical and judgmental. I criticized my family and others for not thinking the way I did, and I continually judged their actions based on my perspective. For instance, as I traveled I mentally criticized people for the way they maintained their homes, yards, and cars, and when I interacted with others I mentally judged their appearance, manners, motives, and intentions.

I now recognize that my actions were very wrong. Since I can't see into another's heart, I can't tell if he or she is motivated by the "world's self-esteem" or "God's self-esteem." Besides, what value is there in criticizing or judging another person's actions? "Who am I to judge another when I walk imperfectly?" (Susan Evans McCloud, "Lord, I Would Follow Thee," *Hymns*, no. 220.) I believe I do it to justify my own actions so that I will feel better about myself. I now know that judging unrighteously contributes to the "world's self-esteem," hardens my feelings toward my fellowmen, and is nonproductive. Furthermore, I will be judged as I judge others (see Moroni 7:18).

Another aspect of "judging not" is that I must not compare myself with others or wish I were someone else. Since each of us has different strengths and weaknesses and a different mission in life and is at a different stage of eternal development, I must learn to love myself as Elder Packer counseled:

> Be glad that you are you. Never, never wish that you were someone else. You *are* you. Accept that. You will always be you.
>
> You may complain about your lot in life. Your social or economic inheritance may not be to your desire. You may think yourself limited mentally. . . . You may not like the body you are inhabiting—but remember that ultimately it may be perfected. You are you—a separate, individual intelligence. You are a spirit inhabiting a body. . . . Sometimes we make an appraisal of ourselves in comparison with another and foolishly wish we were somebody else. Never do that. Thank the Lord for who you are and what you may become. (*Let Not Your Heart Be Troubled*, pp. 97–98, emphasis in original.)

Not only is it detrimental to compare myself to others and wish that I were someone else, but it is also detrimental to wish I were born in a different place or time. Nephi, the son of Helaman, who lived almost six hundred years after Lehi left Jerusalem, said:

> Oh, that I could have had my days in the days when my father Nephi first came out of the land of Jerusalem, that I could have joyed with him in the promised land; then were his people easy to be entreated, firm to keep the commandments of God, and slow to be led to do iniquity; and they were quick to hearken unto the words of the Lord—

Yea, if my days could have been in those days, then would my soul have had joy in the righteousness of my brethren.

But behold, I am consigned that these are my days, and that my soul shall be filled with sorrow because of this the wickedness of my brethren. (Helaman 7:7–9.)

As Nephi did, I must resign myself to live in my days, because Satan wants me to wish that I were someone else or had different opportunities. He wants me to compare myself with others to entice me to pursue the counterfeit success associated with the "world's self-esteem." Therefore, I must not compare my opportunities, my trials, my blessings, or anything else, for as Elder Packer stated: "We get conditioned to the idea that only one team or one person can win. This is not true of spiritual things. There is plenty of room in the Celestial Kingdom for everyone. We are not in competition for some few spaces. The only one we are in competition with is our former self." (As quoted in Maxwell, *Wherefore Ye Must Press Forward,* p. 107.)

Comparing my trials with others' trials is also unproductive and frustrating, for I feel that God has a unique plan for each of His children. Elder Neal A. Maxwell said, "Just as no two snowflakes are precisely alike in design, so the configurations of life's challenges differ also. We must remember that while the Lord reminded the Prophet Joseph Smith that he had not yet suffered as Job, *only the Lord can compare crosses."* (*All These Things Shall Give Thee Experience,* p. 48, emphasis in original.) I believe each person's plan of life, or curriculum, has been specifically tailored to meet his individual needs, strengths, and weaknesses, and to provide personal growth and development.

Studying, Not Reading

Because I began reading the scriptures at an early age, and because I read them many times after serving a mission, I thought I knew a lot about the gospel. However, not until my heart was softened did I realize that generally I had been *reading* the scriptures, but not really *studying* them with the Spirit. I understood many stories, facts, and histories, and some of the principles, but because of my pride, my understanding was actually very limited. Not until my heart was softened did the weightier knowledge come. Now, with an expanded insight, I see that the words of the prophets—especially those found in the Book of Mormon—can help me draw close to the Lord.

One thing that significantly enhanced my study of the scriptures was the edition introduced in 1981. Although I initially didn't appreciate the new footnotes, chapter headings, and cross references, I now love them and truly understand Elder Boyd K. Packer's comments: "These references constitute the most comprehensive compilation of scripture information on the mission and teachings of the Lord Jesus Christ that has ever been assembled in the history of the world" ("Scriptures," p. 53).

I now find my study of the scriptures to be much more enjoyable and insightful than ever before. Even the words of Isaiah have been opened to my understanding—not via a commentary, but by the Spirit. Although I know I can't force spiritual things, I have learned that I can greatly enhance the likelihood of receiving spiritual insights if I study the scriptures. As Elder Spencer W. Kimball testified: "I find that when I get casual in my relationships with divinity and when it seems that no divine ear is listening and no divine voice is speaking, that I am far, far away. If I immerse myself in the scriptures the distance narrows and the spirituality returns. I find myself loving more intensely those whom I must love with all my heart and mind and strength, and loving them more, I find it easier to abide their counsel." (*The Teachings of Spencer W. Kimball*, p. 135.)

Seek Inspired Counsel

While Jo and I were suffering from our adversity, it was suggested that we seek professional counseling to help us cope with our stress and discouragement. Twice we attended parent support groups for parents of handicapped children, but I found them to be of little value because no one struggled with three severely handicapped children and no one understood how I felt. As a result, the only counselors we ever confided in were priesthood leaders.

In retrospect, I am grateful for those leaders' help and guidance. Perhaps professional counselors could have helped me overcome my pride, selfishness, and unrighteous dominion, but I doubt it. I needed to humble myself, repent, and ask Jo for forgiveness before I could find peace in our relationship.

Regarding the use of counselors, Elder Packer advised:

> We have reached a state when evidently we cannot get any considerable number of people together in school, business, society, the military, or anywhere else without having them attended by a sufficient number of counselors, psychologists, and psychiatrists. I look with concern on the increased dependency upon psychologists and psychiatrists. Now, explicitly, I did *not* say I look with concern upon the use of them. I said I look with concern upon our growing *dependency* upon them. I have misgivings about the growing tendency to diagnose every aberration of behavior as the beginnings of "psycho-something-or-other."
>
> Let me caution you to be careful. Do not tell your troubles to the wrong people. We do not call a neurosurgeon every time we have a slight headache, and you had better be careful before going to an analyst.
>
> May I say that I recognize the need for professional help from psychiatrists. I have at times referred individuals to them, but I say again that I look with concern upon our growing *dependency* upon them. I would suppose that when there is that measure of difficulty or disorder which requires professional attention, that attention ought to be given on the referral from the bishop and from the medical doctor. But we are at the point now where at the slightest aberration in behavior we are sent for professional clinical inspection.
>
> I am not always sure that the measures that are taken are wise. For instance, I am not sure it is always wise to try to erase grief with sedatives. Perhaps when we know the true nature of man, we may be more discriminating in the administering of sedatives in an attempt to ease grief or bring peace to broken hearts, and we may be more careful in the buffering of individuals from life through the use of tranquilizers. (*Let Not Your Heart Be Troubled,* pp. 249–250, emphasis in original.)

Describing life's challenges, Elder Packer stated:

> It was meant to be that life would be a challenge. To suf-
> fer some anxiety, some depression, some disappointment,
> even some failure is normal.
> Teach our members that if they have a good, miserable
> day once in a while, or several in a row, to stand steady and
> face them. Things will straighten out.
> There is great purpose in our struggle in life. ("Solving
> Emotional Problems," p. 93.)

> The Lord never told us that life was supposed to be easy,
> comfortable, or convenient. Life is all upstream. It is all up-
> hill. If we quit the struggle, we will be washed downstream.
> (*That All Might Be Edified*, p. 249.)

> When someone is discouraged and feels that he cannot
> solve a problem on his own, he may be right, but at least he
> is obligated to try. Every personal resource available to him
> should be committed before he takes another step. (*Teach Ye
> Diligently*, p 203.)

With the counsel of Elder Packer and other Brethren in
mind, I have compiled the following step-by-step process for
solving future personal problems:

1. I will try my hardest to solve my problems myself, always
remembering to accept help from those who are inspired to assist me—and always remembering the counsel of Elder George
Q. Morris: "The answer to all the problems in the world is the
gospel of Jesus Christ, which enables us to overcome all adversities, sin, and death, and go back into the presence of God (as
quoted in Doxey, *Latter-day Prophets and the Doctrine and
Covenants*, vol. 1, p. 325.) Also, the counsel of Elder Packer:
"True doctrine, understood, changes attitudes and behavior.
The study of the doctrines of the gospel will improve behavior
quicker than a study of behavior will improve behavior. . . . That
is why we stress so forcefully the study of the doctrines of the
gospel." ("Little Children," p. 17.)

And finally, the advice of Elder Richard G. Scott, who spoke
of overcoming serious transgressions—even addictions: "If you

are trapped and there seems to be no way out, . . . the way through is based on faith in Jesus Christ and obedience to His commandments. It is the only way to permanently cure the damage to mind and spirit caused by unrighteous acts. It also provides healing, within the bounds of eternal law, to a body devastated by the effects of transgression." ("Healing Your Damaged Life," p. 61.)

2. If I need additional help I will seek assistance from a trustworthy friend who truly understands the meaning of repentance, the power of the Atonement, and the relationship between truth and agency. In the process I will remember Elder Scott's counsel that "a true friend is not one that always encourages you to do what you want to do, but one who helps you do what you know you ought to do" (ibid., p. 62).

3. I will seek the help of my bishop. As Elder Packer taught, although most bishops haven't been trained as counselors, the mantle of the bishop provides them with inspiration and guidance for those within their stewardship. "The mantle is far, far greater than the intellect; the priesthood is the guiding power" (*Let Not Your Heart Be Troubled*, p. 103). Further, bishops "have a power to soothe and to sanctify and to heal that others are not given" ("Solving Emotional Problems," p. 92). Occasionally, as Jo and I felt impressed, we asked our bishop for guidance, but only after carefully considering Elder Packer's admonition to avoid the spiritual dole (see ibid., pp. 91–93). Parenthetically, many years ago when Jo and I were concerned about caring for Cindy, Heather, and Mark when we became old, our most helpful advice came from a wise priesthood leader: "Don't be overly concerned about the future. Just take one day at a time, and don't cross your bridges before you get to them."

4. If, on rare occasions, I encounter a problem I can't solve myself or with the help of priesthood leaders, I will choose a professional counselor who:

- Understands repentance, the Atonement, divine parentage, and man's eternal nature.
- Believes in revelation, since that is the only means to receive answers to individual problems. Typically counselors give solutions in the form of techniques that are

based on large population samples, but they usually are not in a position to give solutions based on personal, eternal needs. Such needs are discerned only through the Holy Ghost.

- Follows Elder Packer's counsel to avoid "sensitivity training, self-actualization, training groups, . . . simulation, transactional analysis, encounter groups, marathon counseling sessions, . . . value clarification, character education, and so on," because "there are major emotional and spiritual dangers involved in such procedures, and members of the Church would do well to be very cautious, even to leave them alone" (*Teach Ye Diligently*, p. 201). One of the many reasons his counsel feels correct is that there is no group repentance. Repentance must be done on an individual basis.

- Heeds Elder Packer's counsel regarding emotional and psychological disorders and addictions:

> Sometimes study can magnify rather than reduce these problems, particularly when they are psychologically oriented. Again, I repeat: Any position which ignores the revelations of the Lord pertaining to the nature of man must ultimately prove to be inadequate, if not downright false and destructive. Virtually none of the writers on these subjects are sensitive to such revelations.
>
> I have almost come to believe that the chances of rescuing people from these addictions are inversely proportional to the number of books they have read on the subject. (*Let Not Your Heart Be Troubled*, p. 251.)

Thankfully, Jo and I found strength and comfort from Church leaders who did not trust in man's wisdom or in the arm of flesh (see 2 Nephi 28:31) but who understood that the Savior is man's ultimate source of peace and comfort.

Don't Step on the Gas
When You're Going Around a Curve

One of the catalysts that helped me slowly overcome the frustrations that accompanied my previous bitterness occurred while a friend and I were talking. I had explained that I felt extremely frustrated because I could never do all that I needed to do, since caring for Cindy, Heather, and Mark was so time-consuming. His reply was cryptic and unexpected: "Don't step on the gas when you're going around a curve." Then he continued:

> Bruce, you're a wonderful person and a fine example. You're doing what you're supposed to be doing. When you're going through a period of stress in your life, like you are now because you are caring for Cindy, Heather, and Mark, don't do more than you can. In other words, don't run faster than is needful. When you're going around a curve in life, let up on the gas. Then, when you're around it, step on the gas again. Right now you are going around a curve. Your most important responsibility is to care for your family. Don't worry about all the other things you think need to be done. Heavenly Father understands that you can't do everything you want to do. He truly understands.

Although my friend's comments were comforting, later I wondered which commandments or counsel I shouldn't worry about. Didn't I have to keep all of the commandments and follow the admonition of the Brethren all of the time? The Savior said, "Be ye therefore perfect, even as your Father which is in heaven is perfect" (Matthew 5:48), and that He couldn't "look upon sin with the least degree of allowance" (D&C 1:31). Didn't I need to worry about how I was falling short of their expectations?

My answer came early one Sunday morning in July 1987, when I awakened with the thought that I should worry only about my two worst sins and not about all the things that my family circumstances made it impossible for me to do—the Lord knew the desires of my heart. Although that idea seemed strange, the thought continued that I should remain steadfast and work to overcome my worst sins first.

As I contemplated my desires, the words of King Benjamin reminded me that the desires of my heart must be correct: "I would that ye say in your hearts that: I give not because I have not, but if I had I would give. And now, if ye say this in your hearts ye remain guiltless, otherwise ye are condemned. . . ." (Mosiah 4:24–25.) Similarly, the Lord told Joseph Smith that gifts of the spirit "are given for the benefit of those who love me and keep all my commandments, and him that seeketh so to do" (D&C 46:9). And later He said, "For I, the Lord, will judge all men according to their works, according to the desire of their hearts" (D&C 137:9). Those words were comforting, but I realized I must not rationalize my responsibilities and duties.

With those ideas in mind I began in earnest to repent of my two worst sins—repentance that I had procrastinated for a long time. In the process I remembered my friend's counsel: "Don't step on the gas when you're going around a curve. . . . Father understands that you can't do everything you want to do." I finally understood his sound advice. As long as I was striving to overcome my worst sins and kept doing the basic things I had been doing, such as attending church and serving when possible, keeping financial obligations to the Lord, and ensuring that the intents of my heart were righteous, I felt very much at ease. A settling peace filled my heart, and the anxiety and frustration I felt as I tried to complete an endless checklist of rules and responsibilities was removed. I no longer felt guilty if I had to miss church to watch Cindy so Jo could attend, and I wasn't despondent if I couldn't participate in a ward activity.

Recently, while reflecting on my feeling of comfort, I understood my mission president's counsel: "When Satan can't successfully tempt people who are living the best they can, he points out everything they are supposed to do but aren't doing, to make them feel guilty and discouraged." I also remembered prophets and priesthood leaders who reaffirmed the idea that the Lord doesn't expect me to be perfect all at once—that I must work on my worst sins first.

Not Perfect Immediately

Even the Savior continued from grace to grace until He received a fullness (see D&C 93:13). President Lorenzo Snow noted:

When Jesus lay in the manger, a helpless infant, He knew not that He was the Son of God, and that formerly He created the earth. When the edict of Herod was issued, He knew nothing of it; He had not power to save Himself; and His father and mother had to take Him and fly into Egypt to preserve Him from the effects of that edict. Well, He grew up into manhood, and during His progress it was revealed unto Him who He was, and for what purpose He was in the world. The glory and power He possessed before He came into the world was made known unto Him. (In Doxey, *Latter-day Prophets and the Doctrine and Covenants,* vol. 3, p. 266.)

King Benjamin taught: "And see that all these things [service to our fellowmen] are done in wisdom and order; for it is not requisite that a man should run faster than he has strength. And again, it is expedient that he should be diligent, . . . therefore, all things must be done in order." (Mosiah 4:27.) The Lord didn't prescribe how fast I should run to accomplish everything He has prescribed, only that I should be diligent—and as Elder Neal A. Maxwell said, "anxiously engaged" but not "hectically engaged" (see *Men and Women of Christ,* p. 24).

Worst Sins First

President Spencer W. Kimball said: "What are your eccentricities, if any? I think nearly all people have some. If so, then go to work. Classify them, weigh them, corral them, and eliminate them one at a time." (*Come unto the Father in the Name of Jesus,* p. 60.) This process was clarified further in the same priesthood manual:

Make a list of your most serious sins and temptations. . . .

Next, classify the things you have written on your list. Rank them in order of seriousness or difficulty. The Lord can only bless you to the level of your most serious personal sin. So if you work on less serious matters first, you will not receive the blessing you desire. Sometimes men repent of less serious matters, outward things, and then complain that they do not feel any more spiritual, when in reality they should start with the most serious sin or temptation in their lives. (Ibid., pp. 60–61.)

I finally understood why I hadn't been able to get as close to the Lord as I wanted. I had been working to correct my "minor" sins while doing very little to eradicate my worst sins.

Clearly, the Lord does not expect perfection immediately. Instead He expects me to stay on the path and to press forward to the tree of life, and He requires only that which I am capable of giving. It's my diligence and the direction I am moving along the path that is highly important, not how fast I am running. In the words of Stephen E. Robinson: "The Savior requires from each of us a specific percentage: all that we have, or one hundred percent. Yet each individual's one hundred percent will be a different quantity from everyone else's, depending on the spiritual knowledge and maturity of the individual. What a marvelous flexibility—he never requires more than I am able to give, and what he does require of me is always appropriate to my knowledge and circumstances." (*Believing Christ*, p. 49.)

Not Everything Worth Doing Is Worth Doing Well

One day at work, as I struggled to complete a large, unexpected assignment on a tight schedule, a friend remarked, "Remember, not everything worth doing is worth doing well." His comment puzzled me, so he explained, "Not everything needs to be done perfectly or with A-grade quality—sometimes C-grade quality is sufficient. Our challenge in life is to determine which is which."

My friend's explanation confused me. Perhaps it was the Savior's words to be perfect (see Matthew 5:48). Maybe it was the 4-H motto to "make the best better." Possibly it was the admonition "Anything worth doing is worth doing well." Perhaps I was born with a perfectionist mentality. Whatever the reason, from the time I turned twelve until I left to serve a mission, I had perfect church attendance at all required meetings. I fulfilled Moroni's specified requirements perfectly (see Moroni 10:4–5) and easily received a testimony. In high school I had perfect grades, I was "perfect" in many student activities, and I succeeded in being "perfect" in scouting and 4-H. In fact, I was such a perfectionist that when I left home to serve a mission, my brother, who inherited my bedroom, pinned a note on the bedroom door which read, "Don't look for perfection here—it left." The net effect of my youthful behavior was that I developed a "perfectionist-checklist" mentality. Not only had I forgotten the Savior's role, but I thought I could get to heaven on my own if I completed all the items on my "to do" list before I died.

Later, as I pondered my friend's advice, I realized that the same task might be performed with different degrees of quality, depending on the circumstances. For instance, when I made my bed during military basic training I had to pull the sheets and blanket so tightly that a quarter bounced off the blanket, but now I don't make my bed with that same degree of perfection. Certainly I could make my bed as I did earlier, but unless I get a particular satisfaction from it, my time could be better spent doing something else. Likewise, such tasks as cleaning snow off the driveway, shining my shoes, or cleaning the house don't need to be done perfectly. In many cases, I now feel that a job done is a job well done. The challenge I have is to make the most of the time the Lord has given me to accomplish my life's mission without getting sidetracked by unimportant details.

Practices or Principles

As I pondered my checklist mentality I realized that I had been somewhat like the ancient Jews—a list of do's and don'ts governed my life. I worried more about the practices and the letter of the law than I did about the principles and the spirit of the law.

That idea was forcefully communicated to me during a family home evening several years ago. We were talking about things we had taught our children, when one of the girls said, "Dad, all I can remember you teaching me is to 'turn off the light' and 'shut the refrigerator door'!" Later, as I pondered her comments, I realized that my harping about practices had hindered my ability to teach my children the principles of the gospel.

As I continued to ponder I also realized that the family traditions I enjoyed when I was young were practices, not principles. Jo and I were free to develop our own traditions as we felt impressed. Although it is much easier to follow a checklist than to heed the still small voice and apply gospel principles, surely the key to influencing my family is to follow the Spirit rather than a checklist.

A fuller understanding of the differences between practices and principles came when I read Bishop Glenn L. Pace's words: "As great as the various programs of the Church are, they carry with them a potential danger. If we are not careful, it is possible to get so wrapped up in the plan that we forget the principles. We can fall into the trap of mistaking traditions for principles and confusing programs with their objectives. . . . Programs blindly followed bring us to a *discipline* of doing good, but principles properly understood and practiced bring us to a *disposition* to do good." ("Principles and Programs," pp. 23–24, emphasis in original.)

Bishop Pace explained further about following the Spirit:

> One Saturday morning I was on my way to fulfill an assignment on a welfare farm. We were to clean the weeds out of an irrigation ditch. My route took me past the home of an elderly widow in my ward, who was weeding her front yard. The temperature was already in the mid-eighties, and she looked like she was near to having sunstroke. For a fleeting moment I thought I should stop and lend a helping hand, but my conscience allowed me to drive on by because, after all, I had an assignment on the welfare farm. I wonder what would have happened if I had followed the spontaneous prompting of the Spirit and unleashed the genuine compassion I was feeling. I wondered what would have happened to her; I wonder what would have happened to me. But I couldn't do that because I hadn't been assigned. (Ibid., pp. 23–24.)

Truly, it is following the Spirit and the principles of the gospel that enables me to find peace and eventually achieve salvation.

Wickedness or Happiness

Unlike Heather and Mark, I never realized that I choose happiness by the decisions I make—that the key to happiness, and eventually peace, is found in keeping the commandments. From my early youth I could recite Alma's counsel to his son Corianton, "Wickedness never was happiness" (Alma 41:10), but I only gave it lip service. Unfortunately, I learned by trial and error that President Spencer W. Kimball's observations were correct: "Whoever said that sin was not fun? . . . It promises immunity from restrictions, temporary freedoms. It can momentarily satisfy hunger, thirst, desire, urges, passions, wants, without immediately paying the price." (*The Teachings of Spencer W. Kimball,* p. 152.) Additionally, President Benson helped me understand why I didn't worry about sinning: "One of the trials of life is that we do not usually receive immediately the full blessing for righteousness or the full cursing for wickedness. That it will come is certain, but ofttimes there is a waiting period that occurs, as was the case with Job and Joseph. In the meantime, the wicked think they are getting away with something. The Book of Mormon teaches that the wicked 'have joy in their works for a season . . .' (3 Nephi 27:11)." (*The Teachings of President Ezra Taft Benson,* p. 352.)

After my heart softened, a fuller understanding of happiness came when I learned a principle that Elder Neal A. Maxwell expressed: We are free to choose wickedness or happiness, but we are not free to choose wickedness *and* happiness (see "Insights from My Life," p. 199). It was then that I realized that I was trying to make wickedness and happiness coexist in my life, that I had a rather casual attitude about sin. I had earlier thought I must not commit major sin, but "minor" sins could be easily repented of later—God would overlook them for the time being. Consequently, I didn't worry about the swear words that I read in spy novels, about the movies I saw as long as they weren't rated R; or about suggestive lyrics in beautiful songs. After all, I was a mature adult.

Unfortunately, I didn't realize that even "minor" sins weaken my will to live righteously and predispose me to sinning! President McKay quoted William James: "We are spinning our own fates good or evil. . . . Every smallest stroke of virtue or of vice leaves its ever so little scar. The drunken Rip Van Winkle, in Jefferson's play, excuses himself for every fresh dereliction by saying, 'I won't count this time.' Well! he may not count it . . . but it is being counted none the less. Down among his nerve-cells and fibers the molecules are counting it, registering and storing it up to be used against him when the next temptation comes." (In *Come unto the Father in the Name of Jesus,* p. 76.)

With that understanding, Elder Boyd K. Packer's strictness was no longer puzzling: "I will not consent to contamination of the slightest single spot from a perverse source. . . . I will not consent to any influence from the adversary." (*That All May Be Edified,* pp. 271–72.)

With a clearer insight, I now see that the commandments are not restrictive or limiting but are a guide to help me through mortality. Elder Spencer W. Kimball noted: "He truly is free who is master of situations, habits, passions, urges, and de-sires. If one must yield to appetite or passion and follow its de-mands, he is truly the servant of a dictator." (*The Teachings of Spencer W. Kimball,* p. 153.) And President Benson explained further, "Satan would tell you that these commandments re-strict your freedom, that they are oppressive and unpleasant, that they prevent you from finding happiness, but his whisper-ings are lies" (*The Teachings of Ezra Taft Benson,* p. 402). The commandments are like a mariner's chart to help me navigate the treacherous waters of my mortal probation. By heeding them I can steer clear of the dangerous reefs of momentary pleasures, avoid the misery of wickedness, and find the happi-ness that comes from righteous living.

CHAPTER 17

Peace Finally Comes!

As the Lord continued to soften my heart, several experiences helped me find the peace I so desperately sought.

He Is Listening!

During the time I struggled to understand why my prayers weren't answered, I read the words of many prophets, but I still wasn't comforted. Several times I read President Spencer W. Kimball's statement: "Should all prayers be immediately answered according to our selfish desires and our limited understanding, then there would be little or no suffering, sorrow, disappointment, or even death, and if these were not, there would also be no joy, success, resurrection, nor eternal life and godhood" (*Faith Precedes the Miracle,* p. 97). His words were logical and clear, but I wasn't consoled.

I also wondered why some of Joseph Smith's prayers went unanswered. Certainly he was righteous, yet when he was unjustly imprisoned and cried to the Lord for deliverance, the Lord's response was to tell him to endure to the end (D&C 121:7–8). It was not a response of liberation. Why? Why weren't the Prophet's requests granted? Surely he deserved to have his prayers answered.

Then one Sabbath morning after many years of struggle, I finally understood. I awakened early and discovered my mind and heart filled with the knowledge that even worthy people don't always have their petitions answered as they desire. I knew that logically many years earlier, but I never *felt* it. That testimony was strengthened when I read a talk by Elder Melvin J. Ballard, who explained that the prayers of the First Presidency—righteous prophets—were not always answered as they hoped:

> I remember speaking at the funeral of Richard W. Young who had been in the path of danger many times in the [first] World War where his life might have been taken. And yet he was preserved to die from an infection. Why was not the warning which saved him in the time of battle around him to inspire him to have the necessary operation performed before it was too late? There was no warning or impression given. He was left absolutely without the protection he had previously had. And then I recall the great anxiety of the President of the Church [Heber J. Grant], his nearest friend, that his life might be preserved; and with the Presidency we went to the House of the Lord and pleaded that his life might be spared, and told the Lord every reason why this man should be healed and allowed to live. And I recall that night that there came to me the strongest impression that all our arguments, all our appeals, had been weighed, listened to, and the judgment rendered against us. He was to go. (*Melvin J. Ballard . . . Crusader for Righteousness,* p. 273.)

My testimony increased as I read the words of Elder Spencer W. Kimball: "It is evident that even the righteous will not always be healed and even those of great faith will die when it is according to the purpose of God. Joseph Smith died in his thirties as did the Savior. Solemn prayers were answered negatively." (As quoted in Doxey, *Latter-day Prophets and the Doctrine and Covenants,* vol. 2, p. 34.) I then remembered that the petitions of the Savior, the only sinless person to live on this earth, were denied. Elder Neal A. Maxwell testified of Christ's suffering and pleas:

The awful arithmetic of the atonement fell upon him. Beginning to intensify in Gethsemane and in Calvary, we find Jesus groaning under the weight thereof. . . . Even though He was intellectually brilliant—uniquely so, even though He was the Creator of this and other worlds—knowing beforehand what he had to do, when the moment came, since He had never passed personally through an atonement Himself, it was much worse than even He, with his brilliant mind, could possibly have imagined. Jesus, in Gethsemane pleading to the Father, asked that the cup pass from him. Jesus also said, "Father, all things are possible unto thee, take this cup from me," (Mark 14:36), reflecting to the Father that which He, as Jehovah, had said to Abraham, "Is anything too hard for the Lord." A number of times in His mortal Messiahship, Jesus said to him that believeth, all things are possible. So great was His agony as He felt the weight of the atonement, that He made such a special pleading.

Then, in spiritual submissiveness, "Nevertheless, not my will but thine be done." ("If Thou Endure Well," p. 11.)

Elder Dallin H. Oaks further clarified the Savior's requests: "The Father's answer was to deny the plea of his Only Begotten Son. The Atonement had to be worked out by that lamb without blemish. But though the Son's request was denied, his prayer was answered. The scripture records: 'And there appeared an angel unto him from heaven, strengthening him' (JST, Luke 22:43). Strengthened from heaven to do the will of the Father, the Savior fulfilled his mission." ("Faith in the Lord Jesus Christ," p. 100.)

Additional insight came from Elder George Q. Cannon:

And, if they [the Saints] will exercise their faith aright, there is not any good thing which they can desire, that will be withheld from them. Because you do not get all your prayers answered and your desires granted immediately, you must not therefore be disheartened. Remember the instruction upon this point imparted by Jesus through the parable of the importunate widow [D&C 101:81–94; Luke 18:1–9], and remember, also that though your prayers may not be answered immediately if they are offered in the name of Jesus and in faith, nothing being left undone by you that is required, they will live on the records of heaven and in the remembrance of the Lord, and yet bear fruit. The Ancient fathers asked for blessings in their prayers, which are even now being granted thousands of years after the death of their mortal bodies. (As quoted in Doxey, *Latter-day Prophets and the Doctrine and Covenants,* vol. 3, pp. 176–77.)

I now know that God answers all sincere prayers—some even after we leave mortality. He evaluates them from His perspective and, within the limits of our agency and true desires, answers them in a way that is best for us. That is what He meant when he said: "Or what man is there of you, whom if his son ask bread, will he give him a stone? . . . If ye then, being evil, know how to give good gifts unto your children, how much more shall your Father which is in heaven give good things to them that ask him?" (Matthew 7:9, 11.)

Clearly, Heavenly Father sees my life from an eternal perspective, and I see it from a temporal perspective. From my limited mortal perspective I do not know what is best for me, nor do I know what decisions, commitments, or promises I made before coming to earth. Consequently, when I pray I must trust Heavenly Father and do as President J. Reuben Clark Jr. counseled: "I think that . . . we should never pray, particularly when we pray for specific things, that we do not repeat and present to the Lord, even as Christ prayed in the Garden, 'Nevertheless, not my will, but thine, be done (Luke 22:42)' " (in Conference Report, April 1960, p. 21). Unfortunately, before my heart was softened I lacked the faith to do that. In essence I had been saying, "Father, I know what is best for my family. I want Cindy, Heather, and Mark healed!" Surely I must remember that God answers my prayers according to His perspective, not mine.

My questions about prayer and spiritual manifestations were further clarified when President Ezra Taft Benson explained that the spiritual manifestations of Enos, Alma the Younger, and Saul are the exception rather than the rule (see "A Mighty Change of Heart," p. 5). That understanding helped me realize that I had been looking for unusual, miraculous answers to my prayers rather than being content with the quiet promptings that I occasionally received. I had falsely believed that if I kept the commandments I would receive revelation continually. Unfortunately, I had overlooked Elder Boyd K. Packer's counsel:

> We are expected to use the light and knowledge we already possess to work out our lives. We should not need a revelation to instruct us to be up and about our duty, for we have been told to do that already in the scriptures; nor should we expect revelation to replace the spiritual or temporal intelligence which we have already received—only to extend it. We must go about our life in an ordinary, workaday way, following the routines and rules and regulations that govern life.
>
> Rules and regulations and commandments are valuable protection. Should we stand in need of revealed instruction to alter our course, it will be waiting along the way as we arrive at the point of need. The counsel to be "anxiously engaged" is wise counsel indeed. (See D&C 58.) ("The Candle of the Lord," pp. 53–54.)

Later, the words of Dallin H. Oaks, then president of Brigham Young University, provided additional insight:

> We do not always receive inspiration or revelation when we request it. Sometimes we are delayed in the receipt of revelation, and sometimes we are left to our own judgment. . . . It must be so. Our life's purpose to obtain experience and to develop faith would be frustrated if our Heavenly Father directed us in every act, even in every important act. We must make decisions and experience the consequences in order to develop self-reliance and faith.
>
> Even in decisions we think very important, we sometimes receive no answers to our prayers. This does not mean that our prayers have not been heard. It only means that we have prayed about a decision which, for one reason or another, we should make without guidance by revelation. ("Revelation," p. 26.)

Looking back on my life, I believe that the reason I didn't get immediate answers to my sincere prayers was that I would not have obtained the experience and developed the faith I needed if Heavenly Father had directed my every step. I also now see that before my heart began to soften, most of my prayers were routinely mechanical and insincere. Although I prayed at least each morning and evening, my prayers were usually little more than a memorized list of things I was thankful for and things I wanted. It was as if I were an airplane pilot going down a long checklist prior to flight. The duration of my mechanical prayers was always about the same, since my checklist varied little, even when I encountered new experiences. Only when I was confronted with a major problem or a crisis did I set aside my "pre-flight checklist" and earnestly seek the Lord's help and guidance.

I now approach prayer differently. I no longer use a mental checklist; I spend considerable time thanking the Lord for blessings; I pray more for other people; and there is no set duration. My only criterion is that my prayers must be meaningful and sincere. Then, I try to remember the counsel of Elder H. Burke Peterson: "Answers from the Lord come quietly—ever so quietly. . . . We must be listening so carefully or we will never recognize them. Most answers from the Lord are felt in our heart as a warm comfortable expression, or . . . as thoughts to our mind. They come to those who are prepared and who are patient." ("Adversity and Prayer," p. 19.) What a difference that approach has made!

I am thankful that the Lord helped me learn to pray—that He blessed me with the understanding that I don't need miraculous answers to know that He lives and cares about me, and that He cares about each of us. I now rejoice and am not bitter when another's prayers are answered affirmatively.

A Greater Miracle

As I reflected on how the bitterness was lifted from my soul and how my trust in Christ increased, I realized that the softening of my heart was a major turning point in my life. Only recently, however, did I recognize how significant that event was. While preparing a talk on keeping the Sabbath day holy, I was led to the words of Elder Spencer W. Kimball:

Miracles are of many kinds. Perhaps the greatest miracle is the testimony—an experience which . . . transcends our knowledge of the known laws of nature. To know that God the Father lives, that Jesus of Nazareth is the very son of God and that the doctrines promulgated by Him are divine and exalting is a phenomenon inexplicable by human reasoning; for the testifier may be unable to prove his assertion or demonstrate his sureness by any physical senses. He may never have seen, heard, nor touched a Deity, nor have seen nor heard anyone who had; yet, with a total conviction amounting to an absolute knowledge, he bears witness that he knows. ("The Significance of Miracles," p. 396.)

As I pondered his words, I wondered why a testimony would be a greater miracle than a healing. Wouldn't having a spiritual manifestation or seeing a person healed be more convincing? Then I remembered that Laman and Lemuel saw an angel but murmured after the angel left (see 1 Nephi 3:29–31). They observed the miracle of the Liahona but were "slothful, and forgot to exercise their faith and diligence" (Alma 37:41). They were shaken by the Lord when Nephi stretched forth his hand (see 1 Nephi 17:53–55), but they subsequently treated Nephi harshly and forgot that the Lord had prospered them. They saw the winds and the storm cease after Nephi prayed (see 1 Nephi 18:20–21), but they were not convinced that he was a prophet. Later, Nephi said of his brethren, "Their anger did increase against me, insomuch that they did seek to take away my life" (2 Nephi 5:2). Each time they experienced a miracle they were pacified for a time, but their animosity toward Nephi increased because the miracles they witnessed did not produce a testimony of the truth in their hearts. Mormon noted the same: "Nevertheless, and notwithstanding all these miracles, the people did harden their hearts, and did seek to kill them [the disciples of Christ], even as the Jews at Jerusalem sought to kill Jesus" (4 Nephi 1:31).

The more I pondered on miracles, the more I knew that a testimony can be strengthened by a miracle, but a miracle does not produce a testimony. Elder Boyd K. Packer said, "I have come to know that the witness does not come by seeking after signs. It comes through fasting and prayer, through activity and testing and obedience. It comes through sustaining the servants of the Lord and following them." (*That All May Be Edified,* p. 314.) As I considered Elder Packer's counsel, I remembered a baby born in Mississippi and another born in Utah many years later. Each baby was born with serious health problems and, at the request of their parents, each was healed by a priesthood blessing. Although both couples were comforted by the miracles, unfortunately they both strayed from the Church when they encountered new trials. Truly, miracles do not cause conversion to take place or hearts to change. That occurs only "after the trial of your faith" (Ether 12:6).

When I pleaded for a healing miracle for Cindy, Heather, and Mark, a miracle eventually occurred, but not as I wanted. Instead, it was what I needed, and that miracle was greater than a healing miracle. That miracle occurred when the Lord softened my heart and removed my bitterness. It continued when He blessed me with a greater testimony of moral agency, the plan of salvation, and the value of adversity in my life; and also when He blessed Michelle, Lara, and Heidi with testimonies of the gospel. Now, after putting the events of my life in proper perspective, I know that it was much more important for our healthy daughters to have testimonies of His restored gospel than it was for Cindy, Heather, and Mark to be healed.

Because the Lord softened my heart and gave me the faith to trust Him, I now can say, "Father, I'm glad Thou knowest what is best for me. I'm glad Cindy, Heather, and Mark weren't healed as I pleaded. If I could have healed them, I would have frustrated Thy plan." This understanding came in part from President Spencer W. Kimball's explanation:

> The power of the priesthood is limitless but God has wisely placed upon each of us certain limitations. I may develop priesthood power as I perfect my life, yet I am grateful that even through the priesthood I cannot heal all the

sick. I might heal people who should die. I might relieve people of suffering who should suffer. I fear I would frustrate the purposes of God.

Had I limitless power, and yet limited vision and understanding, I might have saved Abinadi from the flames of fire when he was burned at the stake, and in doing so I might have irreparably damaged him. He died a martyr and went to a martyr's reward—exaltation.

I would likely have protected Paul against his woes if my power were boundless. I would surely have healed his "thorn in the flesh." And in doing so I might have foiled the Lord's program. Thrice he offered prayers, asking the Lord to remove the "thorn" from him, but the Lord did not so answer his prayers. . . .

I fear that had I been in Carthage Jail on June 27, 1844, I might have deflected the bullets that pierced the body of the Prophet and the Patriarch. I might have saved them from the sufferings and agony, but lost to them the martyr's death and reward. I am glad I did not have to make that decision.

With such uncontrolled power, I surely would have felt to protect Christ from the agony in Gethsemane, the insults, the thorny crown, the indignities in the court, the physical injuries. I would have administered to his wounds and healed them, giving him cooling water instead of vinegar. I might have saved him from suffering and death, and lost to the world his atoning sacrifice. (*Faith Precedes the Miracle,* pp. 99, 100.)

I am so grateful that God is always in control of the outcome of priesthood blessings, and that I now know that I didn't fail that spring day in Camarillo when I blessed Heather. The words of the blessing were fulfilled, and if I had been given limitless power and had healed her, I would have frustrated God's plan for our family and for those whose hearts have been touched by the story "Jesus, Listening, Can Hear."

Lasting Peace and Comfort

Another blessing that came as my heart was softened is best explained by relating an incident that occurred while I was serving a mission in Germany. I remember talking with a large, robust German woman who showed us deep, ugly scars on her ankles and feet, which had been severely burned by phosphorus bombs during World War II. She explained that her parents were killed and she was burned as they ran for a bunker. "I don't believe in God anymore," she said bitterly. "If there were a God, He wouldn't have allowed the horrible destruction to occur. You wouldn't believe how we suffered."

My missionary companion and I reasoned with her that from an eternal perspective, our life on earth is like act 2 of a three-act play. We arrived late for the play and missed act 1, and had to leave before act 3 began. The plot can be very confusing after seeing only act 2. So it is with life. We don't remember what happened before we were born, and we don't know what will happen after we die. Consequently, this life often seems unfair. She said the analogy made sense but it didn't comfort her.

Later my companion and I talked to others who also experienced the war first-hand and who no longer believed in God. If they sincerely searched for understanding, we told them about the suffering Alma and Amulek witnessed as wicked leaders killed faithful Christians by fire:

> And when Amulek saw the pains of the women and children who were consuming in the fire, he also was pained; and he said unto Alma: How can we witness this awful scene? Therefore let us stretch forth our hands, and exercise the power of God which is in us, and save them from the flames.
>
> But Alma said unto him: The Spirit constraineth me that I must not stretch forth mine hand; for behold the Lord receiveth them up unto himself, in glory; and he doth suffer that they may do this thing, . . . according to the hardness of their hearts, that the judgments which he shall exercise upon them in his wrath may be just; and the blood

of the innocent shall stand as a witness against them . . . at the last day. (Alma 14: 10–11.)

After hearing that scripture, the Germans usually said it made sense but it didn't make them feel any better. I couldn't understand why they weren't comforted, because our teachings were true and seemed so sensible to me. Unfortunately, it wasn't until I personally suffered the grief, agony, and heartache when Cindy, Heather, and Mark became handicapped that I finally understood why my companion and I couldn't comfort those suffering with grief. When we experience adversity in our lives, logic cannot provide lasting peace or comfort. That comes only from the Savior, because of His atonement.

Previously I thought that there were only two purposes for the Atonement: one, Christ died so all mankind would be resurrected—all would overcome physical death and become immortal; and two, Christ atoned for the sins of each of us if, and only if, we repent of them. However, I recently discovered as I read Alma 7:11–13 that Alma actually described three purposes for the Atonement. Referring to the Savior, Alma said:

- "He will take upon him death."
  Why? "That he may loose the bands of death which bind his people."
- "He will take upon him their infirmities."
  Why? "That his bowels may be filled with mercy, according to the flesh, that he may know according to the flesh how to succor his people according to their infirmities."
- "He might take upon him the sins of his people."
  Why? "That he might blot out their transgressions according to the power of his deliverance."

As I read and reread Alma's words, I was surprised to learn how clearly he explained that the Savior can comfort us because of His atoning sacrifice. Then I remembered other scriptures that supported Alma's words.

- *Hebrews 2:18:* "For in that he himself hath suffered being tempted, he is able to succour them that are tempted."

- *2 Nephi 9:21:* "He suffereth the pains of all men, yea, the pains of every living creature, both men, women, and children, who belong to the family of Adam."
- *Mosiah 14:4:* "Surely he has borne our griefs, and carried our sorrows."
- *D&C 88:6:* "He that ascended up on high . . . descended below all things, in that he comprehended all things."

I had read those scriptures many times, but they never came together with such force as they did after I studied Alma's words. It was the Savior who had comforted me, removed my bitterness, and brought peace to my troubled heart! Elder Neal A. Maxwell confirmed that testimony: "Since not all human sorrow and pain is connected to sin, the full intensiveness of the Atonement involved bearing our pains, infirmities, and sicknesses, as well as our sins. Whatever our sufferings, we can safely cast our 'care upon him; for he careth for [us]' (1 Peter 5:7)." (*"Not My Will, But Thine,"* p. 51.) Stated differently, we can safely cast our care upon Him because "he knows more of the dark side than any of us. In fact, he knows more about pain, grief, loneliness, contradiction, shame, rejection, betrayal, anguish, depression, and guilt than all of us combined." (Robinson, *Believing Christ,* p. 116.) Plainly, He even understands the feelings of guilt and pain associated with sinning because He experienced all of the negative consequences and ramifications of sin in Gethsemane.

Yes, through Him I can find peace in adversity—but I must remember the counsel of Elder Neal A. Maxwell: "Paul observed, 'Now no chastening for the present seemeth to be joyous, but grievous: nevertheless afterward it yieldeth the peaceable fruit of righteousness.' (Hebrews 12:11.) Such 'peaceable fruit' comes only in the appointed season thereof, after the blossoms and the buds." ("Endure It Well," p. 33.)

Equally Yoked Together

As Jo and I reflected on the things we learned from our adversities and the blessings that came as a result of changed hearts, we recognized that one of the greatest blessings is that we now have a fulfilling, romantic, and happy marriage. It might be said that we are now equally yoked together.

The Apostle Paul told the Corinthian Saints that they should not be "unequally yoked" with unbelievers (see 2 Corinthians 6:14). Jo and I believe Paul's counsel may be applied to the marriage relationship in different ways. From our perspective, although we enjoyed a temple marriage we were "unequally yoked" because the focus of our lives was different. Jo's focus was usually on God and Christ, while mine was on the Church, family, employment, and myself.

I now realize that to make our marriage better I needed to change my focus. I needed to focus my life on God and His Son and then allow the Holy Ghost to give me the proper perspective. As President Ezra Taft Benson counseled: "When we put God first, all other things fall into their proper place or drop out of our lives. Our love of the Lord will govern the claims for our affection, the demands on our time, the interests we pursue, and the order of our priorities. We should put God ahead of *everyone else* in our lives." ("The Great Commandment—Love the Lord," p. 4, emphasis in original.) And as President Spencer W. Kimball noted: "If two people love the Lord more than their own lives and then love each other more than their own lives, working together in total harmony with the gospel program as their basic structure, they are sure to have this great [marital] happiness" (*The Teachings of Spencer W. Kimball,* p. 309).

And from the manual *Teach Them Correct Principles:*

> As husbands and wives come unto Christ, becoming one with him and casting their burdens upon him, they find peace in the midst of trial, and as they become one with him, they find themselves becoming one with each other and bearing one another's burdens. But when they do not seek the Lord, then many of life's experiences seem unbearable. Unfortunately, because of the "hardness of their hearts," couples all too often reject his invitation by the choices they make and the methods they use to address the challenges of life. . . .

We will not escape trials. They may come from the behavior of others, from health or economic difficulties beyond our control, from our own lack of wisdom, or from sin.
But the Savior's invitation to come to know him and his
Father (see John 17:3) is an offer of liberation, an offer of
peace. As we take his offer seriously, we become one in
marriage, and that oneness is a key to the fullness of joy.
(Pp. 98–99.)

I believe that when Jo and I each put God first, He becomes
our advocate with each other, and He helps us resolve our differences and difficulties. We don't need a long list of man-made
techniques to make our marriage successful. Instead, to achieve
a oneness in marriage Jo and I must each strive to be humble;
repent when we offend God, each other, our children, or others;
and forgive, even if we have been wronged. As C. Richard
Chidester, a marriage counselor and bishop, wrote: "To develop
that oneness [in marriage], we must first be humble enough to
look at the flaws in our character and to eliminate them through
faith in the Lord and through repentance" ("No Place for Pride,"
p. 16). And as Elder Boyd K. Packer explained:

To those who are married and not in love—and in our
society this is not an infrequent circumstance—the remedy
for your dilemma was prescribed in these words by President Stephen L Richards:
"I made the statement, and I hope you will approve of
it, that the remedy for domestic problems and irritations is
not divorce, but repentance. . . ."
. . . If there is trouble, you stay married—both of you.
You repent—both of you. You be worthy—both of you. You
be prayerful—both of you. You be forgiving—both of you.
Love can grow again from the same root stalk and bloom
again with blossoms sweeter still. (As quoted in *Achieving a
Celestial Marriage*, p. 138.)

Furthermore, I must continually guard against pride, for it
can destroy my marriage. C. Richard Chidester wrote:

As marriage and parenthood begin to reveal our faults to us, we may be tempted to strike out and blame others— our parents, our spouse, our children, or our circumstances—for our unhappiness. But if we get no further than blaming others, we will become deadlocked in the vicious grip of pride. . . .

As a marriage counselor, I believe that pride is the reason for the mass marital failure in our society. But if you look at marriage books on the world's market today, you'll never see *humility* at the top of the list of ways to improve marriage! . . .

In my experience, there is no real hope for lasting improvement for those who refuse to humble themselves. Humility is a major ingredient of genuine spirituality—the foundation of a happy life and a happy marriage.

Because of pride, we get embarrassed and uncomfortable when we realize we need to repent. But if we look for less-demanding ways to improve, all we can find are man-made techniques that focus on changing outward behavior only. If we rely on these methods alone, we are relying on the arm of flesh rather than on God. Outward behavior can be changed through techniques and skills, but the changes that really need to take place are in our hearts. . . .

. . . We must have faith in the Savior's power to help us—and then truly allow him to change our hearts and purify them. This means that he will cleanse us of pride and selfishness—the major impurities of our hearts. ("No Place for Pride," pp. 18, 19–20.)

I know that the preceding statements are true! Many times I tried to work on our marriage relationship by being more kind, considerate, patient, and complimentary, but it never lasted. As soon as we had a financial setback, someone became sick, or Jo or I had a bad day, I couldn't sustain the effort, and the negative feelings and behavior returned. No matter how hard I tried, I couldn't change those ill feelings on my own. Only after I humbled myself, apologized for my mistakes, and turned my heart to Christ did Jo and I develop a happy relationship—even when the outside problems and pressures remained.

In retrospect, Jo and I are especially thankful that we both desired to repent and make our marriage successful. We are also grateful to understand that there is peace when we forgive each other for things that happened in the past. Every day is happier, and we both better understand and appreciate the differences between men and women, and each other. We are slower to criticize and find fault, and we both try to consider the other's needs, comfort, and feelings before our own. Now if either of us hurts the other, repentance and forgiveness take place in a matter of minutes instead of days, weeks, or never at all.

I believe one of the reasons we get along so much better is that our vision of life is nearly the same. It is as if we now are looking through the same spiritual lenses, and we see the world, gospel topics, adversity, and a host of other things in the same way. What a blessing that is! Now we see eye to eye on most everything except my "cruising" the TV channels with the remote control! Another personal blessing is that although I had always found it hard to accept Jo's counsel, after my heart was softened I realized that she had helped me better understand gospel principles. Because of her faith and ability to explain spiritual concepts, she is a great gospel tutor, and I appreciate her tutelage.

An Unexpected Blessing

Although Cindy, Heather, and Mark underwent many medical tests prior to Heather's death, doctors never determined why they became handicapped. So when our pediatrician suggested a detailed autopsy after Heather died we were skeptical that it was of value, but we consented. Samples of Heather's vital organs were sent to a laboratory in Colorado, where, coincidentally, they were analyzed by a researcher studying a rare disease known as glutaric acidemia. To our great surprise, he confirmed that Heather suffered from that disease, and subsequent testing revealed that Cindy and Mark also suffer from it. The mystery was over! After more than eighteen years we learned that our children have a genetic disorder that many Amish children also have "in which the body fails to produce enzymes needed to break down two of the 20 amino acids that make up protein. As a result, a toxic byproduct—glutaric acid—builds up. Normally, the kidneys can flush the buildup away, but any illness that leads to dehydration . . . halts the removal. In a matter of hours, the acid buildup attacks the brain, and a seemingly healthy child suffers a spastic type of paralysis." (Wolkomir, "The Doctor Who Conquered a Killer," pp. 162–63.)

We later learned that the number of people with glutaric acidemia in the United States is unknown. However, in Europe one person in 600,000 is afflicted, and in the Scandinavian countries, where some of Jo's and my relatives originate, one in 30,000 people has it. Unfortunately, since very little is known about the disease there is no known cure, treatment, life expectancy, or explanation for the extremes in severity among patients. But we were told that Cindy is one of the oldest living patients in the United States. Although we were disappointed that Cindy and Mark could not be helped, it is comforting just to know the name of their illness.

Even If I Could, I Wouldn't Change Them

Hopefully I haven't conveyed the impression that once my heart began to change, my adversity and trials ended, or that I have become nearly perfect. Such is not the case. I still struggle with weaknesses of the flesh and continually work to overcome pride, selfishness, anger, and impatience. My trials just change from time to time as Heavenly Father continues his eternal polishing process. For instance, Cindy became allergic to her antiseizure medication, and before an acceptable substitute was found she had major seizures many times each day. During much of that time when I was home I held her in my arms as she shook uncontrollably. I thought my heart would break as I suffered with her day after day.

More recently my heart aches as I watch Mark's health deteriorate. His back becomes more deformed, and his muscles and joints ache under constant tension. At times he is so tense that I can't pry his fingers open or straighten out his arms without hurting him. Often when he cries out in the night I find him with his arms and legs twisted in a painful, pretzel-like fashion. It's frustrating to helplessly watch his limited speech slowly erode, witness his increasing struggles to communicate, see him longingly watch friends play without being able to participate, and fail to answer his questions about when he or Cindy will die.

I now know that, as Elder Packer said, our testing is more equal than we might believe, because many of our trials are custom-tailored to meet our needs, and because God will take all factors into account when we finally appear before Him for His perfect judgment. He will not test us beyond our limits to endure. After quoting 1 Corinthians 10:13, Elder H. Burke Peterson said: "Did you get the significance of that scriptural promise—we will have no temptation or trial beyond our ability to overcome—he will provide a way for us to rise above—whatever it may be" ("Adversity and Prayer," p. 19). I also know that Heavenly Father *was* giving me bread all the time I was complaining. Unfortunately, because of my pride I perceived His chastening to be a stone. He simply had a different plan for me than I had expected.

I also know that the Lord gives us agency and provides experiences to help us overcome our weaknesses and grow. For instance, I exercised my agency to have children, but once I exercised that agency, Heavenly Father had the right to bless me with the children He felt would increase my spiritual growth and development. Similarly, I was free to keep Cindy, Heather, and Mark at home or put them in an institution, but once I exercised that agency, He had the right to make it difficult for us to care for them so I could overcome my pride and selfishness, develop stronger faith, and learn to sacrifice for others.

With a heart softened by my adversity, and a stronger testimony because of it, I testify to the truthfulness of Elder Boyd K. Packer's words:

> You are going to have some troubles in your life. You know, if I had all the power that the Almighty has, and it was within my province to make your way so straight that there would be never a bend and to make it so smooth that there would be never a rut and to make it so clear that there would be never an obstacle, for your sakes I would not do it;

for from your troubles there will come growth. You will find moments of disappointment, even despair. You will not be free from illness or even death, and even stark tragedy may visit you in this great adventure of family living. But from these things your love will deepen, your testimony will increase, your faith will grow, your knowledge of the Lord will become more firm. (*That All May Be Edified,* p. 234.)

As I review my life, I can say honestly that if I had it to live again, I would not want my trials removed or changed, as I now know that "earth has no sorrow that heav'n cannot heal" (Thomas Moore, in *Hymns,* no. 115).

Endure to the End

My life is very different now! I am no longer haunted by unanswered questions. I no longer feel that God treated me unfairly, that He gave me stones instead of bread. I no longer question His wisdom, judgment, or motives. He not only calmed my troubled heart and helped me "feel" the answers to my questions, but He gave me a fresh view of life and its purpose. He provided insight to help me apply gospel principles in my life, and, most important, He blessed me with the faith to trust Him as He polishes the rough edges of my soul. Furthermore, He taught me that I can find peace in any adversity, because He has blessed me with the peace "which passeth all understanding" (Philippians 4:7).

Through the help and blessings of the Lord, I now have the faith to accept challenges and trials as a necessary, though often unpleasant, part of my life. My test now is to live so He will bless me with sufficient faith to overcome future adversity. To receive that blessing I must continually work to overcome pride and selfishness and to keep my heart centered on Him (see Mosiah 4:26). My greatest concern is maintaining sufficient faith to endure to the end, because I am certain that if I don't do His will, my faith will diminish and my former bitterness will return. Regarding that, Elder George Q. Morris stated: "So, in adversity we may have that which will exalt us, or we may have that

which will degrade us. We may have that which, 'if we endure it
well,' will ennoble us, and we may have that which, if we in-
dulge in self-pity and bitterness, may destroy us. In all our adversities there are these two elements, and the determining factor is how shall we endure them? Shall we endure them well? If
not, they may destroy us." (As quoted in Doxey, *Latter-day
Prophets and the Doctrine and Covenants*, vol. 4, p. 199.)

Elder Neal A. Maxwell counseled:

> There are so many things to be endured: illness, injus-
> tice, insensitivity, poverty, aloneness, unresponsiveness,
> being misrepresented and misunderstood, and, sometimes,
> even enemies. . . .
>
> . . . Endurance is more than pacing up and down within
> the cell of our circumstance; it is not only acceptance of the
> things allotted to us, but to "act for ourselves" by magnify-
> ing what is allotted to us. (Alma 29:3,6.) . . .
>
> Therefore, true enduring represents not merely the pas-
> sage of time, but the passage of the soul. . . .
>
> . . . Sustaining correct conduct for a difficult moment
> under extraordinary stress is very commendable, but so is
> coping with sustained stress subtly present in seeming rou-
> tineness. Either way, however, we are to "run with patience
> the race that is set before us" (Hebrews 12:1), and it is a
> marathon, not a dash. . . .
>
> Thus, enduring is one of the cardinal attributes; it simply
> cannot be developed without the laboratory time in this
> second estate. Even the best lectures about the theory of
> enduring are not enough. All the other cardinal virtues—
> love, patience, humility, mercy, purity, submissiveness, jus-
> tice—they all require endurance for their full development.
> ("Endure It Well," pp. 33, 34.)

What will I do in the future? Will I trust Father to be my
"Gardener"? Will I keep His commandments by continually
working on my marriage relationship, exercising faith in Christ,
repenting of my sins, and enduring to the end, or will I suc-
cumb to my weaknesses and lose my soul in bitterness? The
choice is mine!

PART V

Conclusion

Joyce J. Erickson

CHAPTER 18

An Expression of Gratitude
and Testimony

As Bruce and I look at our lives today, we have much to be thankful for. Michelle has graduated from college and is happily married. Lara and her husband, Jereck, have graduated from college and are living nearby. Heidi is attending college away from home and is learning the real joy of the gospel. And thankfully, all our children continue to help us whenever they're home. Also, our extended families give us unwavering love and support. How grateful we are for our family!

Bruce and I are also thankful for our much improved marriage. Oh, we still have some disagreements and times when things don't run smoothly, but for the most part selfishness and pride have been replaced by repentance and humility, and our goals and focus are much the same now. Because we both have learned to focus on Christ and exercise faith in His atonement, we usually see eye to eye and now have a happy, loving relationship. What a difference that has made when meeting our daily challenges!

We are also very thankful for the many people outside our family who have helped us over the years and who continue to help us now. We are thankful for teachers, bus drivers, aides, doctors, specialists; for Mark's friends who come to our home and play with him, include him in their activities, and spend much time and effort trying to decipher his limited speech; and for the adults in his life who continue to remember him. We are grateful, too, for the wonderful people who come to visit Cindy, who tend her while the rest of us attend church together each Sunday, and who sit with her while I run errands during the week.

And, of course, we are especially grateful for a loving, kind, and omniscient Heavenly Father who knows us so well that, within the bounds of our agency, He allows those things to happen that will be for our best good. He is the one who teaches us important truths "line upon line and precept upon precept," and who makes our trials bearable. For instance, although it has been difficult caring for severely handicapped children, I have thought many times how grateful I am that God placed me here on earth during this time when I have access to so many modern conveniences—like running water, medical treatments, sanitation devices, and carpeted floors on which to lay my children. How difficult it would have been to care for three handicapped children even fifty years ago!

Bruce and I are also extremely grateful for everyone who continues to help us bear our burdens, for surely our adversity hasn't ended. We are still tied down and unable to get away by ourselves for more than about six hours at a time. Cindy is still bedridden, and she and Mark are still ours "to keep, to hold, and to nourish." There are still six special meals to prepare daily, hours of feeding, teeth to brush, hundreds of pills to crush and diapers to change, difficult baths to give, unending doctors' appointments, sore joints and muscles to rub and treat, long nights with little sleep, and much lifting into wheelchairs, through narrow doorways, and into and out of bathtubs and cars. And, of course, we all still miss Heather.

An example of how our challenges remain but how Heavenly Father continues to send us peace and understanding took place a short time ago. Mark had just arrived home from school—a time that is usually happy for him—and I could tell when I saw him coming down on the bus wheelchair lift that he was ready to cry. Sure enough, as soon as I got him into the living room the tears came quickly and freely. I immediately took him out of his wheelchair, held him close, and let him cry for a couple of minutes.

Finally I interrupted his crying and said, "You really feel bad, Mark. Did something happen at school today?"

"Yes," he said as he began to cry hard again.

I said, "Mark, I can't understand you while you're crying. You'll have to quit if you want me to understand you."

He said, "Okay," and finally quit crying. Then he said, "Mom, the boys at school are so lucky."

"Why do you think they're lucky, Mark?"

"They can run, play football. They can run fast and run races." With those words, he started to cry once again. My heart ached for him. I held him close and let him cry while I tried to think of something to say.

Without knowing beforehand exactly what I would say, I began, "Mark, you think the boys at school are really lucky, don't you?"

"Yes, " he said.

"Well," I said, "they are lucky, Mark. But do you know something? Everyone is lucky in some way. Did you know that?"

"No," he said.

"Well, they are."

Then, without ever having thought about it before, I held up my left hand, and, pointing to each finger as I spoke, I said, "Mark, your friends are lucky because they can run, play football, ride bikes, play computer games, write—"

"And draw," Mark said.

"Yes, and draw. But do you know what, Mark? You're lucky too." I held up my right hand. "You're lucky because you got to go into the BYU locker room and meet the BYU football players, and you're lucky because you got to go into the BYU locker room and meet the basketball players; you got to sing with the Tabernacle Choir and meet Brother Ottley—"

"And go on the U.S.S. *Nimitz*," Mark said.

"Yes, and do you know how else you're lucky, Mark?"

"No," he said.

"You're lucky because *everyone* likes you. I don't know of anyone who doesn't like you. Did you know that one of your friends once said to me, 'Mark is so lucky. I wish I had as many friends as Mark has.' And when you were running for governor of the fourth grade, a girl who was running against you said, 'It really isn't fair. Everyone knows Mark, and everyone likes him.' Did you know that?"

"No," he said again as his whole countenance brightened.

"And do you know how else you're lucky, Mark? You're lucky because Satan can't tempt you. He can tempt your friends to disobey their parents, to steal, to cheat, to be mean to other people—but he can't tempt you to do any of those things. Did you know that, Mark?"

"Yes," he said in a happy tone.

"Everyone's just lucky in different ways. Your friends are lucky in these ways," I said as I held up my left hand, "and you're lucky in these ways," I said, holding up my right hand.

Mark readily agreed, but for some reason I continued one step further. I held up both hands and asked, "Mark, if you had a choice, which hand would you choose? Would you choose to be lucky like your friends?" I held up my left hand. "Or would you choose to be lucky like you are now?" I held up my right hand.

Without hesitating, Mark looked directly at my right hand and said, "I choose that hand."

"Well, Mark," I said, "that's the one I think you chose before you were born, when you lived with Heavenly Father."

"Yeah, I know," Mark replied happily.

I was so thankful that the Spirit had inspired me with the right words to say, because finally Mark was comforted. He felt peace because he understood and was touched by the Spirit, and I felt peace because I was able to comfort and console him through the help of the "still small voice."

How grateful Bruce and I are for such sweet experiences! Not only do they sustain us from day to day, but they also enhance our understanding of ourselves, our children, and the world around us. Most important, however, they help us feel with our hearts the goodness of God, the value of His great plan of salvation, the importance of adversity, and the peace "which passeth all understanding" (see Philippians 4:7).

Our Testimony

Regarding the great plan of salvation, it is our testimony that when all of mankind lived as spirit children in the premortal world, our heavenly parents loved us so much that they wanted us to enjoy the life that they enjoy. Consequently, they made sure we were taught the gospel, the great plan of happiness. They taught us about eternal progression, the Creation, the Fall, and the necessity of an atonement. They taught us about faith, obedience, sacrifice, temptation, opposition, repentance, forgiveness, baptism, the gift of the Holy Ghost—and about adversity. In addition, they taught us that in order for us to progress further and fully understand and appreciate godhood, it was not enough just to know the gospel. We needed to experience mortality and prove our faithfulness. We needed to develop our faith by leaving their presence and experiencing pain, disappointment, temptation, sickness, death—afflictions of all kinds—in order to become like them and enjoy the life that they enjoy.

Because of our training in the premortal existence, we knew then that there would be challenges in mortality. Perhaps, like Christ, we knew what challenges we would have but didn't realize how difficult our ultimate tests would be. Maybe we even chose our adversity. Perhaps we simply agreed to accept the tests God determined would be best for us, or those that happened to come our way due to the uncertainties of mortality. Whatever the case, we were fully aware that there would be adversity and trials here. Yet we chose to come anyway. We approved, because we wanted to become like God and to live with Him again.

In the case of our family, because of what Heather told us when she was seven years old, and because of Bruce's patriarchal blessing, we have a very strong feeling not only that Heather agreed to come here with her handicap, but also that the rest of our family probably said, "We'll help each other. Send us together."

Since experiencing adversity is an essential part of knowing God and returning to His presence, none of us is exempt from suffering—the Savior wasn't, prophets aren't, and we aren't.

But how do people withstand trials and prove themselves worthy to live with God again? How do they find peace in the midst of adversity?

As Bruce and I analyzed how we eventually found peace in our relationship, we concluded that difficult marriage problems are seldom solved quickly; that it is impossible to force another person to change; that until both partners feel a compelling need to change, or until they experience a "Pearl Harbor Day," the only person one can effectively change is himself. We then realized that the key to our finding peace was when each of us repented of our own sins and forgave the other of his. That, in turn, enabled God to bless us with His gifts of love (charity), patience, and true joy. King Benjamin, a great king and prophet in the Book of Mormon, explained the process this way:

> Believe that ye must repent of your sins and forsake them, and humble yourselves before God; and ask in sincerity of heart that he would forgive you. . . .
>
> . . . And humble yourselves even in the depths of humility, calling on the name of the Lord daily, and standing steadfastly in the faith of that which is to come. . . .
>
> And behold, I say unto you that if ye do this ye shall always rejoice, and be filled with the love of God, and always retain a remission of your sins; and ye shall grow in the knowledge of the glory of him that created you, or in the knowledge of that which is just and true.
>
> And ye will not have a mind to injure one another, but to live peaceably. (Mosiah 4:10–13.)

Stated differently, Bruce and I now realize that the way we found peace in our relationship was by discarding our own carnal desires to be selfish, proud, dishonest, stubborn, and disobedient to God—which, in scriptural terms, means putting off the "natural man" (see Mosiah 3:19)—and that we accomplished that task by submitting our own will to the will of the Father, or becoming humble; exercising faith in Jesus Christ and His atonement; repenting of our own sins; forgiving our fellowmen of their trespasses against us; and continuing to be as obedient as we knew how.

Now, after much studying, we realize that because of Christ's atonement, that same "peace process" of humility-faith-repentance-forgiveness-obedience is the way to find peace in every instance, even when we are the victims. For example, it will work if one suffers because of divorce, a wayward child, the death of a loved one, loss of employment, old age, financial ruin, childlessness, or even abuse. And the reason it is a universal solution is that when we go through the "peace process" we make ourselves worthy to receive a remission of sins, which brings God's mercy, a "peace of conscience," and "exceedingly great joy [to our] souls" (see Mosiah 4:3, 10–11). In the words of Elder Spencer W. Kimball, "It is not easy to be at peace in today's troubled world. . . . It can be attained only through maintaining constantly a repentant attitude, seeking forgiveness of sins both large and small, and thus coming ever closer to God." (*The Miracle of Forgiveness*, p. 366.) Incidentally, we believe that same "peace process" is also the key to happy relationships among parents, children, siblings, roommates, neighbors, church members, co-workers, and even nations.

We testify that the "peace process" works for everyone simply because we all sin, and "there is no peace, saith the Lord, unto the wicked" (1 Nephi 20:22). Also, it works for everyone because the way to come closer to God and make the Atonement individually meaningful is to repent and forgive. In a very real way, through repentance and doing all we can do we qualify ourselves to receive God's mercy, love, and peace.

Finally, Bruce and I know for a surety that life *is* unfair, because trials, by their very nature, are unfair. But we also know that if we continually and diligently follow the "peace process," we can find comfort during our trials, and we can find the strength to endure to the end. We will become sanctified and perfected and will be able to endure the trials of the latter days if we follow the prophet Moroni's counsel: "Deny not the power of God; for he worketh by power, according to the faith of the children of men. . . . And again I would exhort you that ye would come unto Christ, and lay hold upon every good gift, and touch not the evil gift, nor the unclean thing. . . . Yea, come unto Christ, and be perfected in him, and deny yourselves of all ungodliness; and if ye shall deny yourselves of all ungodliness, and love God with all your might [spiritually], mind [mentally], and strength [physically], then is his grace sufficient for you, that by his grace ye may be perfect in Christ." (Moroni 10:7, 30, 32.) And as the prophet Alma testified, "Whosoever shall put their trust in God shall be supported in their trials, and their troubles, and their afflictions" (Alma 36:3).

It is our hope and prayer that we all might understand that there is value in adversity, that the Lord doesn't care nearly as much about changing our circumstances as He does about changing our hearts, and that our adversities can help us grow. It is also our hope that we all might find comfort and peace as we are tutored by a loving Father who wants us to be like Him and to live with Him again.

Works Cited

Achieving a Celestial Marriage [student manual]. Salt Lake City: The Church of Jesus Christ of Latter-day Saints, 1976.

Ashton, Marvin J. "A Pattern in All Things." *Ensign* 20 (November 1990): 20–22.

Ballard, M. Russell. "Be an Example of the Believers." *Ensign* 21 (November 1991): 95–97.

———. "Purity Precedes Power." *Ensign* 20 (November 1990): 35–38.

Benson, Ezra Taft. "Beware of Pride." *Ensign* 19 (May 1989): 4–7.

———. "Cleansing the Inner Vessel." *Ensign* 16 (May 1986): 4–7.

———. "The Great Commandment—Love the Lord." *Ensign* 18 (May 1988): 4–6.

———. "A Mighty Change of Heart." *Ensign* 19 (October 1989): 2–5.

———. *The Teachings of Ezra Taft Benson.* Salt Lake City: Bookcraft, 1988.

———. "To the Fathers in Israel." *Ensign* 17 (November 1987): 48–51.

Brown, Hugh B. "The Currant Bush." *New Era* 3 (January 1973): 14–15.

Cannon, George Q. *Gospel Truth.* Compiled by Jerreld L. Newquist. 2 vols. Salt Lake City: Deseret Book Co., 1975.

Chidester, C. Richard. "No Place for Pride." *Ensign* 20 (March 1990): 16–21.

Come unto the Father in the Name of Jesus [Melchizedek Priesthood study guide]. Salt Lake City: The Church of Jesus Christ of Latter-day Saints, 1990.

Covey, Stephen R. *The Divine Center.* Salt Lake City: Bookcraft, 1982.

Cowley, Matthew. "Miracles." *New Era* 5 (June 1975): 38–44.

Doxey. Roy W., comp. *Latter-day Prophets and the Doctrine and Covenants.* 4 vols. Salt Lake City: Deseret Book Co., 1978.

Ernstrom, Jean. "Jesus, Listening, Can Hear." *Ensign* 18 (June 1988): 46–47.

Father, Consider Your Ways [pamphlet]. Salt Lake City: The Church of Jesus Christ of Latter-day Saints, 1973.

Faust, James E. "The Refiner's Fire." *Ensign* 9 (May 1979): 53–59.

———. "The Works of God." *Ensign* 14 (November 1984): 54–60.

Follow Me [Relief Society personal study guide]. Salt Lake City: The Church of Jesus Christ of Latter-day Saints, 1988.

Grant, Heber J. "Dream, O Youth! Dream Nobly and Manfully." *Improvement Era* 44 (September 1941): 524.

Hill, Napoleon. *Think and Grow Rich.* New York: Fawcett Crest, 1970.

Hunter, Howard W. "Being a Righteous Husband and Father." *Ensign* 24 (November 1994): 49–51.

Kimball, Spencer W. "The Abundant Life." *Ensign* 8 (July 1978): 2–7.

———. *Faith Precedes the Miracle.* Salt Lake City: Deseret Book Co., 1972.

———. "The False Gods We Worship." *Ensign* 6 (June 1976): 2–6.

———. "Hope and Encouragement for Cancer Cure." *Relief Society Magazine* 56 (April 1969): 244–47.

———. "Listen to the Prophets." *Ensign* 8 (May 1978): 76–78.

———. "Listen to the Prophet's Voice." *Improvement Era* 64 (December 1961): 936–41.

———. *The Miracle of Forgiveness.* Salt Lake City: Bookcraft, 1969.

———. "The Significance of Miracles in the Church Today." *Instructor* 94 (December 1959): 396–97, 400.

———. "Small Acts of Service." *Ensign* 4 (December 1974): 2–7.

———. *The Teachings of Spencer W. Kimball.* Edited by Edward L. Kimball. Salt Lake City: Bookcraft, 1982.

———. "Tragedy or Destiny." *Improvement Era* 69 (March 1966): 178–80, 210–14, 216–17.

———. "Welfare Services: The Gospel in Action." *Ensign* 7 (November 1977): 76–79.

Kushner, Harold S. *When Bad Things Happen to Good People.* New York: Avon Books, 1981.

Larsen, Dean L. "Looking Beyond the Mark." *Ensign* 17 (November 1987): 11–12.

Lay Hold Upon the Word of God [Melchizedek Priesthood study guide]. Salt Lake City: The Church of Jesus Christ of Latter-day Saints, 1988.

Lee, Harold B. "Understanding Who We Are Brings Self-Respect." *Ensign* 4 (January 1974): 2–6.

Lewis, C. S. *Mere Christianity*. New York: Macmillan, 1952.

Maxwell, Neal A. *All These Things Shall Give Thee Experience*. Salt Lake City: Deseret Book Co., 1979.

———. "Endure It Well." *Ensign* 20 (May 1990): 33–35.

———. "If Thou Endure Well." Address given at Brigham Young University, December 2, 1984; typescript, Church Historical Department, Salt Lake City.

———. "Insights from My Life." In *1976 Devotional Speeches of the Year*. Provo, Utah: Brigham Young University Press, 1977, pp. 187–201.

———. *Men and Women of Christ*. Salt Lake City: Bookcraft, 1991.

———. *"Not My Will, But Thine."* Salt Lake City: Bookcraft, 1988.

———. *Wherefore, Ye Must Press Forward*. Salt Lake City: Deseret Book Co., 1977.

———. "Wisdom and Order." *Ensign* 24 (June 1994): 40–43.

McConkie, Bruce R. "The Salvation of Little Children." *Ensign* 7 (April 1977): 2–7.

———. "Stand Independent above All Other Creatures." *Ensign* 9 (May 1979): 92–94.

Melvin J. Ballard...Crusader for Righteousness. Salt Lake City: Bookcraft, 1966.

Mitchell, David. "Thousands of Saints Left Homeless by Idaho Flood." *Ensign* 6 (August 1976): 69–76.

Monson, Thomas S. *Favorite Quotations from the Collection of Thomas S. Monson*. Salt Lake City: Deseret Book Co., 1985.

Nelson, Russell M. "Reverence for Life." *Ensign* 15 (May 1985): 11–14.

Oaks, Dallin H. "Faith in the Lord Jesus Christ." *Ensign* 24 (May 1994): 98–100.

———. "Our Strengths Can Become Our Downfall." In *Brigham Young University 1991–92 Devotional and Fireside Speeches*. Provo, Utah: University Publications, 1992.

———. "Revelation." In *Brigham Young University 1981–82 Fireside and Devotional Speeches*. Provo, Utah: University Publications, 1982.

Pace, Glenn L. "Principles and Programs." *Ensign* 16 (May 1986): 23–25.

Packer, Boyd K. "An Appeal to Prospective Elders." *Ensign* 5 (May 1975): 104–6.

———. "Balm of Gilead." *Ensign* 17 (November 1987): 16–18.

———. "The Candle of the Lord." *Ensign* 13 (January 1983): 51–56.

———. "The Choice." *Ensign* 10 (November 1980): 20–22.

———. "Faith." *Improvement Era* 71 (November 1968): 60–63.

———. "Funerals—A Time for Reverence." *Ensign* 18 (November 1988): 18–21.

———. "'I Say Unto You, Be One.'" In *Brigham Young University 1990–91 Devotional and Fireside Speeches,* pp. 81–91. Provo, Utah: University Publications, 1991.

———. *Let Not Your Heart Be Troubled.* Salt Lake City: Bookcraft, 1991.

———. "Little Children." *Ensign* 16 (November 1986): 16–18.

———. "Marriage." *Ensign* 11 (May 1981): 13–15.

———. "The Moving of the Water." *Ensign* 21 (May 1991): 7–9.

———. "The Mystery of Life." *Ensign* 13 (November 1983): 16–18.

———. "The Pattern of Our Parentage." *Ensign* 14 (November 1984): 66–69.

———. "Prayers and Answers." *Ensign* 9 (November 1979): 19–21.

———. "The Saints Securely Dwell." *Ensign* 3 (January 1973): 88–90.

———. "Scriptures." *Ensign* 12 (November 1982): 51–53.

———. "Self-Reliance." *Ensign* 5 (August 1975): 85–89.

———. "Solving Emotional Problems in the Lord's Own Way." *Ensign* 8 (May 1978): 91–93.

———. "Spiritual Crocodiles." *Ensign* 6 (May 1976): 30–32.

———. *Teach Ye Diligently.* Salt Lake City: Deseret Book Co., 1975.

———. *That All May Be Edified.* Salt Lake City: Bookcraft, 1982.

Perry, L. Tom. "The Joy of Honest Labor." *Ensign* 16 (November 1986): 62–64.

Petersen, Mark E. "Salvation Comes Through the Church." *Ensign* 3 (July 1973): 108–11.

Peterson, H. Burke. "Adversity and Prayer." *Ensign* 4 (January 1974): 18–19.

———. "Unrighteous Dominion." *Ensign* 19 (July 1989): 6–11.

Robinson, Doug. "Kozlowski's Injury Isn't Holding Him Back." *Deseret News,* 12 November 1985, sec. D., pp. 1, 6.

Robinson, Stephen E. *Believing Christ.* Salt Lake City: Deseret Book Co., 1992.

Romney, Marion G. "Welfare Services: The Savior's Program." *Ensign* 10 (November 1980): 92–93.

A Royal Priesthood [Melchizedek Priesthood study guide]. Salt Lake City: The Church of Jesus Christ of Latter-day Saints, 1975.

Scott, Richard G. "Healing the Tragic Scars of Abuse." *Ensign* 22 (May 1992): 31–33.

———. "Healing Your Damaged Life." *Ensign* 22 (November 1992): 60–62.

——. "Obtaining Help from the Lord." *Ensign* 21 (November 1991): 84–86.

Smith, Joseph. *Teachings of the Prophet Joseph Smith.* Compiled by Joseph Fielding Smith. Salt Lake City: Deseret Book Co., 1976.

Smith, Joseph F. *Gospel Doctrine.* Salt Lake City: Deseret Book Co., 1939.

Smith, Joseph Fielding. *The Way to Perfection.* Salt Lake City: Deseret Book Co., 1972.

Taylor, Jean. "The Case of the Missing Car." *New Era* 8 (December 1978): 45.

Teach Them Correct Principles: A Study in Family Relations. Salt Lake City: The Church of Jesus Christ of Latter-day Saints, 1987.

To Make Thee a Minister and a Witness [Melchizedek Priesthood study guide]. Salt Lake City: The Church of Jesus Christ of Latter-day Saints, 1990.

Tuttle, A. Theodore. "On Being a Father." *Improvement Era* 70 (June 1967): 86–91.

Wolkomir, Richard, and Joyce Wolkomir. "The Doctor Who Conquered a Killer." *Reader's Digest* 139 (July 1991): 161–66.

Young, Brigham. *Discourses of Brigham Young.* Selected by John A. Widtsoe. Salt Lake City: Deseret Book Co., 1954.

Jesus, Listening, Can Hear

(Especially for Heather)

Words and Music by
Janice Kapp Perry

1. God did not give me voice to speak, And yet my faith is
(2. He) did not give me voice to sing, But in my heart sweet
(3. I) can - not speak to tes - ti - fy, But faith shines bright - ly

quite com - plete. When I pray I have no fear, For
mus - ic rings. Mel - o - dies that no one hears Rise
in my eyes. In my heart it's ver - y clear The

in my mind the words are clear, And Je - sus
from my soul to heav'n - ly spheres, And Je - sus
tes - ti - mo - ny I would bear, And Je - sus

lis - ten - ing can hear.＿＿＿＿＿ 2. He
3. I

hear.＿＿＿＿＿ When I need to

feel Him near, I think His name through si - lent tears,

And Je - sus, lis - ten - ing, can hear.＿＿＿＿＿

8va bassa

Index